How to Make Clothing for Poser

A step by step guide covering every aspect of creating clothing for Poser from design sketch, through modeling, rigging, texturing, morphing, packing and troubleshooting issues.

Contents

Prologue – Getting Ready

A brief discussion of the purpose of this book, and the tools and thoughts you will need to bring with you into your project

So you have been using Poser or DAZ studio for a while and you want to make some clothing items of your own. Perhaps you have made some textures, or some props, but as you may have found out already, creating clothing is a long and complicated process. No one step is all that tricky, the problem is that there are literally hundreds and something done in step 5 can directly effect step 400.

The workflow and methods I use are merely how I am comfortable working. After you have followed this tutorial once or twice and have a firm grasp of the theory then you can start experimenting with doing things in a different order or with different tools available to you.

I have done some sections twice in different programs to give a variety of approaches, but of course there are dozens of modeling programs, uvmapping solutions and image editors. So by all means don't feel yourself bound to using exactly what I use. For one thing my copy of C4D7 is exceedingly old, and newer ones have newer and more flexible tools. Always remember to use what you have.

When reading tutorials try not to focus on the names of tools or the specific programs, but instead pay the most attention to the concepts – these can be adapted to any similar program and by keeping an open and flexible mind you can adapt my modeling tutorial to any modeling program that can extrude and cut polygons.

Programs needed by Type

A 3d modeling program: Cinema4D, 3D Studio Max, Wings3d, Hex, Carrara, etc.

A uvmapping program: UVLayout, UVmapper, Roadkill, and many modelers have mapping solutions built in.

An image editor: Photoshop, Photoshop Elements, GIMP, Painter, PaintshopPro, etc preferably one that allows you to work in layers in one document.

Poser: preferably the newest version you can lay hands on, but you can go as far back as Poser4ProPak without serious issues. In fact, for DS users the technology of p4PP is comparable as far as compatibility issues go, except for shader issues. Can you rig in DAZ studio? These days, yes but in DAZ studio 4 things changed a great deal and that should be the subject of its own tutorial. However, since DAZ studio still reads Poser content, barring a few things, anything you rig in Poser should work in DAZ studio. Genesis (1, 2 3) content can only be rigged in DS 4.5, as Genesis does not work in earlier versions.

A cr2 editor – Poser File Editor, cr2edit, Wordpad.

And lastly copious amounts of time and patience. This is not the easiest task you have set yourself, but if you are careful and patient you will eventually succeed. Your first few projects may require you to go back several stages to rip apart and repair things, but do not despair. As in any craft, experience is your greatest teacher.

IMPORTANT: make backups early, and often. I suggest working in incremental saves i.e. Yourfile1, yourfile2. That way when you find an error (and you will) you can go back with a minimum of bad language and continue from there. This book contains a section on troubleshooting issues, as well as a chapter on making edits for issues found by a Quality Control check.

Language

As I go through this guide there are some specific terms I will use. Many of them are common to all 3D programs, and some are specific to Poser. Like any technical field there are specific technical terms that mean certain very specific things, so understanding the language will make following this and any other instructions much easier. It will also make communicating with other people using Poser much easier, when it comes to collaborations, customer support or troubleshooting issues.

Modeling

vertice or vert = a point in space defined by its 3 coordinates.

poly or polygon = a mesh section defined by 3 or more vertices.

tri = triangular (3 point) polygon.

Quad = square or quadrangular (4 point) polygons.

Ngon = any polygon with more then 4 sides. Usually a bad thing.

Normal = polygons are one sided. The normal indicates the direction it is facing.

Loop = a row of vertices that forms a complete circle around the object.

Edgeloop = a row or loop of vertices creating a line close to the edge of an object or shape.

Poser

cr2 = a character or figure file in Poser. This is an articulated figure, with various parts that move. It can be a base figure (a human or animal), an articulated prop or a conforming clothing item. It can be placed in the Characters folder with the file extension .cr2 or it can be in the Props folder with the extension .pp2, though the internal structure is still that of a cr2.

pp2 = a static prop figure. File extension is .pp2 and they are saved in the Props folder. Props can contain morphs. Props can also be saved as Smart props, which load already parented to a bodypart of a figure. Sometimes an articulated prop can be saved with the .pp2 suffix but they will behave as cr2 do when loaded.

Parenting = any figure or prop can be parented to another figure. Think of it as simply gluing it in place. This means that if you for example parent a sword to the left hand, when the hand is moved the sword goes with it. Some clothing items like hats or wings are best used as parented rather than conformed, since this means they can be used on any figure.

Hr2 = An hr2 is a special form of prop which is saved in the Hair folder. It loads parented to the head and is single group. Articulated hairs are conforming cr2's.

MAT pose = a pz2 format pose that applies material (surface) settings to the selected cr2 or smartprop.

Pz2 or Pose file = a .pz2 file is saved in the pose folder. There are many subtypes such as pose files, MAT poses, MOR poses, INJ poses and SET poses. Although the default is simply a list of bodypart transformations to load a specific pose, over the years, creative content makers have figured out how to make the simple pz2 file do all sorts of odd things. I have not listed them all here.

Binary Morphs or PMD = Morphs stored in an exterior file (.pmd) by Poser, starting in Poser6, rather than in the cr2 as in previous formats. Generally not used, for various reasons including lack of inter program compatibility.

Mt5 = Introduced in Poser 5 with the debut of the Material room, the mt5 or Material setting saves the surface settings of a single material zone and can be applied universally to a single material zone of any prop or figure. These are usually used for universally applied materials such as generic textiles, latex, glass, or metals. They are in the Materials folder.

Mc6 = Material Collections are Posers internal answer to the hacked MAT pose. They save a collection of material settings for a specific prop or figure. They are in the Materials folder, along with the mt5 shaders, which can be confusing. Generally the created thumbnail is a picture of the scene, rather than a sphere, which can help tell them apart.

Shader = the general term for any procedural, or mathematically, created surface material in most 3d programs. Poser's shaders are called Materials and are saved in the Materials folder natively.

Dynamic = dynamic cloth or hair are items that go through a simulation process in order to be affected by gravity and other impacts. Poser creates it own hair internally, which does not export, and can dynamically drape most cloth mesh as long as they follow certain constraints. Draped cloth can be exported or saved as morphs.

Magnets = Magnets are special objects in Poser that deform meshes. They have three sections, a target, a zone and a proxy. By manipulating these you can distort meshes in a number of ways. Magnet presets are saved collections of magnets, that distort to a certain shape.

Magnetise poses = Magnetise poses are used on clothing for figures that have joint magnets, in order to add the magnets effects to the clothing item.

Joint Magnets = Some figures have built in joint deformers to aid in fixing bend issues. These can complicate the clothing fitting process.

Merchant Resources = Merchant Resources are purchasable items where you are paying for the license to modify and redistribute. These are usually seamless textures, or figure skin bases, but can be almost any sort of resource used in creating content.

DevKits = Developers Kits are usually kits set up to get developers for a new figure started faster. These can include such essentials as a donor rig, base mesh for clothing, and so forth.

Quicksuits = a quicksuit mesh is a basic (usually low poly) clothing mesh for a figure, usually a bodysuit or long dress, that you can modify into a new clothing item. Some can be licensed for commercial use. Often found in Devkits, but not always.

Copyright Issues

I strongly suggest you look up copyright laws in your country. However the global community tends to default to American/European union copyright laws.

In general it is always best to make everything from scratch yourself: mesh, textures, so forth.

However not everyone has the ability or time to make everything themselves so here are some simple things to keep in mind, to keep yourself out of legal trouble.

Clothing Designs from Reality

In general the fashion design industry decided quite some time ago that clothing patterns/designs cannot be copyrighted. So even in the real world if you take apart your old jacket and make 20 copies of it, there are no legal consequences. The exception here is any textile or notion (buttons, etc) that incorporate logos and trademarks. Those Chanel buttons are copyrighted, not for the button, but for that interlocked C logo.

So as far as Poser clothing goes – have fun. You can recreate any clothing item in 3d that you can legally do in reality.

Clothing/Costume designs from Games/Movies

This starts to enter a fuzzy area. On one hand all costume/fashion designs are fair game. On the other hand, trademarked characters (including costuming) are protected by copyright. It is usually a good idea if you are going to make a known costume from a movie or game, to make a similar but not the same design.

Some companies do not mind fan work, as long as no profit is involved. So if you absolutely must make a certain star spangled mans armour and shield, you might be okay releasing it as a freebie. Some companies are okay with this, and some are completely strict.

Also, keep in mind that many artists use Poser content for their commercial illustration, animation and game creation work. There is no way for people to know every movie, game and anime character out there. So it is possible for a perfectly innocent artist to inadvertently copy a companies copyrighted character design in their commissioned image simply because they did not know that the clothing item they are using is a derivative work.

For that reason as well as the legal complications I usually recommend that any derivative works be kept entirely in the realm of free items not for commercial use, and clearly marked as such.

Textile Designs

Like clothing design, real world textile designs are not copyrightable. There are some exceptions, any textile design containing a logo or trademarked image such as the Luis Vuitton logo print or any textile depicting cartoon characters, since those characters are trademarked. In addition copyrighted artwork is being used in textile design, especially by quilting fabric companies, in an effort to cut down on knockoff versions.

So by and large most textile designs can be used freely, with those exceptions.

BUT you are not working directly with the cloth, you are working with a photograph of the cloth. So you must establish the ownership of the photo. As long as you have the permission of the photographer of the cloth, and it does not contain logos or trademarks you should be free and clear as far as using it as a digital resource.

For this reason if you intend to seriously start making clothing assets, I recommend picking up a digital camera or flatbed scanner. If you are the photographer you have the advantage of knowing exactly how and where the image was captured.

Logos and Trademarks

Logos and trademarks are protected by international law. In general, the only ones who can use them are the owners, excepting in certain circumstances. As far as what we do goes ... you don't want to go near this particular legal thicket.

So if a design or textile contains a logo or trademarked character, don't touch it. This includes logo shaped belt buckles and purse clasps, cartoon characters on textiles, and package designs like soda cans and cereal boxes.

I found It On The Internet

'I found it on a website' 'my friend sent it to me' 'I got it from Google sketchup' 'I extracted it from a game'.

Just don't, okay?

In general any image or mesh you find wandering around the internet should be viewed with extreme suspicion. You don't know where it came from, you don't know who took the photo or made it and in general even if your best friend in the world hands it to you, they might not know the items provenance. Save yourself a lot of trouble and Just Don't.

Paper Trails

For every asset you do not make yourself make sure you have a clear paper trail. So for every mesh you use that you didn't make, every textile image you used, make certain you have a clear statement that you purchased or otherwise obtained a license to use and distribute it.

Even if your good friend makes a cloth tile for you, make sure you get an email from them clearly indicating the name of the file and what you are allowed to do with it. Just in case.

Some stores will ask for verification or listing of all assets used in a product.

For assets you make yourself, most stores accept iterated saves with multiple save dates and or layered image files as proof of ownership. So hang onto all your working files, you may need them in the future to prove your copyrights.

Don't Steal

This seems obvious, but it needs to be said. An artist WILL see their own work, no matter how you attempt to disguise it. As much as the shortcut may seem worth the risk, its best if you don't. Once you are found and proven to be plagiarizing someone else work that's pretty much the end of your credibility as a creator. So just don't.

The Difference Between Royalty Free and Common Domain

There is some confusion about these terms. *They are not interchangeable.*

Royalty free. This is an item that you do not need to pay a royalty or license fee to use. This items copyright still remains with its creator (for lifetime + 50 years in the US). Only the owner of the copyright can set use limitations, including commercial use and distribution.

Common Domain or Public Domain. In the most place these are items that are now 50 years past the death of the creator. Some creators place items in the public domain deliberately. These items are fair game for anything, modifying, commercial and non commercial use, and distribution.

NOTE: an item (such as art) may be public domain, BUT the photograph of it itself has copyrights and those rights must be respected as well. Keep that in mind.

How Long do Copyrights last

In general any created work has an automatic copyright of the creators lifetime plus 50 years. This includes music, written work, and images of all sorts. The specifics have been changed many times over the years, and of course are different in various countries.

If you find an item you want to use and its exact status is unclear, make sure to have it checked as much as possible and verify with a copyright lawyer. If you are not sure, most stores should have staff to help you find out if something can be used safely.

MYTH – If its on the Internet it is Public Domain

Absolutely not true. Any and all text and images you find on the internet are protected under copyright laws unless explicitly stated by the original maker. Somebody owns it and will be very unhappy with you if you take it without asking.

Chapter 1 –   Modeling

A step by step walk through of choosing a design,

working from a sketch and modeling clothing items in

Cinema4d over an imported base figure

Before you get started, you need to consider what you are making and the difficulty of rigging the item. Every clothing design has its troublesome points. When you are just starting out I suggest sticking to items that will be simple to rig.

Simple: tight clothing items that follow the body contours, most modern shirts, pants, shoes.

A little complicated: long skirts, loose armor plates, high heels, dangling sleeves, loose shirts and pants, layered items, items with linings.

Very difficult: Kimonos, items with several long articulated strings of parts, ballerina boots.

Impossible: items that connect to themselves across bodyparts such as pants with straps that connect the shins, scarves that attach at both neck and wrist.

Note: some difficult and impossible items are better handled as dynamic cloth.

Note: Some otherwise impossible items can now be handled in weightmapping, but only for certain figures and versions of Poser that support it.

Elf Age Light for Victoria 4

by 4BlueEyes

Eleniel Textures

by Arien

Deceptively simple, this six piece outfit hides a lot of fine detail. The skirt has quite a lot of rigging to control the three draping sections using both EZpose controls and morphs.

0 First step   Decide what you are making. I always work from a pencil sketch. Almost all of my work are original designs which I create on a figure template as you can see.

You can also work from photos or artwork directly, but I usually suggest drawing it out so you can really think out the parts and how it goes together at all angles before you start trying to create the thing in three dimensions.

I've selected a fairly simple design from my backlog of designs. A two part outfit, shirt and top fairly standard in cut and symmetrical. The only tricky part to rig will be that hanging sash on the pants.

1   Now to get my victim ready. You want to model right over the figure so import your model into your modeling program.

ALWAYS USE the OBJ from the Poser geometries folder. I cannot stress that enough. Do NOT work over an exported obj, one not in the default position or one that has been morphed. It will give you nothing but headaches. And trust me, this is rough enough without making your life tougher on purpose.

Here is DAZ 3D's David in all his boring beige splendor. David is a nice simple model, without much in the way of fancy joint magnets or corrective morphs and a good starter.

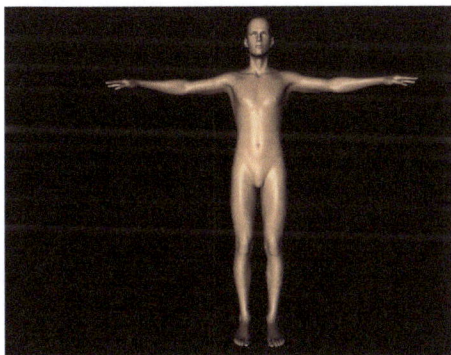

2   And here he is in C4d wireframe, top camera. I am going to start
shaping the base oval that I'll be expand-
ing the rest of the outfit from.

A note on polygon counts: too much
is as bad as too little. A general rule of
thumb is never more polys than the
figure the clothing is for, and in general
the poly sizes should be about the same
as the ones they are covering.

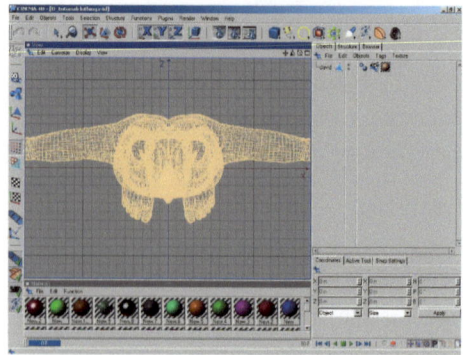

Too few and you get faceting and lack
of detail. Too many and not only will
you have trouble when rigging, but your
system will be working much harder than
it has to. Plan to use displacement and
bump maps to add fine detail like cloth
wrinkles and so forth.

Remember every morph you add adds
about one quarter the file size of the
original obj again.

Also try to avoid too many triangles,
as Poser and Poser users prefer quads,
square polygons. Tris however are essential in some areas, especially any place
where there will be diagonal creasing like
the groin and armpits.

3   Here I'm laying in points to
make my first polygon. I'm going to be
mirroring this so I only need to make
one side.

If your program doesn't allow you to
make loose points like this, make a
square primitive (not a cube) and add
points to it to get the shape you will
need.

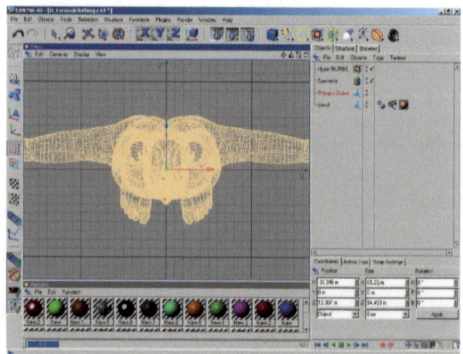

As you can see I've laid out points
roughly around his torso cross-section,
and points on the centerline.

Chapter 1 –   Modeling

4   Here I've hooked my points together to make my base shape. The important part is not the shape of the inner polys, but actually the distribution of the outside vertices. I've found this layout, after subdividing, tends to accommodate most clothing designs very easily. That center poly on the sides makes it easier to shape the armhole when we get that far.

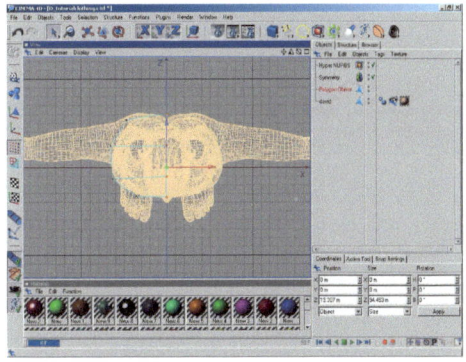

5   As you can see when working in top view the poly gets made on the floor, with its origin center at universe center (0,0,0) This means the centerline is at 0 on the X axis.

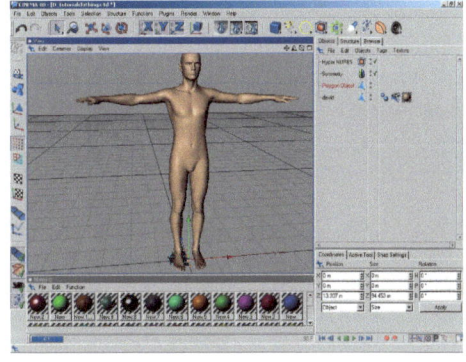

6   I've slid the poly up, leaving its origin center with the center of the poly. In C4D my camera rotates around that origin point.

You can see on the right in the structure tab I have made a 2 level hypernurb divider and a mirror symmetry.

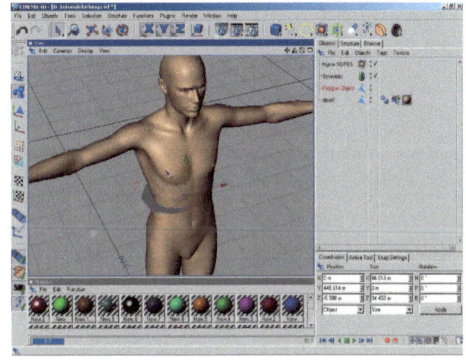

Chapter 1 –   Modeling

7   Here I've mirrored and used that hypernurb subdivider to smooth that poly and make in symmetrical.

The hypernurb modifier makes the mesh smooth, without actually changed my low polygon cage. I can control the level of subdivision it uses. I can't say I've ever gone above 3, and usually use 2.

Subdivision takes each polygon and cuts it in half both ways. This doesn't double the polys in an object, it quadruples them. You can actually subdivide the mesh, but for clothing I don't suggest it until the final finishing stages. After all, 6 big polys are easier to adjust than 24 smaller ones.

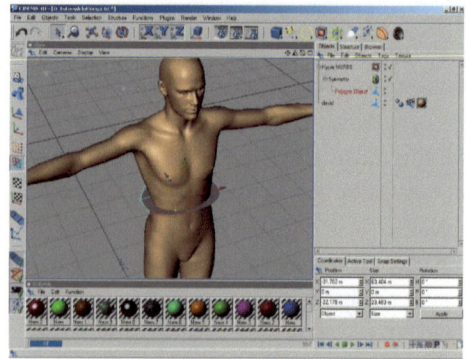

8   I selected all the polys and extruded them upwards. The hypernurb smoothing has smoothed out the top, but that is ok.

Try to get your horizontal loops of polys at place son the torso where your mesh will need to change direction, to move in or out on the figure.

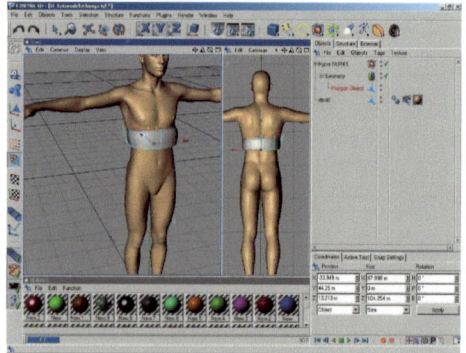

I've split my viewport so I can see the closeup of the area I'm working on as well as a smaller overview. This can be useful when you are working on something large.

9   Here I've extruded it a few more times, making sure to drop a loop of polys at the top of the figures abdomen group, just under the pectorals, at the bottom of the sleeve opening area, and top of sleeve area. I did some simple scaling as I went.

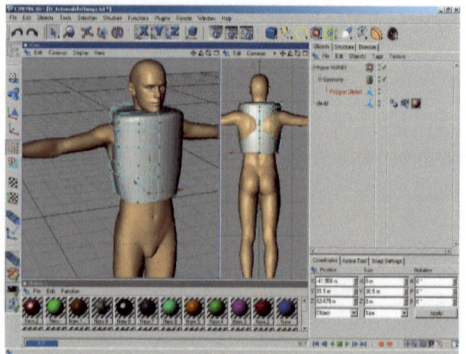

10   Now I've started adjusting the mesh to fit the figure. Looking at the sketch I can see I don't want it to be form fitting, so I keep an eye on the silhouette of my shape as I fit it to David. I haven't cut the hole out where the sleeve will be but you can see I've started to shape the armhole already.

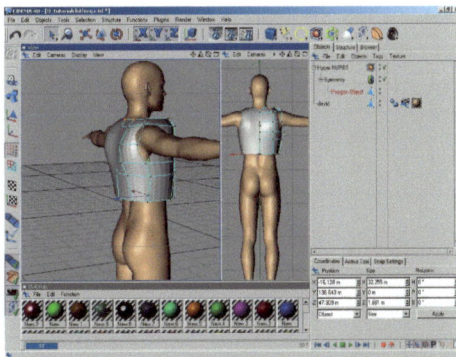

11   And here is the front more shaped. You can see that even with less than 30 polys the hypernurb smoothing has made a nice clean shape.

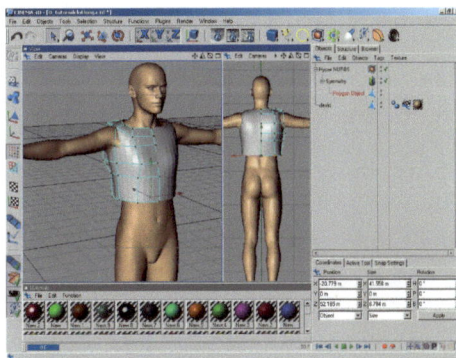

The faceting you see currently is because I have left off a smoothing tag. A smoothing tag smooths out the edges of the facets, and in fact Poser automatically smooths everything, so its a good preview of the finished product. I turn it on and off so I can see how the hypernurb is making the subdivided polygons flow.

12   Now to select the 2 polys that make up the sleeve area and remove them. You may want to nudge the front and back verts that define the armhole to make a more pleasing shape, depending on the style of sleeve you have in mind. Mine is a simple cylinder, slightly oval deformed by gravity.

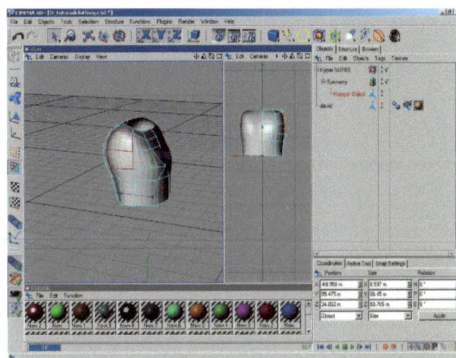

13   As you can see the hypernurb smooths out the edges making a nice round armhole.

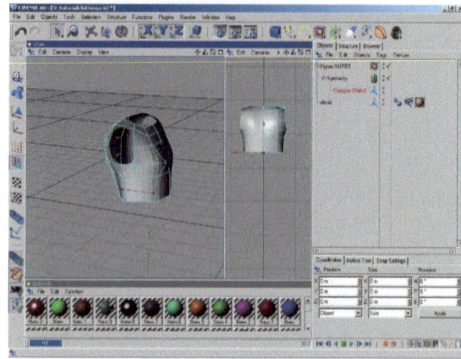

14   Here the armhole verts are selected, to get ready to start the extrusion of the base of the sleeve.

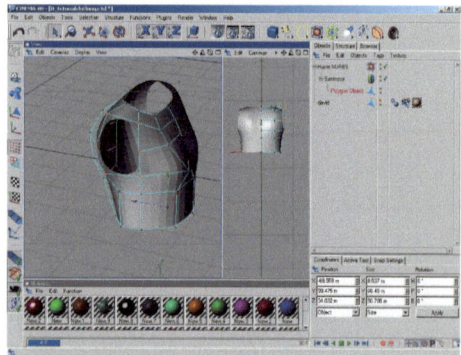

15   And here I've extruded them to start the sleeve.

The farther apart the verts are, means bigger polys. With sub D on, larger polys means softer details, and smaller means crisper. So if you want a nice crisp arm/sleeve join, keep that first row of sleeve polys fairly close to the torso.

If you look at the figures mesh you will see that there are more polys close to the joints for better bending. Giving your clothing about the same poly size and density in the same areas means they will bend like the figure and be easier to fit.

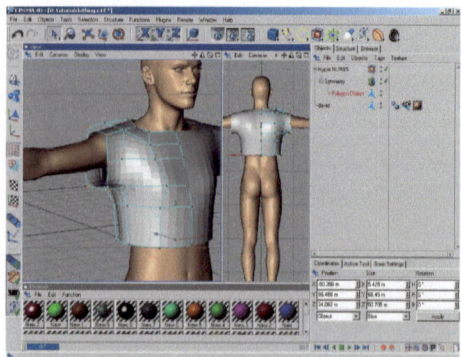

Chapter 1 –   Modeling

16   I decided that the underarm and side were too square, so I selected the polys and cut them to make a new vertical row of vertices. This should make it easier to make a nice round sleeve like in my sketch, and if I want to cut in side seams having a row of verts there already makes it much simpler. If I'd thought about it I would have started this way but eh .. you can't think of everything.

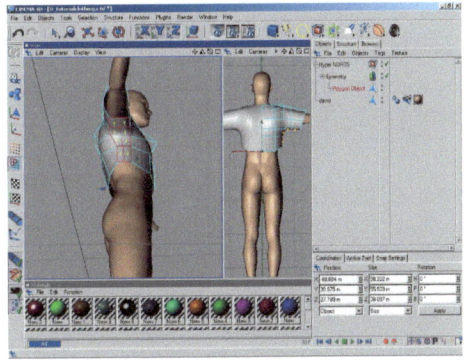

17   I've pulled the new cut out a bit to smooth out my shapes and the bottom of the tunic has shaped up very like my sketch. Its nice when you can see it shaping up so early.

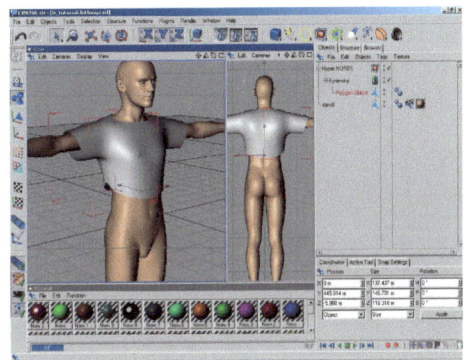

18   I've roughly shaped the top according to my sketch, and now its time to rough out the pants before I cut in any more detail to this mesh frame.

This is also a good place to save a copy in your Bits Bin for later. It would be easy enough to adapt this mesh to a number of different looks and why make something twice if you can recycle?

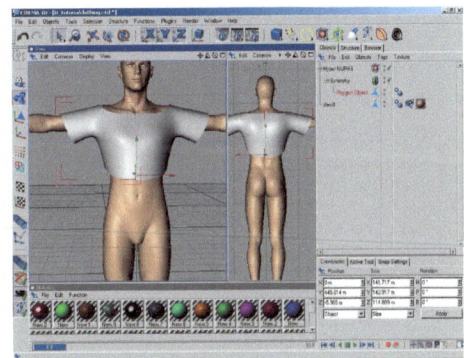

Chapter 1 –   Modeling

19   This should look familiar. Here we are again, but this time see I've made 5 polys going back, so I don't have to cut down the side again. This should give me a nice side seam if I want it, and nice shaping around the butt.

You may laugh at that, but one of the hardest to rig areas on the human figure is the hip/groin joins. Nice clean well fitted mesh makes it much simpler when you get there.

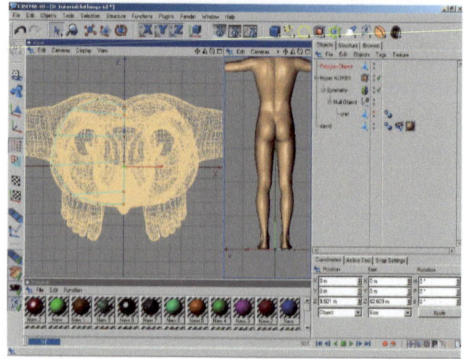

20   I've started extruding my base shape down. As you can see I've dropped a loop at the top of the buttocks, at the peak of the curve and at the groin level.

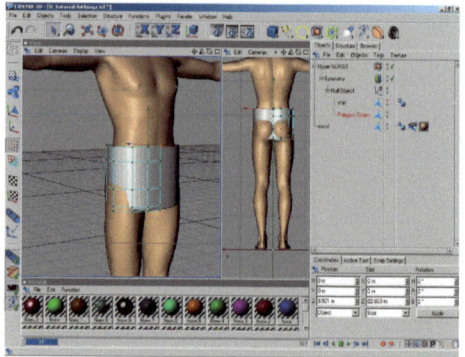

21   I've moved points in and out to shape the hip of the pants over David's butt. As you can see the location of my loops makes it easier to lay the mesh nice and smooth over the complex curves here.

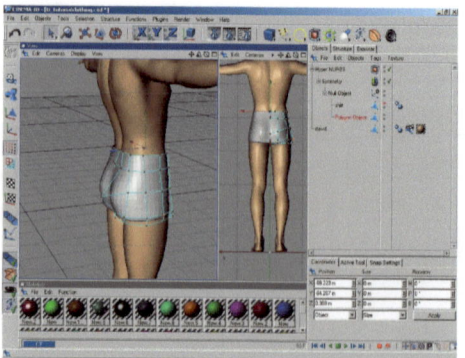

Chapter 1 –   Modeling

22   In Poser, child bodyparts can NOT share an edge and weld properly. They will pull apart and gap. This means that you need to leave a strip of the parent parts mesh in between.

In this case on the hips you have to leave a strip of hip mesh between the two legs so the thigh parts do not touch. This is NOT always an easy task depending on your figure.

As you can see my poly placement has left me a band down the center on purpose.

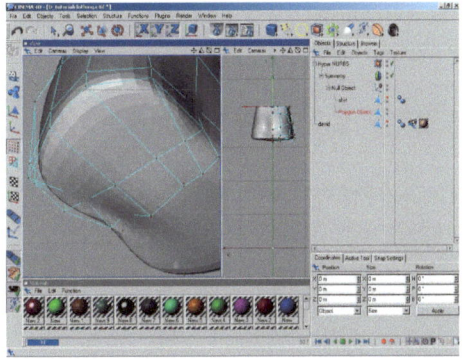

23   Shaping the area to make it ready to extrude the legs downward, and leaving that very important center strip as a buffer zone.

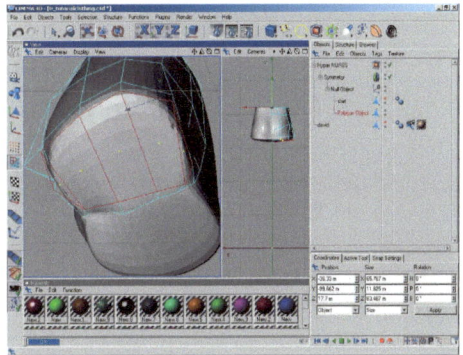

24   I've dropped one loop close to the hips to keep the area nice and crisp and tight and then another loop at the top of the thigh.

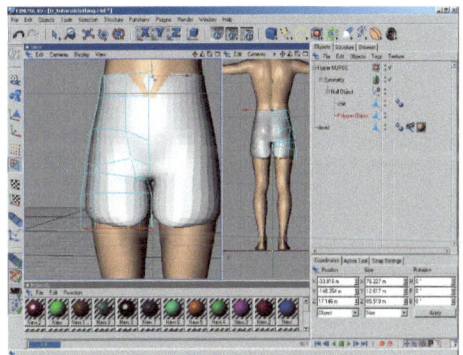

25   Here I've gone back and shaped the groin area a bit. Remember how I said "always use quads when you can?" Well here is a place not to. By cutting that one poly in the front into 2 tris I've started the mesh with a nice natural looking fold radiating outwards from the groin. This also mimics the mesh on the figure underneath, since the body folds there as well.

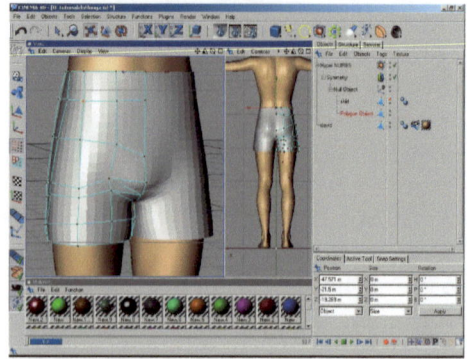

When modeling on the male figure many people think its a good idea to er .. pad the groin out a bit. Well, I don't recommend it. Always try to model close to the actual shape of the figure around the hip, as the rigging is especially difficult here. Add your masculine padding via a morph later.

26   I've continued extruding the pants all the way down to the ankles. Its easier to get a nice smooth silhouette this way, but as you can see I need to do some cutting and shaping.

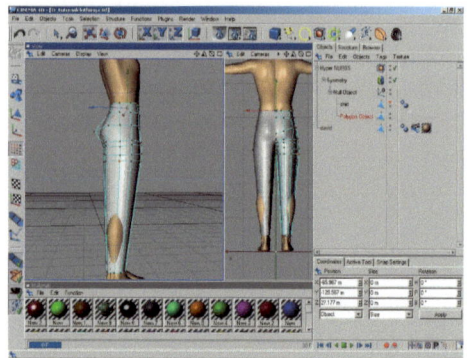

27   Here I've cut in more loops at the joints and peaks of curves.

You can if you rather, extrude down dropping loops and roughly shaping as you go. But I sometimes find it hard to keep a nice clean drape that way.

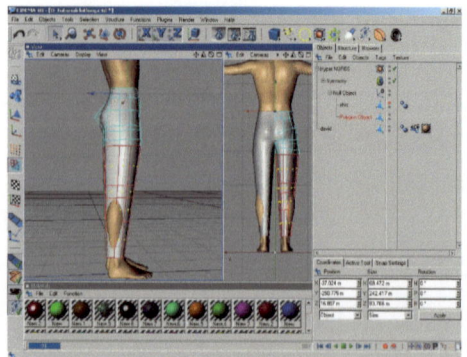

Chapter 1 –   Modeling

20

28   Here I've shaped the legs over the figure and you can see the side line is very smooth.

I use a similar approach for making long skirts, model at as far down as the groin line and then extrude and drop to the floor to get a clean drape.

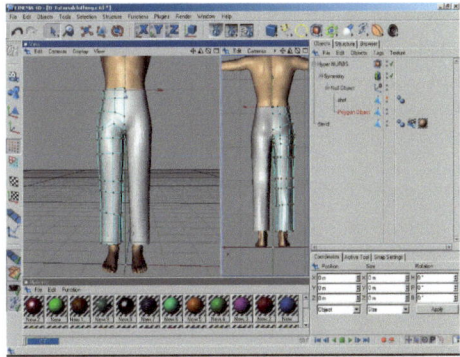

29   To make that inset on the legs I've copied the pants mesh. After shaping this one I can edit the next one to lay just underneath.

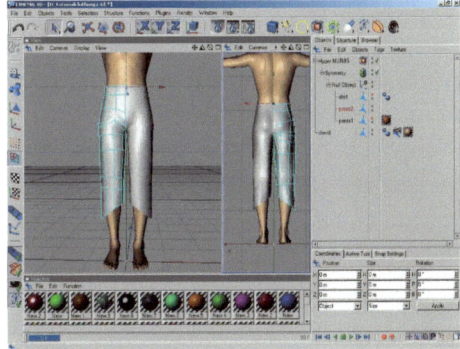

30   The copied pants mesh for the inset, colored orange so I can see it easily. I removed the hip and leg polys I don't need.

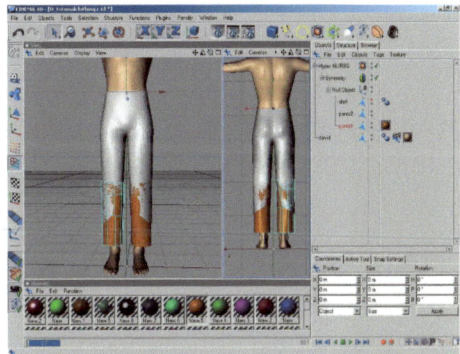

31   A little point editing and the inset lays cleanly under the pants.

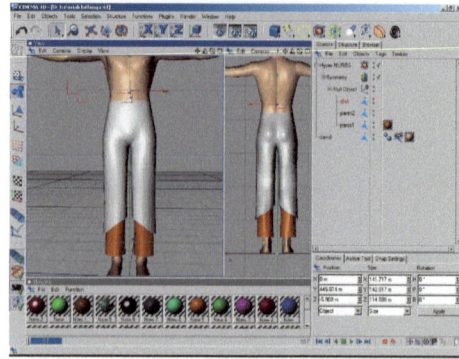

32   To make the belt I copied the pants, colored it red and removed the polys I didn't need. This will ensure me a close and similar fit to the pants. I've made it red so I can see it better. I tend to end up with a lot of vivid solid colors to keep track of things. When you have multiple items and multiple parts it can help.

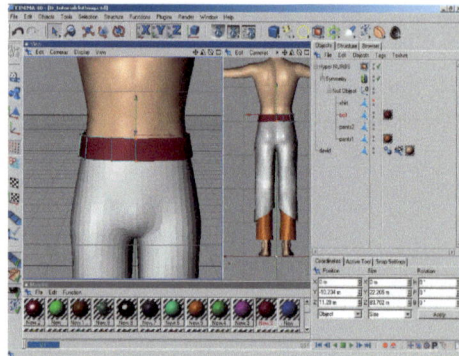

33   The hip drape is made starting with, you guessed it, a copy of the belt. Two loops dropped down to shape it over the top of the hips and butt.

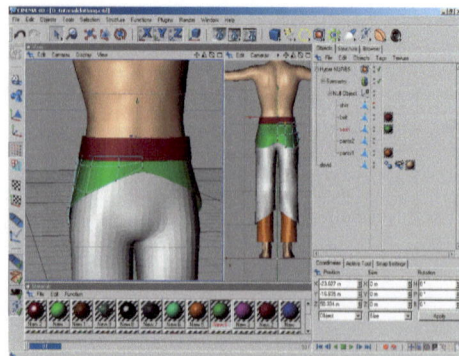

Chapter 1 –   Modeling

34   And again a last time for the
sash. This one gets extruded all the way
down so we can control the fabric drape
more easily.

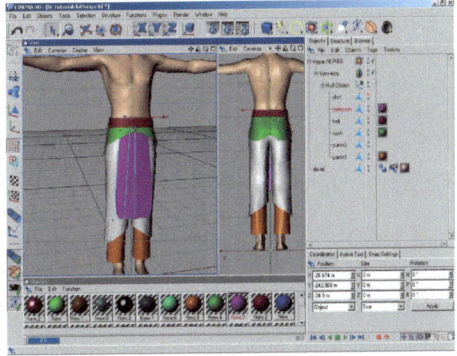

35   Looking at the sketch I count
the direction changes in the bottom line
of the drape. This tells me I will need at
least 5 polys to starting folding the cloth
like the picture. So I cut in some more
polys vertically.

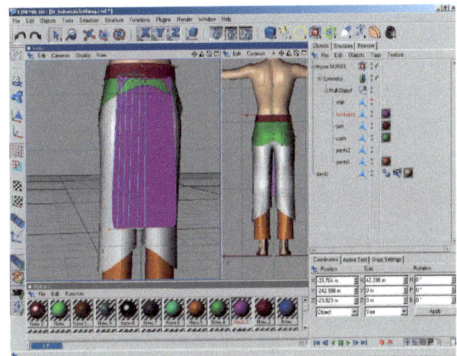

36   I select all the verts but the
center two and slide them forward and
towards the middle. That starts the first
fold.

To start the second fold, deselect the
next 2 verts from the center and slide the
remaining selection forward and towards
the middle. Its just like pleating actual
fabric or paper.

In fact sometimes it helps to take a strip
of paper and fold it a bit to get the feel
for how it the surface goes back and
forth.

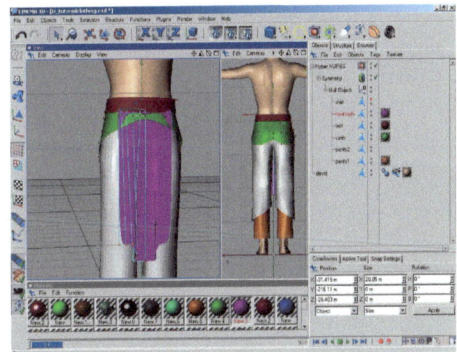

37   I've now finished shaping the folds and I've moved the verts up to get the nice cascade like the sketch.

If you try to mesh this with triangles going up you will not get the same crisp long fabric drape, but something more flared. An interesting effect, but not what I was after.

And that is the last of the basic shaping! Always get the basic shaping to your liking first before adding any fiddly bits you may have to remove or adjust.

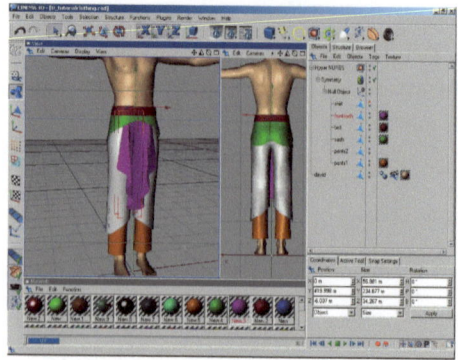

38   Time to start cutting in detail.

On the top I select the polys along my side cut line.

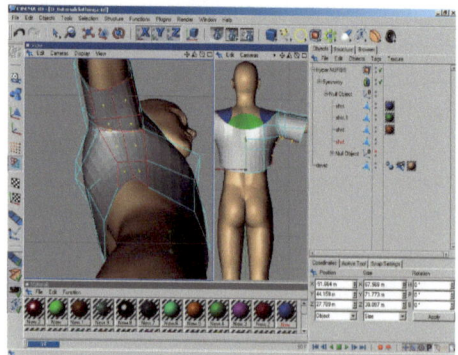

39   And then cut in 2 rows very close to my line. Or I could select that line of polys and Bevel them to get a nice even gutter. Sometimes one method is easier than the other.

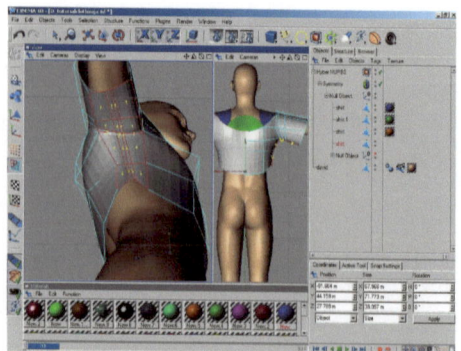

40   With the centerline polys selected and moved up and in, a nice cloth
seam has appeared.

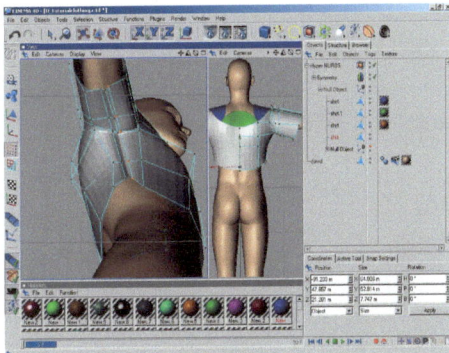

41   I've moved the new points I
made closer to the center to make the
seam nice and crisp. If you need a sharp
edge like an armor plate, then cut another row on the outside of the seam to
keep that corner sharp (or insert an edge
loop if you prefer the technical term).

The reason to do this sort of work
after the basic shape is made is mostly
because trying to select all the point to
edit a line like this cleanly is a pain in the
wossnames. Do the fussy details last so
you don't have to mess with it as much.

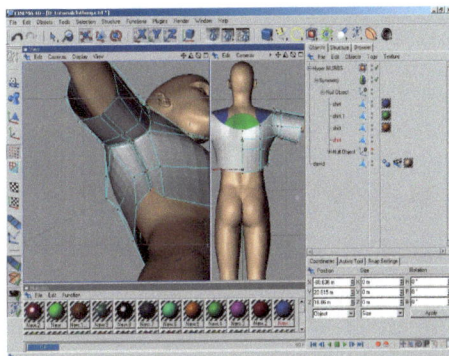

42   Okay jumping down to the
pants I cut in some triangles to make
those inserts on the lower legs. I've cut
a loop at the top of the triangle to keep
the point sharp, and at the cuff to keep
the edge there.

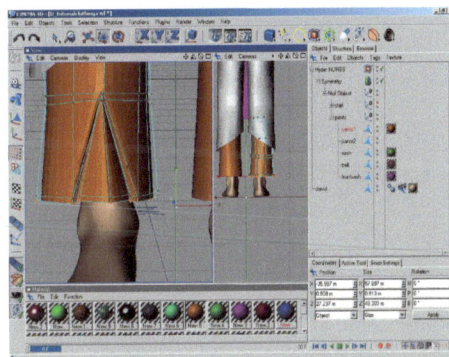

43   The next step is to start rolling my edges to create the illusion of thickness. If you don't then your clothes look paper thin, and not very realistic.

What we want to end up with is kind of a U cross section, with the outside, a flat bottom edge, and then a row inside going back up a little ways to create the illusion of an interior.

Here I've extruded once inwards to create that flat bottom.

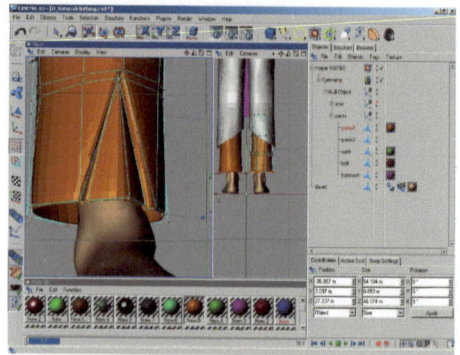

44   And here I've completed the turned edge by extruding once more, straight up.

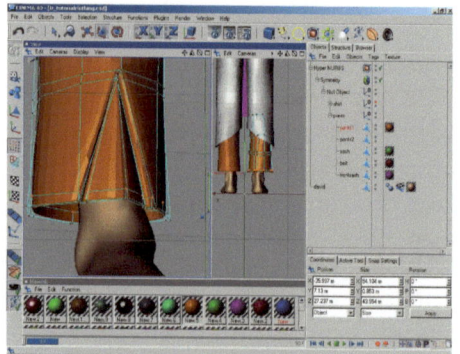

45   Now back up to add detailing and depth to the waist section.

To make the gathered waist drape I'm going to need more mesh to work with. Now I could cut things by hand ....

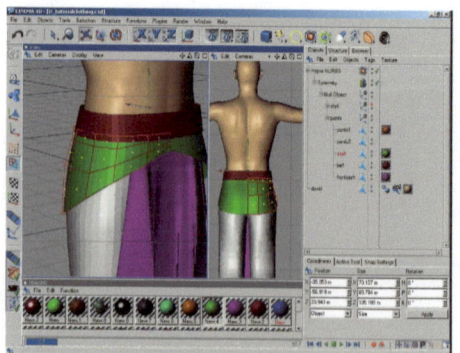

46   Or I could subdivide it once
to get more mesh. With the hybernurb
virtual subdivision still on the mesh gets
much denser. So don't over do it.

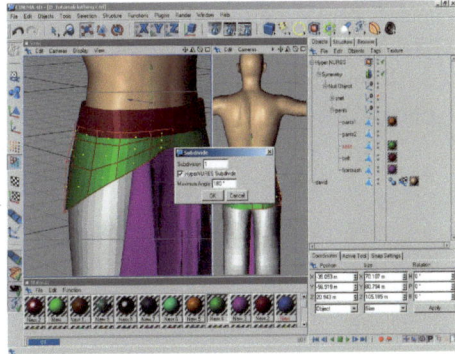

47   After the subdivision some of
my center edges have gotten wonky, so I
select the center verts and set them to 0
on Y.

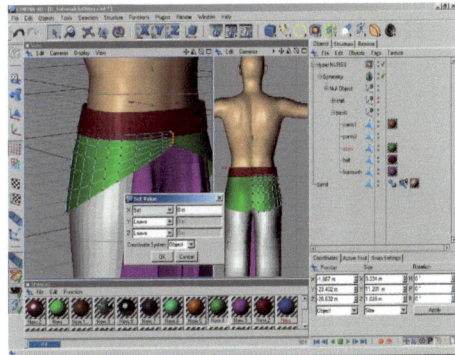

48   I start by moving loops of the
drape in and out to start the long rows
of compression wrinkles. Remember,
a fold is smaller and tighter and more
defined at the point where it is fixed
(sewn down or gathered) and spreads
out and gets softer the further away from
its anchor point. If you don't know what
that means, go get a tissue and a piece of
tape. Gather one edge of the tissue and
tape it to the edge of a table so it hangs.
See? The bottom edge wants to lay
straight again, so it pulls the folds apart.

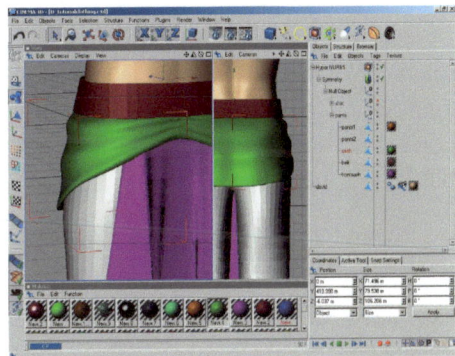

49   I used a Surface command called 'crumple' to randomly rumple up my fabric a little and then adjust it for a fairly natural look.

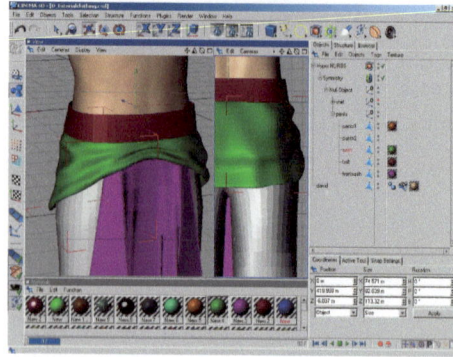

50   On the white pants leg. I cut in 1 loop above the edge to make my banding. I select the polys of the band and extrude them out a little bit to create a seam edge on the inside. This has also created the bottom edge of my turned edge, so I select that last row of verts and extrude upwards once again to complete my turned edge.

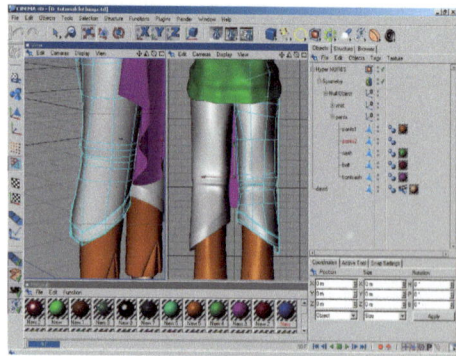

51   You know? I don't like that waist drape at ALL. Its ugly and rumpled and doesn't look as formal as the rest of the outfit.

Ok. Delete it and try again. This time I'm paying more attention to the lines of my folds and not going for the easy but not very good Crumple solution.

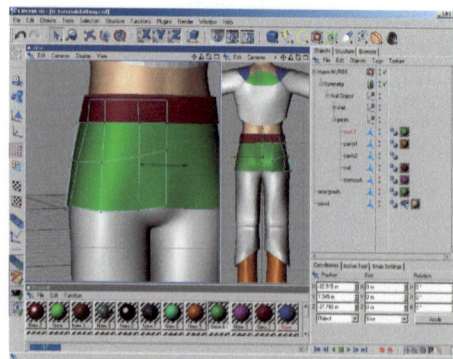

Chapter 1 –   Modeling

52   OK 3 polys rows down, and pull the center vert up to create that V. You can see this time it doesn't meet in the center. I think it will look crisper like this.

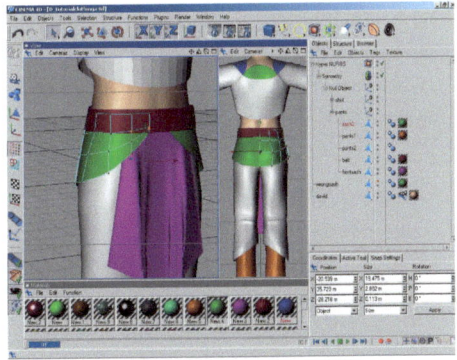

53   Again subdividing the drape to get more mesh to shape.

54   I've turned the bottom edge and shaped that fold and brought out the next fold higher up on the hip. That looks much better and neater, and goes better stylistically with the front sash drape.

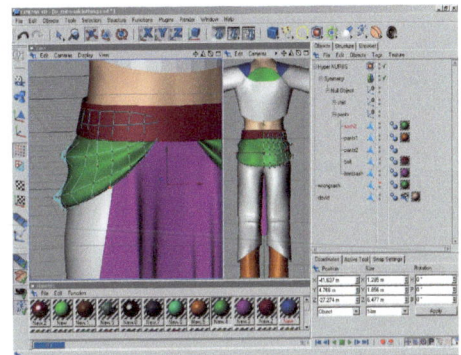

55   Turning the edges on the sash
drape to give it a bit of thickness. You
can see how the edges get very sharp.
I've also cut it once mid thigh to give it
more mesh. I may need to cut it again
later .. a dangly sash like this is going
to need movement of some sort. And
movement needs fairly dense mesh to be
able to move.

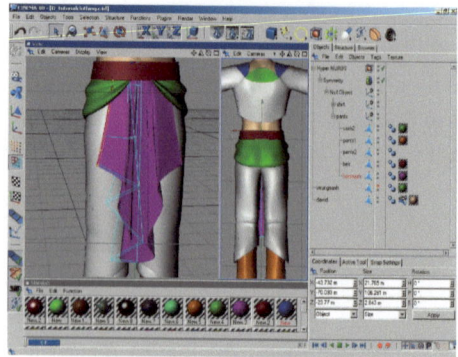

56   Ok turning the belt back on
to fit it. I select all the polys and Move
them on Normal towards the center a
smidge. Lots of pokethrough as you can
see.

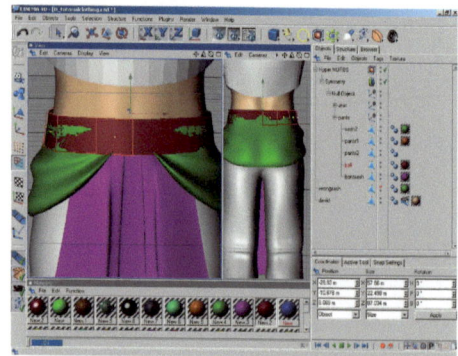

57   Now Extrude once out. This
make your turned edge top and bottom
evenly in one shot. Yes, I am that lazy,
though some people would call it effi-
cient.

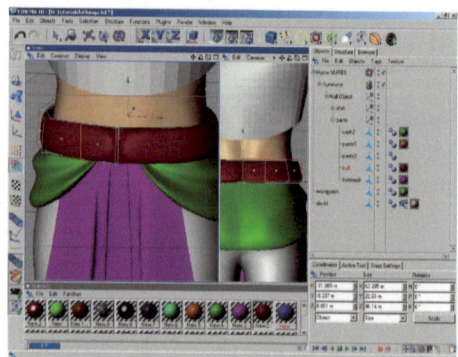

Chapter 1 –   Modeling

58   See that dent front and back? The extrusion has left an extra face there, so remove those 2 faces (front and back) and zero those verts to get a nice solid band for the belt.

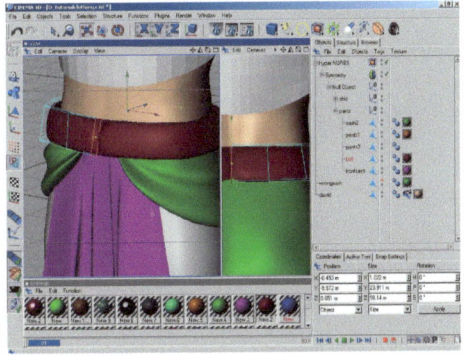

59   Because the belt looks kind of puffy, that hypernurb smoothing at work again, I Extrude Inward once to add a then row of polys around the edges, also known as adding some tight edgeloops.

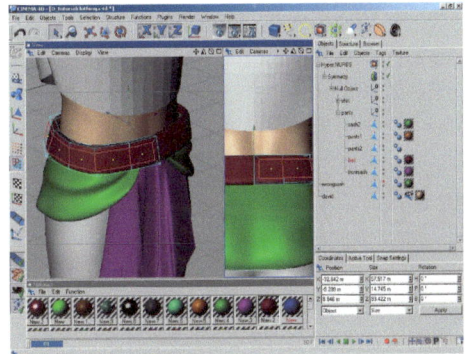

60   To get nice edges on the belt, I Extrude that once inward.

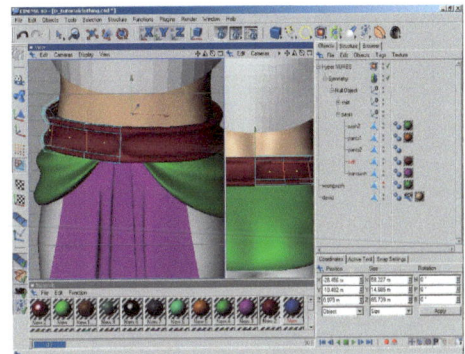

61   Now to clean up the centerline front and back, removing an extra poly or two and align those center verts again.

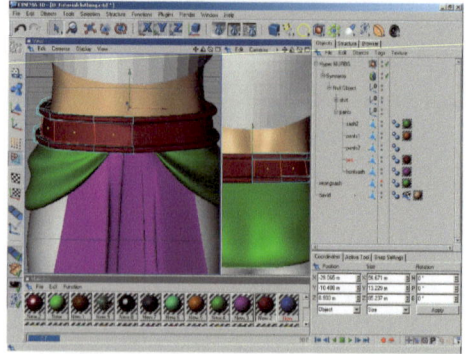

62   Now I've finished turning the top edge by selecting the last loop of verts and extruding them down once. The bottom edge of the belt doesn't need it, nobody will see it with the pants there.

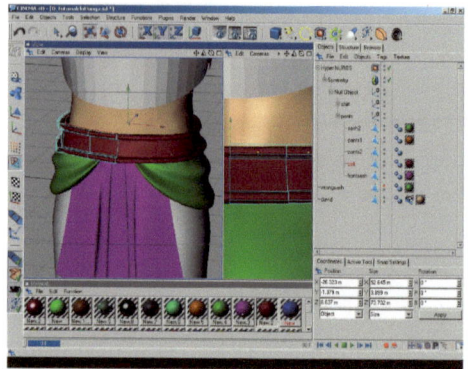

63   Now for a belt buckle. I start with a circle, reduce the polys and chop it in half.

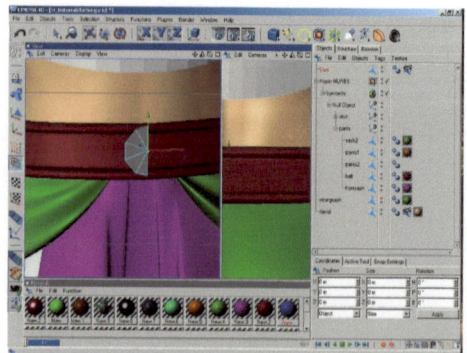

64   Once stuck inside the hypernurb and mirror it make a nice flat disc base to start from.

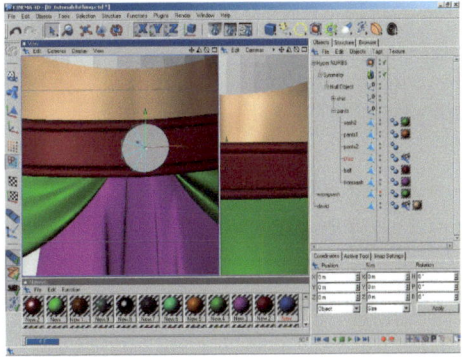

65   I use the same process I just did on the belt to make the edge. Extrude the edge out, then extrude that thin ring of new polys.

I leave the center plain, a design or logo can be added via displacement easily enough and a plain surface leaves more space for variety.

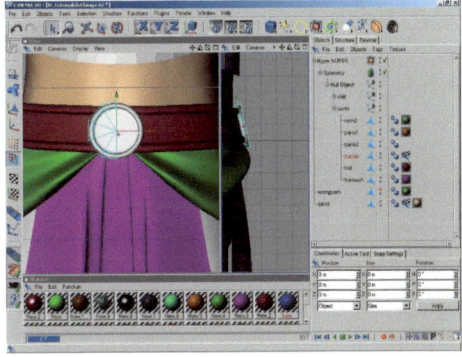

66   Okay back up to the shirt. Time to start cutting in polys to make that edge banding and the base for the triangle inserts.

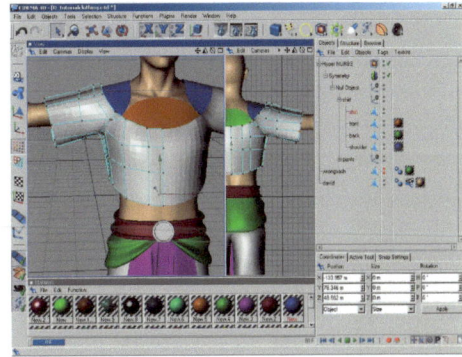

67   I've selected my new polys to show you where the banding will come in, and so I get an idea of what I'll end up with.

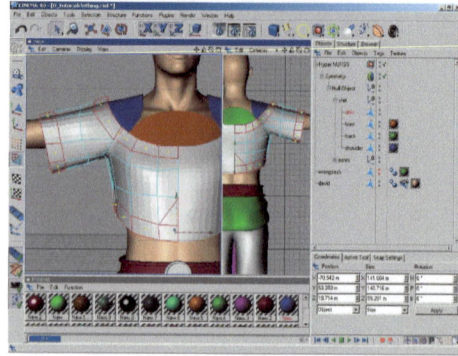

68   I start at the collar and extrude that band once. That won't need a turned edge, the blue and orange circle block it from view.

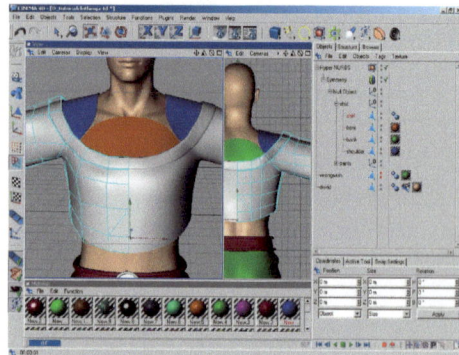

69   Here I've done the same for the waist and cuffs. But this time I have finished the turned edge as well.

On loose cuffs like sleeves where you can see the inside sometimes you need to keep going for a while making a lined sleeve. Try not to go past the elbow, because those bends will drive you mad keeping the lining from popping out.

With bands like these, just go the depth of the trim and stop.

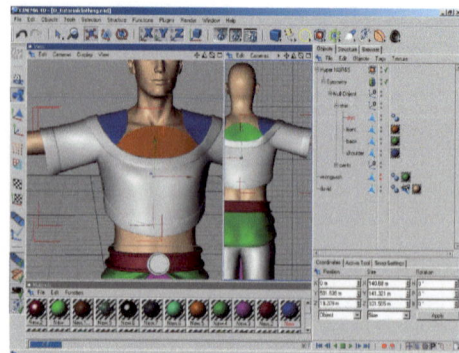

Chapter 1 –   Modeling

70   Now to turn and detail the orange bit. Just the same as all the others, extruding the band and triangle and then extruding the edge to turn it fro thickness.

There are some techniques that you end up using over and over and over. Some programs allow you to define them as scripts or assign to hotkeys, which is a good idea once your workflow is more set.

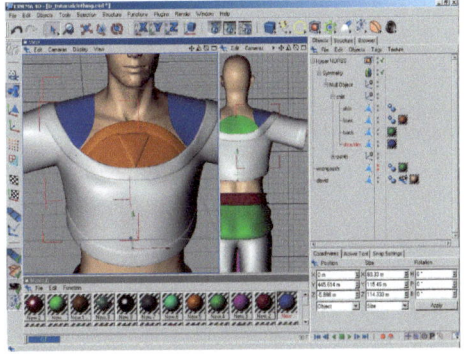

71   I've finished turning all my edges and extruding the triangles on the front and back of the shirt.

A quick once over for look, make sure everything is where I want it.

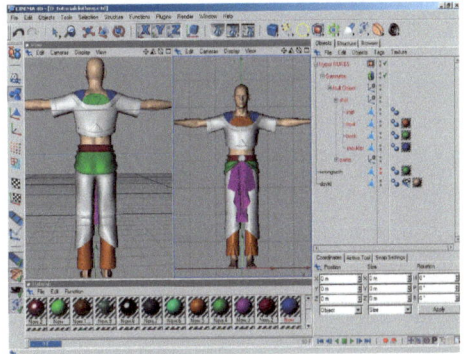

72   Then a check in wireframe mode, especially making sure there is enough mesh for flexibility in that front sash, and at the joints.

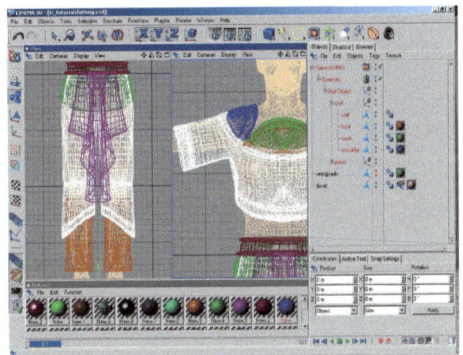

73   Final.

And I'm done!

As you can see with some very basic methods and techniques, with a little attention paid to the reality of cloth draping and the constraints of mesh in Poser you can get a fairly realistic looking set of clothing.

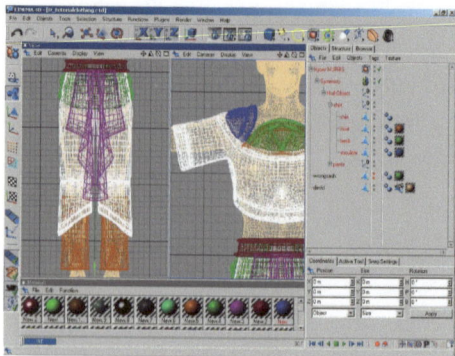

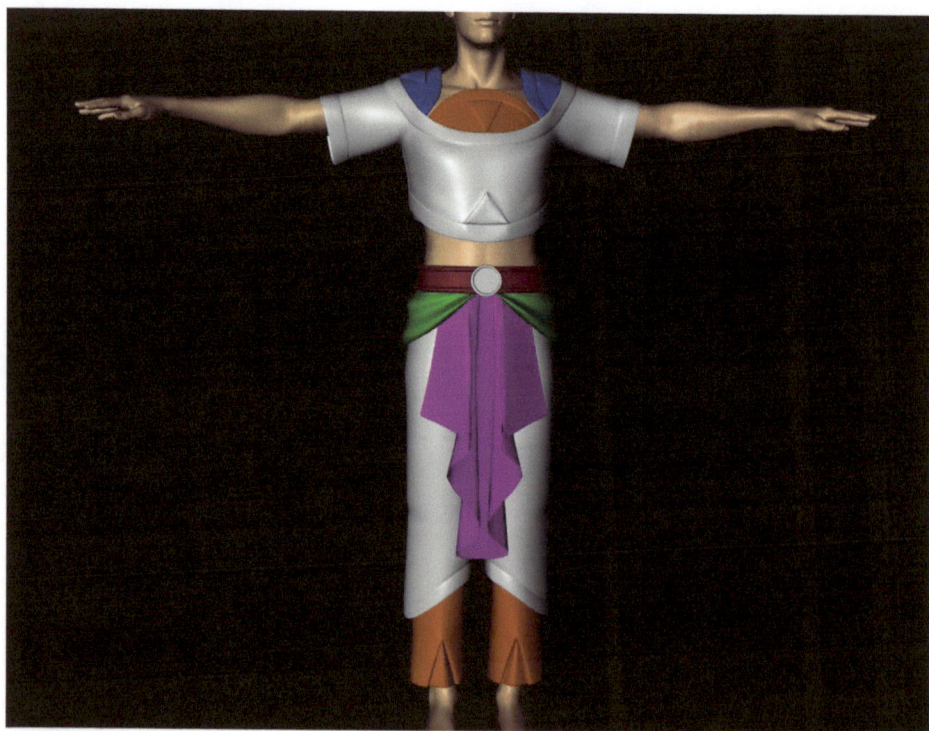

Chapter 2 – Uvmapping with UVLayout

Uvmapping the project mesh using UVLayout

If you do not have UVLayout, skip to the next section on UVmapper. UVmapper's tools are similar to most uvmapping programs and built in UV solutions so you'll have an easier time adapting the methods to your program.

What is Uvmapping? Uvmapping is the process of assigning each polygon to a specific place on a flat plane so you can paint on the flat plane and have it show up in the assigned place on the model.

In general when uvmapping you want to cut apart your model keeping the following things in mind:

Make it as flat as possible with as little distortion of texture as possible.

Make as few pieces as possible.

Cut the pieces in a way to make the texturing and reduction of texture seams easier.

Cut clothing on natural cloth seams.

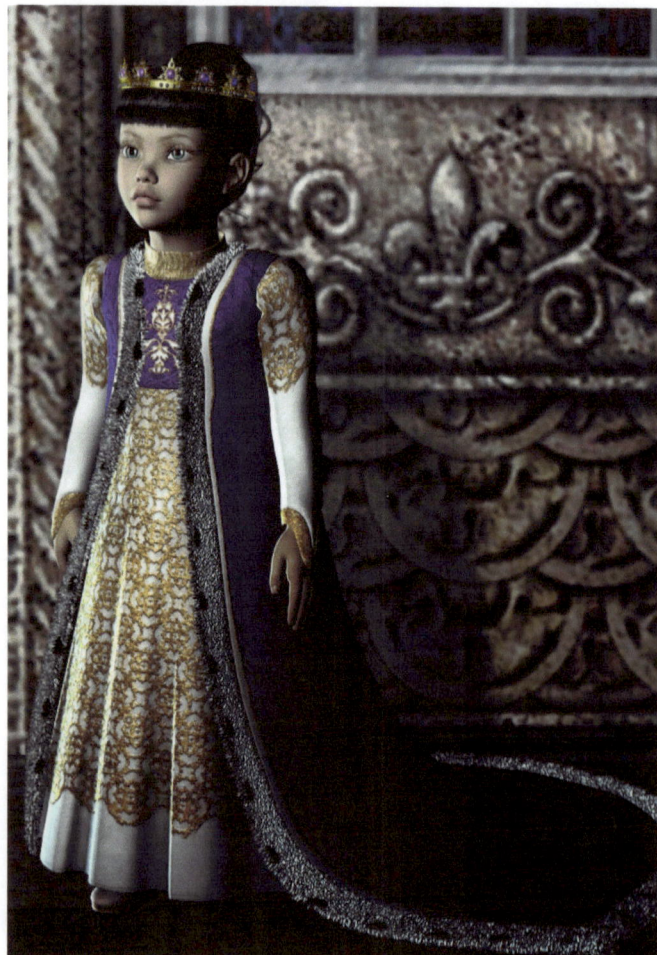

Enfanta for Kids4

By Lyrra Madril

This set contains four items of clothing, three rigged and one prop. Crowns and circlets are often best handled as props, so they can be more easily moved and scaled to adjust for headshapes and hair.

In this set both the dress and over robe have pose control handles, in addition to the extra bones in the train. The fur trim is created with a simple displacement map to simulate the look of short pile ermine.

1   The top as loaded in UVLayout. Please note the blue color means my polys are inverted, with the normal facing in not out. C4d likes doing that. I just need to remember to flip the normal in UVmapper when I'm done here. I could do it now but I'm lazy.

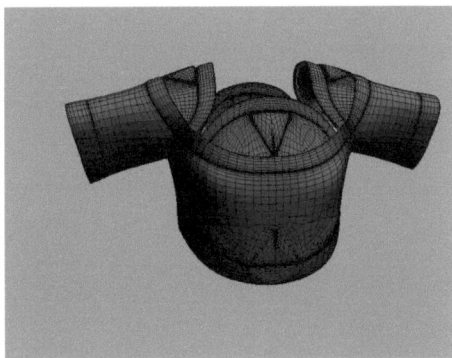

2   I've pulled the base of the top away from the inset bits. Those I use D on and Drop them to uv space so they vanish from the Edit view I'm in.

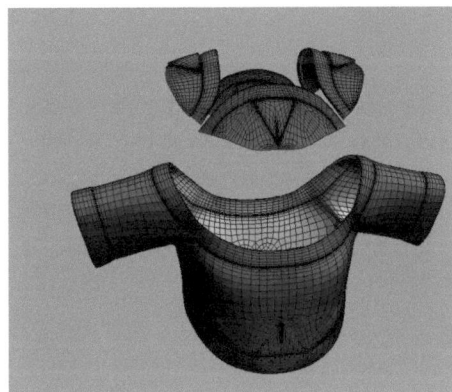

3   Using C I select a cut line up the front and back of the top. You can always weld stuff back together later and it is often easier to flatten smaller pieces of complex shapes and then reweld them.

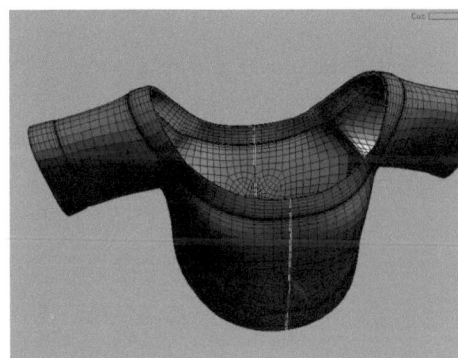

4   I hit enter to finish the cut and the two pieces pop apart.

Depending on your version, if I hadn't finished the cut the line would turn red and nothing else would happen OR the line will turn green and snip apart but the mesh would remain connected somewhere. That's when you zoom in and check along the line to find the poly you missed.

In newer versions of UVL you can make partial cuts starting at one of those hard blue edges, which can show you your problem spot right away.

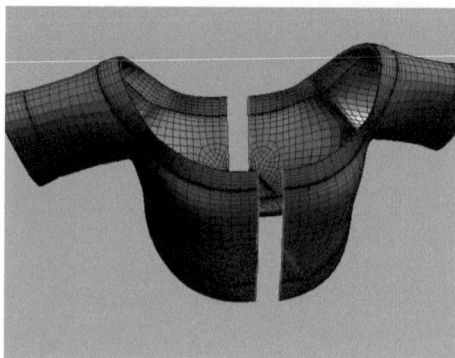

5   Here I've cut the sleeves off and along the top and bottom of the sleeve. Generally its a good idea to cut clothing along seams or where seams would go. Also, any time you can put a UV seam in a hard to see place, like the underside or back side .. do it. Your texture artist will thank you.

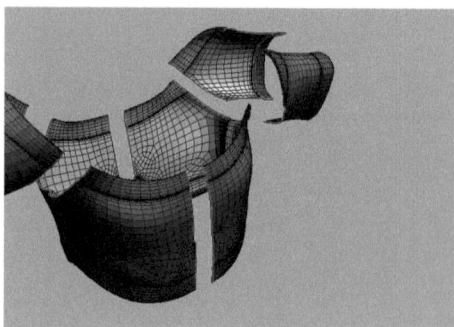

6   Continue cutting up your mesh with the other sleeve and by cutting along the side seam lines.

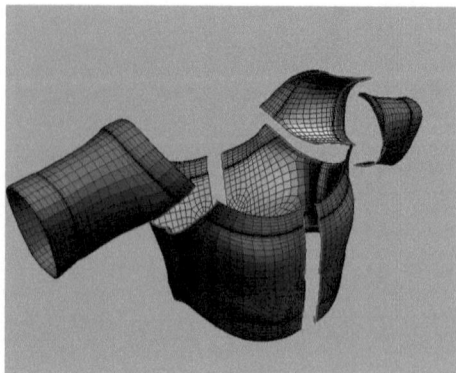

7   I've dropped all my pieces to UV space and now in uvspace I see them as white shapes. This means they haven't been flattened yet at all.

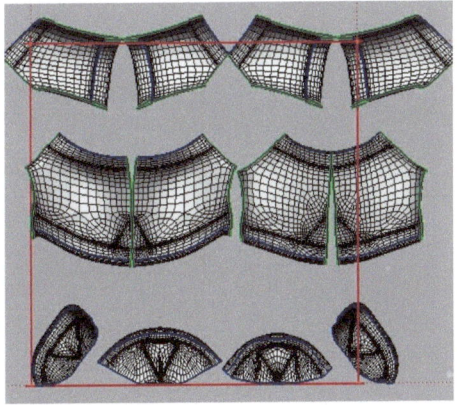

8   I click F and click and drag over the parts and hit enter to flatten them all once. Now they start showing colors.

Green is flat, red is pinched and blue is stretched.

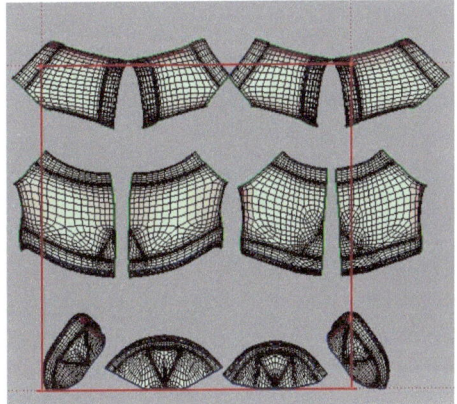

9   I hover the pointer over one part called a 'shell' by UVL and hit F again. It swells up, turns blue and starts to flatten.

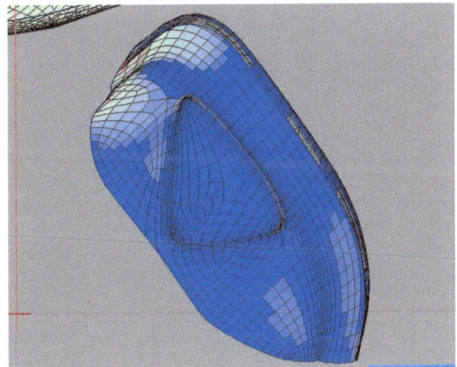

10   As I keep hitting F for flatten, you can see the mesh flatten out. Its like melting a hard plastic shell. The program uses a long complicated set of tension related algorithms to figure out how the mesh pulls on itself and so forth.

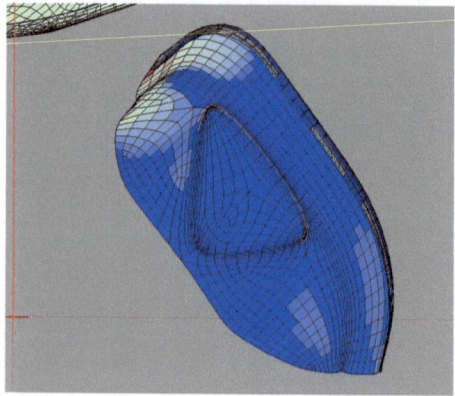

11   Yeah I don't understand it either .. but its the best uvmapping tool I've used, certainly the easiest with the best results.

What I do know is that its fun to watch optimize, and it feels an awful lot like cutting stretched fabrics under tension. If you cut into this shape and then flatten it would peel apart in much the same way as cutting a slash in a pair of spandex pants does.

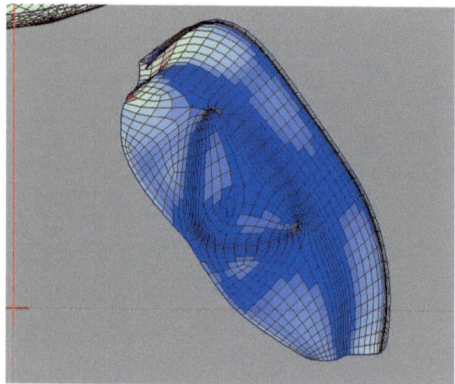

12   Hitting F again.

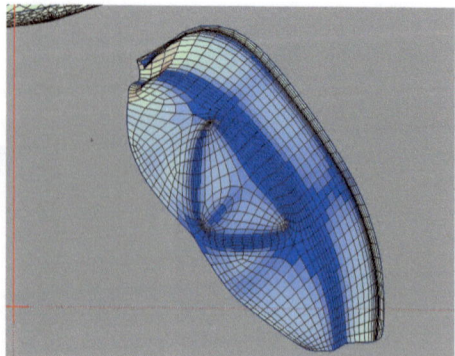

13   And again.

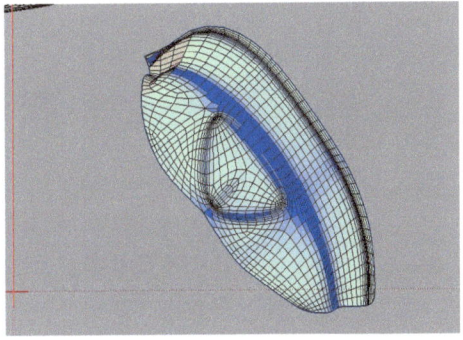

14   And again. See that red compressed area in the corner where it was curved under? Its starting to spring out into shape now. And the blue stretched part is where the indent of the seamline is.

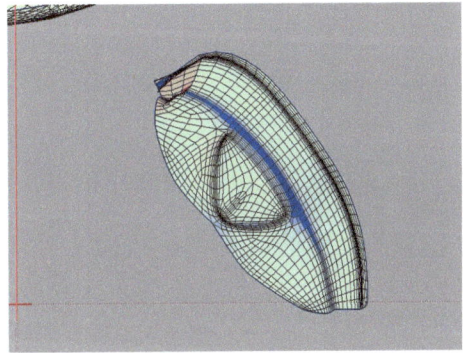

15   F again. The seamline has adjusted more but the turned corner is still working on it.

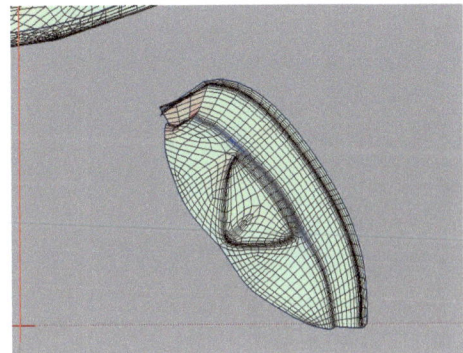

16   F again and finally that corner
pops out and you can see the distortion.

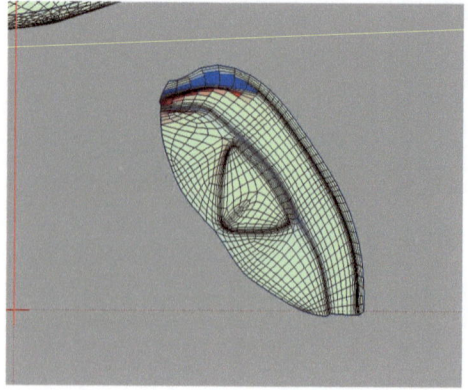

17   One more time and the corner
is much better with a little squeeze left.
The rest has sorted itself out.

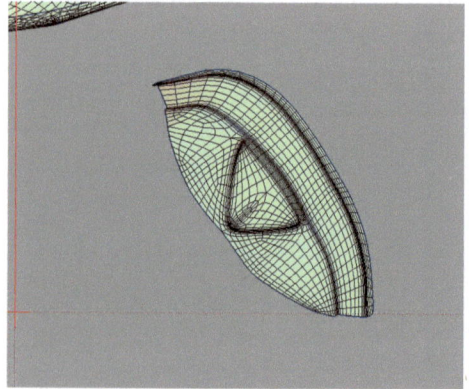

18   Pretty good! I'll be running Optimize later so this is good enough for
the moment.

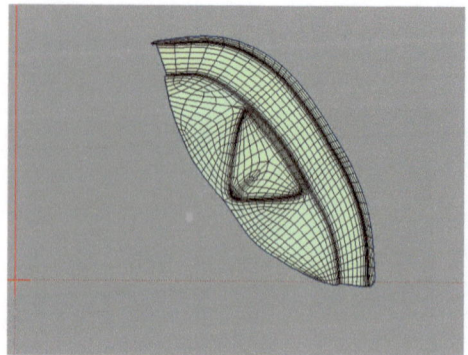

19   The one in the bottom right corner is flat. The rest still need work.

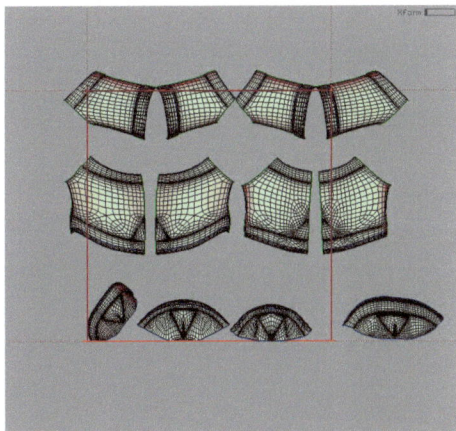

20   OK I've flattened all the parts out now.

But.

Those trim bands and insets should really be separate parts. It will make life MUCH easier for the texture artist.

On a mesh like this, with clear definition of trim bands, cutting the trim off will make it easier to color them in Photoshop.

If you aren't a texture artist yourself, go find an experienced one and ask their opinion. If a model is hard to work on nobody will support it. And support means it gets used.

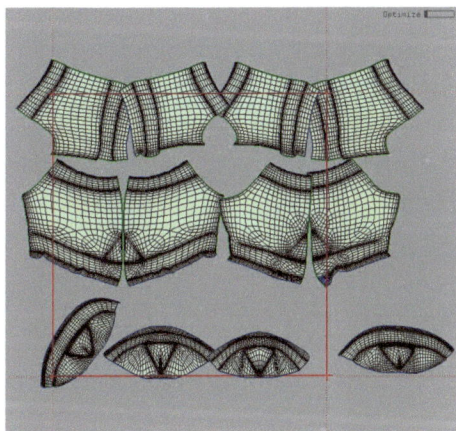

21   In 3d view I've zoomed in on the top of a sleeve. You can see the green cut line and a bit of blue stretching on the mesh.

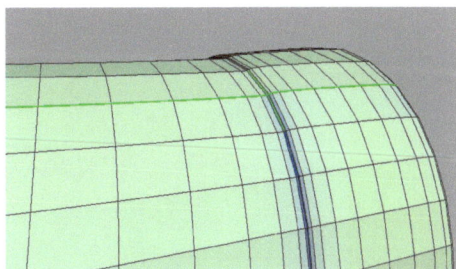

22   You can snip mesh in 3d mode, which is lovely. It's nice to see what you're doing. So I start cutting here to make sure I'm in the right place. To cut mesh you hover over the line and hit C. To weld it hit W.

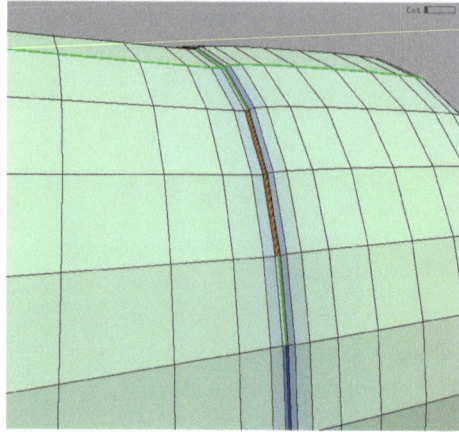

23   And then go back to uv mode to continue cutting my trim off using C.

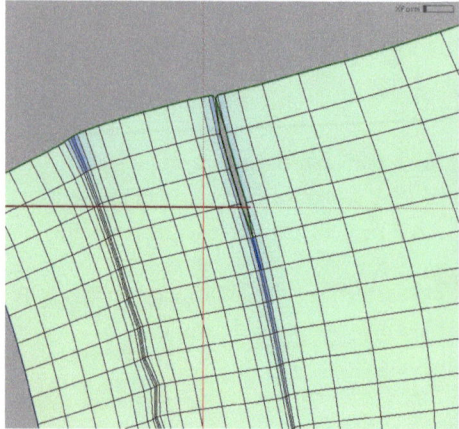

24   Here I've finished the cut and have my trim strip (and rolled under cuff) and the sleeve.

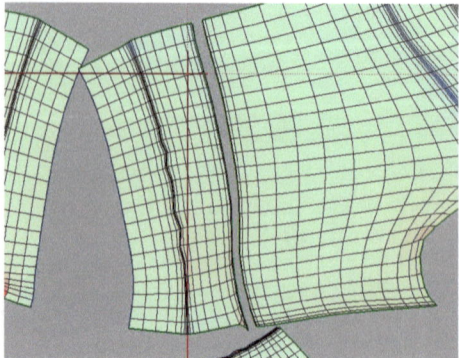

25   With a little flattening things are nice and clean.

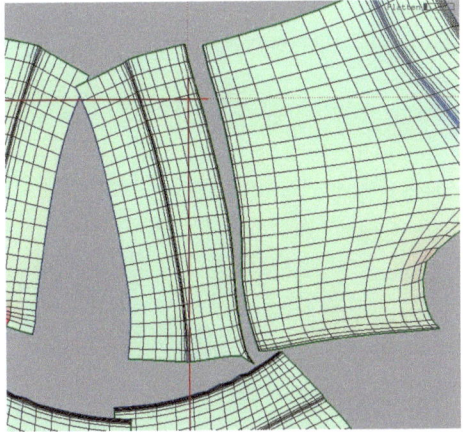

26   To make sure I cut the other half of the sleeve in the same place I use W to select the lines on either side of my cut.

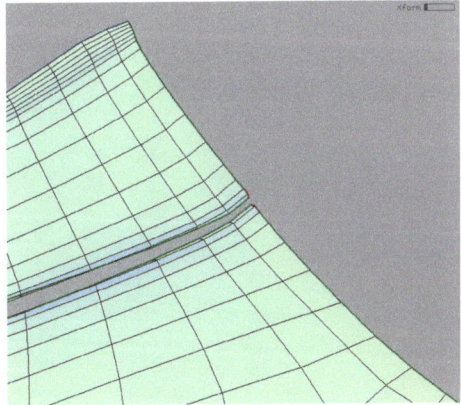

28   On the corresponding piece they also turn red, and I can continue cutting knowing that my parts will line up when I put the halves back together again.

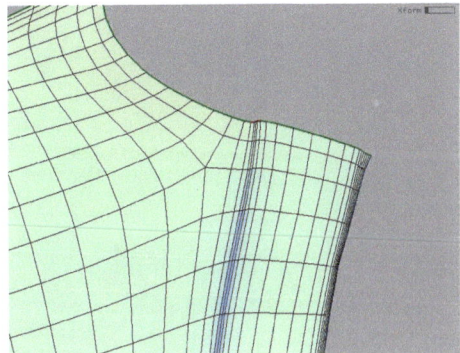

28   Here I've cut the trim bands off the sleeves and shirt body.

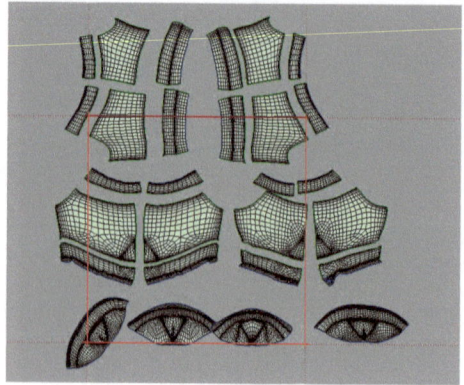

29   And now the inset triangles as well, and flatten them all again.

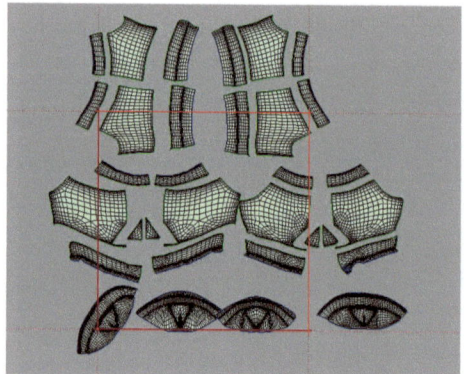

30   Now to start cutting up the half circle inset parts.

Here I've started cutting out the inset triangle by cutting at the peak and then along the sides.

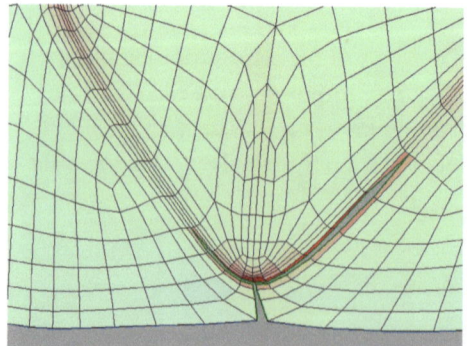

31   The open cut edge is selected.

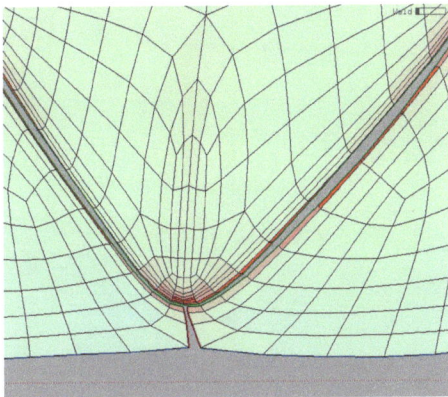

32   And then welded back together
and I continue snipping out the triangle.

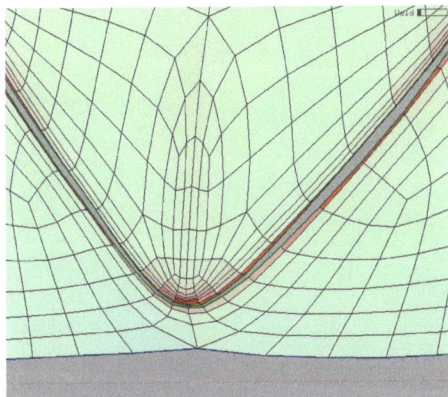

33   Here I've cut the triangle out
and snipped off the trim.

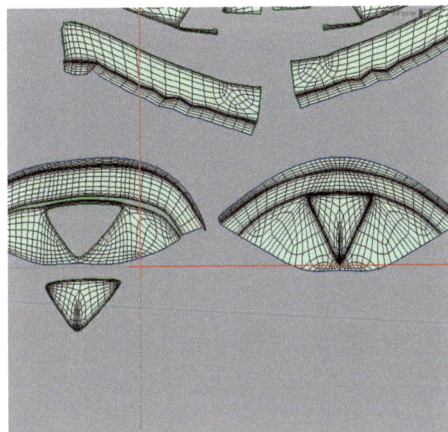

34   Everything is all cut.

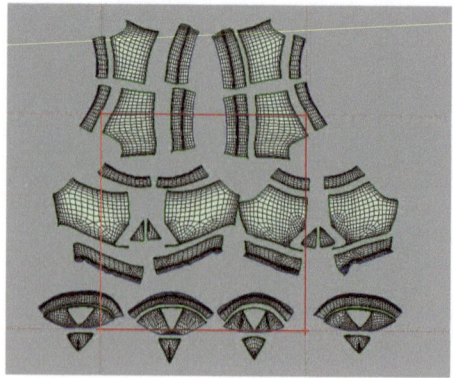

35   And flattened again.

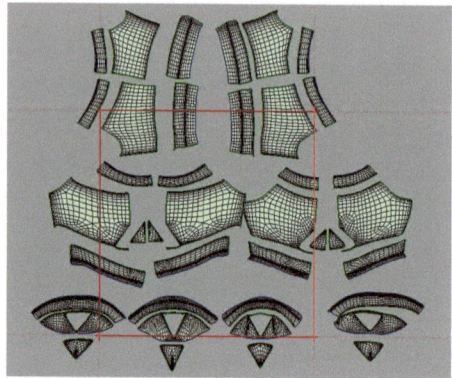

36   Now its time to put the parts
back together into the final configura-
tion. I've welded the sleeves and trim
bands so the remaining cut is underneath
the arm where it will be less noticeable,
and where a seamstress would have put
it in real life.

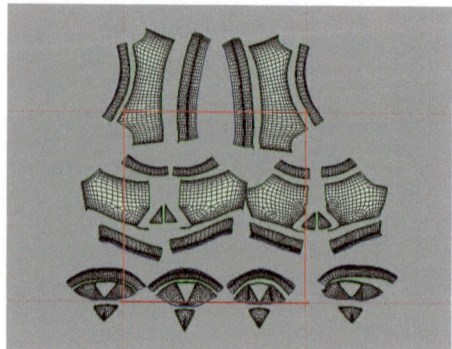

37   The main section is welded down the front, so the cuts are in the seamline I modeled along the sides.

Now I use the Optimize option, set it to run for 120 minutes and then wander off to find some tea.

Ten minutes later when I come back its all done with everything nice and flat.

I can lay out everything inside that red box here (the map space) or I can just save it , knowing I need to use UV-mapper to set the materials and invert normals anyways. So the rough part of the mapping on the top is done.

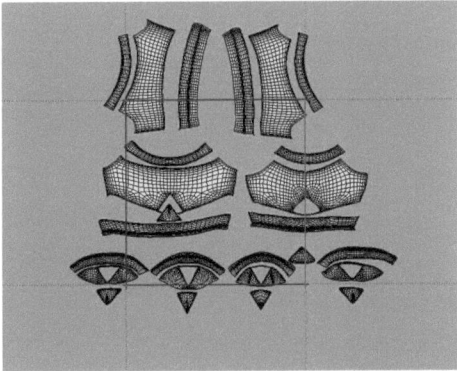

38   Now for the pants!

This one came in right way round for a change.

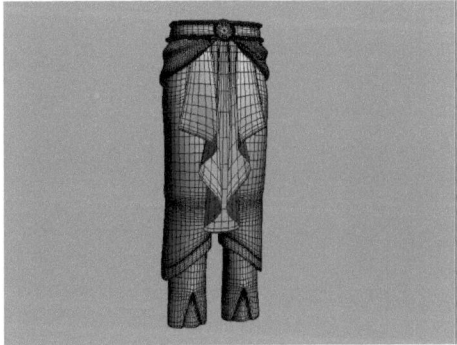

39   I've pulled my parts apart. I use D to drop all the parts that don't need cutting, leaving the pants and leg inserts.

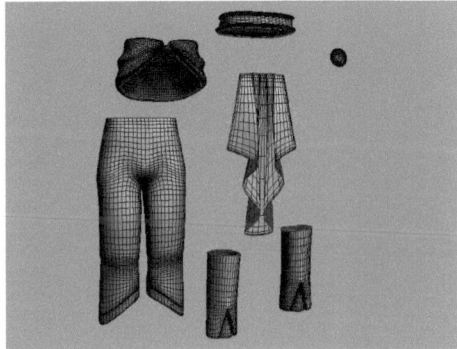

40   Now to cut the parts up starting with the inserts.

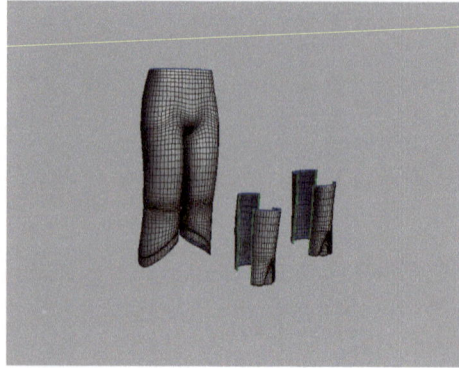

41   And now the main part cut left and right, and then again in half. That groin seam is always trouble, so regardless of how my final parts will be cut, I try to flatten them with the hip cut in four sections.

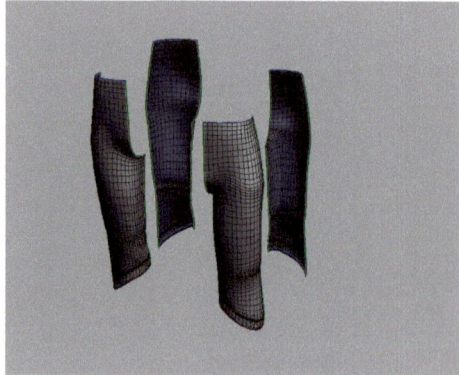

42   Everything dropped to UV space.

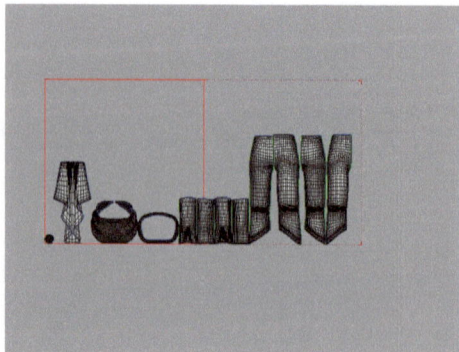

43   F, click and drag to select and then Enter to flatten.

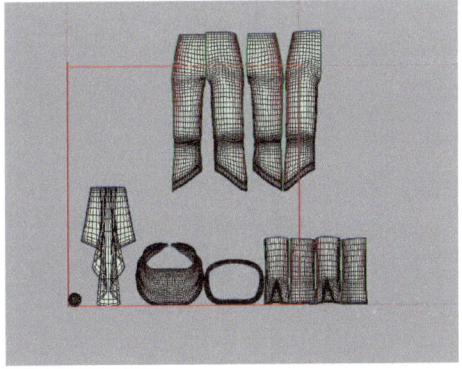

44   And then everything flattened out. See how that drape and sash have flattened out? Those should look great with a nice fabric on them. No nasty stretches.

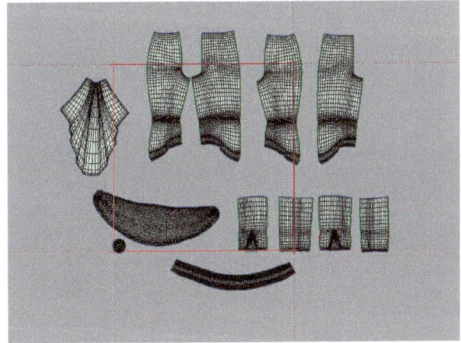

45   Trim strips cut off the pant legs.

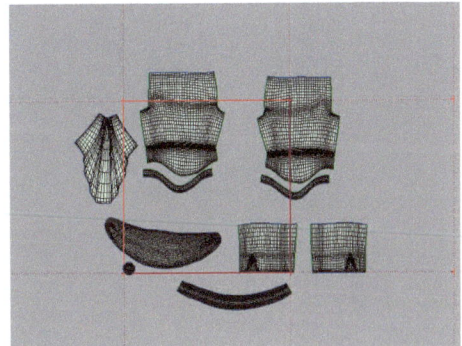

46   And the triangles cut from the insets and everything laid out in the red box.

And that is it! Now the mesh is ready for the next step, grouping

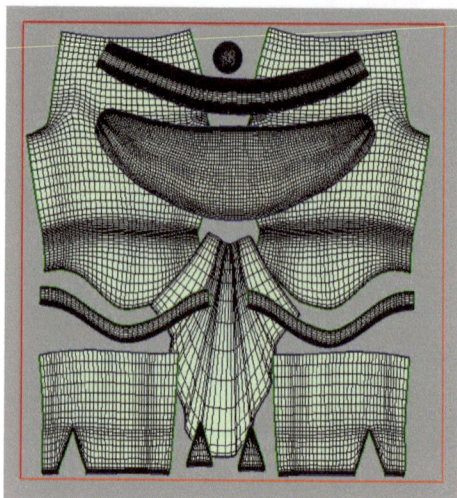

Lost Realms for Victoria4

by Mada and Thorne

Not all conforming items are clothing, although they are rigged the same way. This product contains a conforming mermaid top and jewel as well as a tail fin. Portions of the figure are hidden and with the tightly fitted tail transform Victoria into a mermaid.

The tail rigging starts with Victoria's base rigging, with multiple bones for the tail, with ez pose controls and morphs for both shaping and movement.

Chapter 2A – Uvmapping with UVmapper

Uvmapping the project mesh using UVmapper

Well what if you don't have UVLayout? One program made specifically for Poser users is UVmapper Pro. Its been a round for a while and has a free no-frills version as well as the Pro version that I use.

UVmapper is a more 'classic' uvmapping program and uses the various unwrapping methods that most do. Box, cylinder, planar and so forth. So the commands used here should be roughly similar to most other uvmapping programs and ones built into many modelers. But it is much harder to get cuts where you want them than in UVL. You will have a harder time on more complex organic shapes but UVmapper really shines on hardsurface objects like buildings.

UVmapper Pro does have a basic UV relaxing tool to flatten mesh, but the method I will show here doesn't use the relax method. It does mean more manual work for you though and is harder to get a clean result.

What is Uvmapping? Uvmapping is the process of assigning each polygon to a specific place on a flat plane so you can paint on the flat plane and have it show up in the assigned place on the model.

In general when uvmapping you want to cut apart your model keeping the following things in mind:

Make it as flat as possible with as little distortion of texture as possible.

Make as few pieces as possible.

Cut the pieces in a way to make the texturing and reduction of texture seams easier.

Cut clothing on natural cloth seams

Wistfully Yours for Aiko 3

by Ryverthorn

Although this set is for one of the generation 3 figures from DAZ, Aiko3 still has a great anime style charm enhanced by the details and bold shapes of this design. The long skirt has movement morphs and controls added to the rigging.

1   When opening my obj in UV-mapper pro this is the first error message I get. All this means is that my modeler made uv coordinates that are outside of the bounding box area UVmapper uses. I can say yes or no at this point and it hardly matters since I'll be remapping everything anyway.

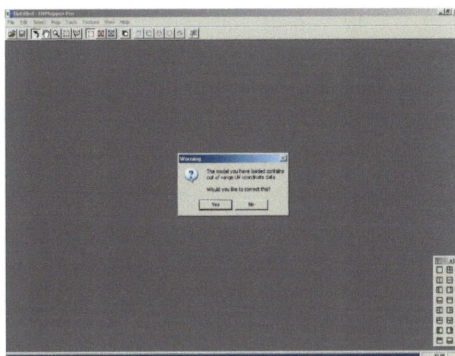

However if I say no then the uvmap will stay as it is. If I say yes everything will be squished down, disproportionately, to fit in the square.. I chose yes, since it doesn't matter at this point.

2   I almost always end up with inverted normals exporting from c4d so the next thing I do is Reverse the normals.

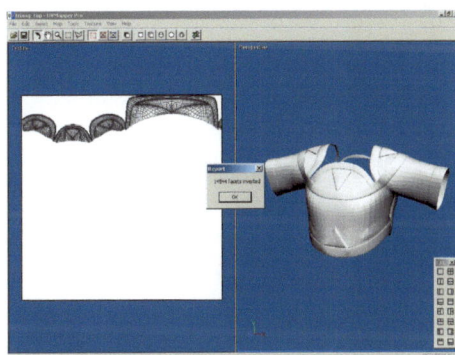

Each facet (square or polygon) has a normal pointing out from its center that tell the modeling program which way the surface is facing and so forth so it renders right. If your thing is loading in invisible in Poser, or renders black on the outside and light on the inside or your 3d preview looks weird in UVmapper... you probably have inverted normals.

3   Depending on your modeling method, and program and a host of other things you might get lucky and have some of your object come in already partly mapped.

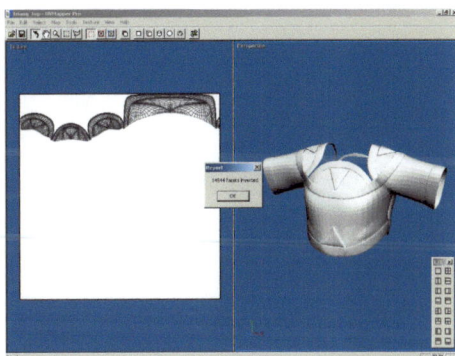

Since the shoulder pieces are partly mapped I'm going to leave them along for the time being and work on the main part of the shirt, which has no UV coordinates at all.

4   Because it has no coordinates that I can select on the map I have to select them the long way .. first I select what I do have mapped and Invert my selection. I can't see it, but now I have the shirt part selected.

First I'll do a quick map just so I have something to work with.

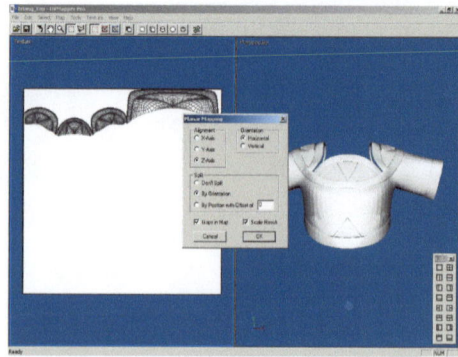

5   I use a planar map to start with. A planar map is like cutting the objects silhouette out of a sheet of paper.

I chose the Z direction, which is front and back on most Poser models. I let it split by orientation, that is to say anything facing front on one map and back on another. You can choose not to split it at all, but I find this makes it easier to grab the front and back parts.

I also chose to have it scale the result. That keeps the map proportional to other parts being mapped, and also to itself so it doesn't get stretched in one direction.

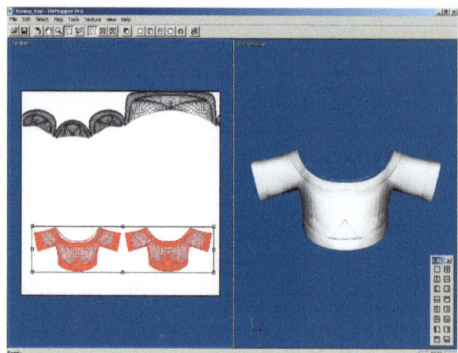

6   Well my next step is to split up the shoulder insets so I have some space in between and fix that one that got the tip lopped off.

I start by marquee selecting part of the section I want to grab.

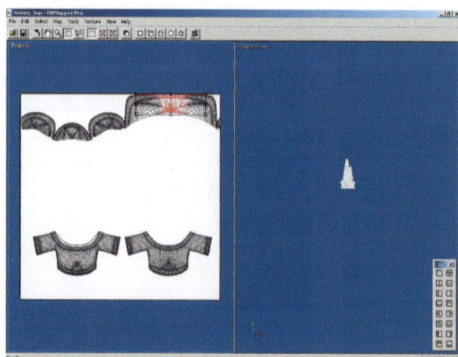

Chapter 2A –   Uvmapping with UVmapper

7   I then press the number 7 which is a shortcut to Select Connected. That selects the whole of the cut off part without having to worry about grabbing that side bit right next to it.

I can now drag it down on the map and repeat the process of moving the center shoulder tab down as well.

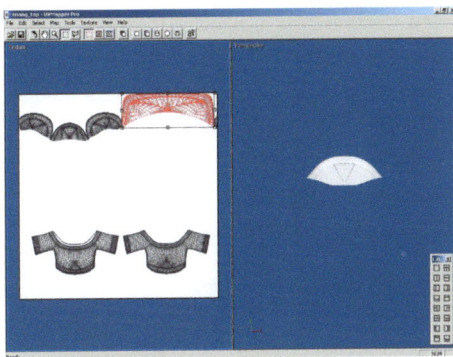

8   Now I can select and move the broken of shoulder corner and fit it to the place where it goes.

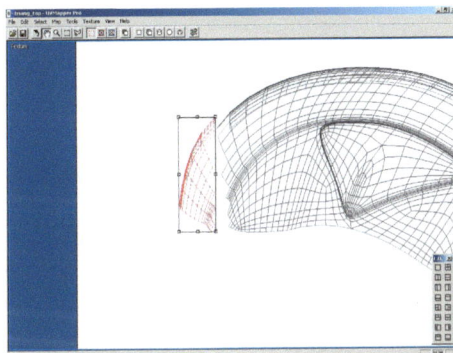

9   After roughly getting the alignment by dragging and dropping I use the arrows keys to gently nudge the selection into the place it belongs. Just like piecing together an eggshell. I'm lucky, all the points have lined up and I won't need to edit anything dot by dot.

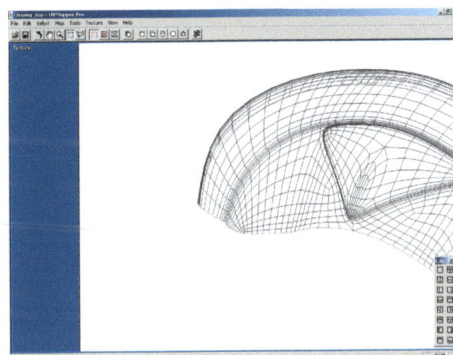

10   Ok now to check it with the built in checkerboard texture. Sometime I find it helpful to expand the size of the clothing map outside the bounding box so I can see smaller checkers on it and therefor a better idea of how the map is distorting.

This is the front.

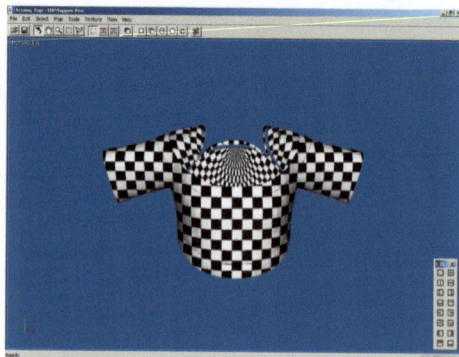

11   And the back.

The shoulder tabs seem ok, but the front and back tabs have this weird polar distortion thing. That is going to have to be fixed.

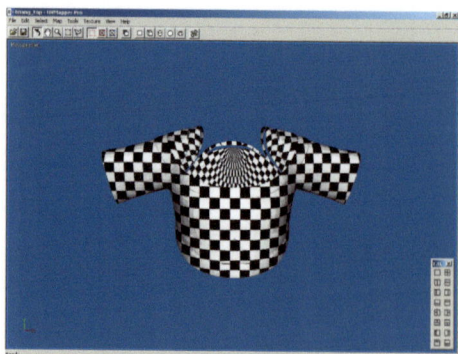

12   And the side. The side is really ugly. You can see all that stretching at the sides and under the arms. You can try relaxing this, but I find there is another method that gets fairly good results.

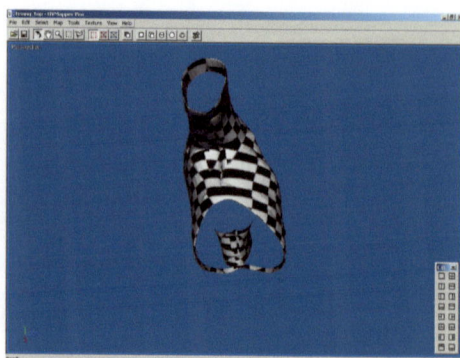

13   I start with the easy part ... I planar map the front tab on Z, using the same settings I had on the shirt but NO split. That gets it nice and even with no weird distortion. Same thing on the back tab.

It does mean any turned under seams will repeat the map since they overlay and double back on themselves.

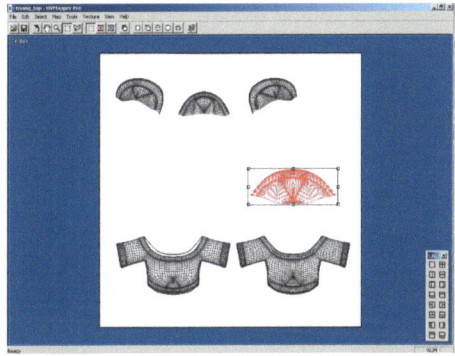

14   Now to carefully rip the sleeves off the shirt .

I have a modeled seamline to divide by so after carefully selecting and deselecting polys I can pull the sleeve right off.

I need to get all 4 parts off so I can remap each sleeve (left and right) separately.

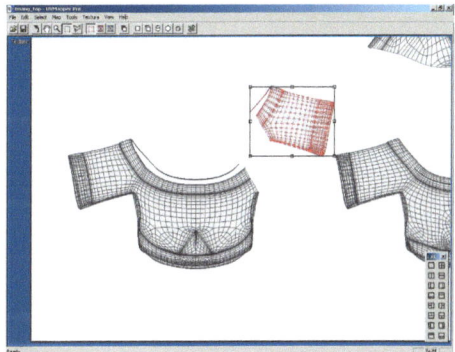

15   Ok now that I have the sleeves nipped off I select one side, by selecting the two parts. I'm dyslexic so sometimes it takes me a minute to get the right bits.

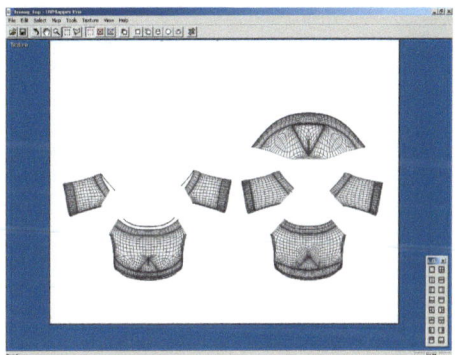

16   Now for the trick ... I'm going to cylinder map the sleeve. I choose X, so its going to approach the sleeve like it is a tube on its side and cut it the long way to unroll it. I choose scale results again to keep it proportional.

Cylinder cap could be used if the sleeve was very thick or had an edge like armor plates. CylCap mapping cuts it open like a tin can, popping the two ends off and slits it the long way to unroll it.

17   Now for the main body of the shirt. If you look at what I had left after the sleeves were taken off you would see that there was this thin rim of loose polys on both front and back sections. That happened because of my rolled over edge .. UVmapper isn't that bright and so when it was Z planar mapped everything facing front ended up on the one side, even if it really belonged to the back.

So to make life easier I select the shirt section and planar map it on Y (up and down) to give me a birds eye view. Now I select just the front. Or possibly back. Hard to say really.

18   Here I've mapped one side and started the next. I could planar map it on Z with no separation, but that would still give me that nasty side distortion.

So instead I cylinder map it again, this time on Y and scale the result.

Chapter 2A –   Uvmapping with UVmapper

19   Checking it now with the checkerboard and you can see the improvement. The front tabs are nice and flat with no distortion.

I adjust the size of all the pieces so that all the checkers are the same size. This means if I apply say a polka dot patten to the whole thing it will all come out the same size, and not have different sized dots in different parts.

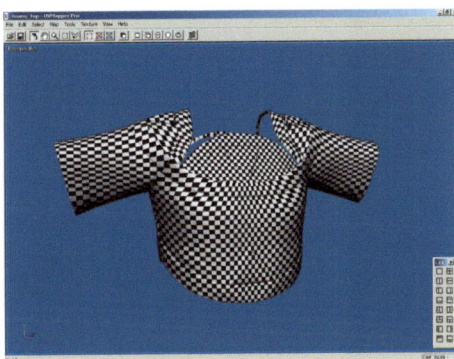

20   Here on the side you can see the difference on the seam areas. There is still some distortion, but its nowhere near as bad is it was.

If you are a perfectionist you can try adjusting this manually or use the relax tool if you have it. But this is pretty good.

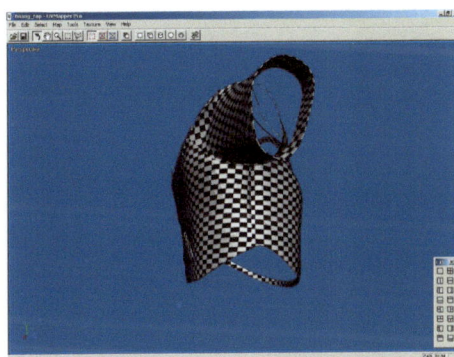

21   The final map all fitted nicely inside the bounding box. I've turned the sleeves so the fabric grain matches the main garment. I find the little things like matching direction and size really make a difference when you get to the texturing.

In theory if you had the patience you could pull all the trim parts off the shirt and in fact in order to set the trim Material zone you may have to.

Now on to grouping.

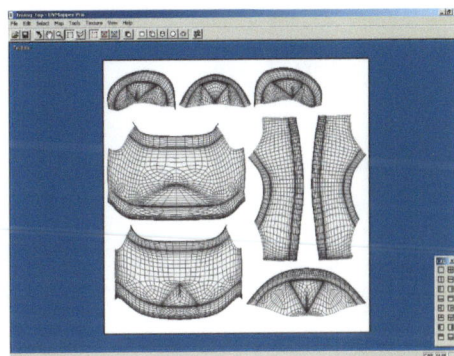

Chapter 2A –   Uvmapping with UVmapper

Chapter 3 – Making a Base Conformer

Preparing a copy of your destination figure file to be a rigging donor.

In order to rig for Poser, and to do some other operations, you will need a donor or Base Conformer.

A base conformer is also known as the donor rig, donor skeleton and so forth. This is a cr2 based on the figure, or a clothing item like a bodysuit that contains only the rigging needed to use as a starter for a new clothing item. When you are making a base conformer there are a few simple things you need to keep in mind.

You can use the figure itself, but it will contain a fair amount of non relevant junk that was made for the original figure which you don't need cluttering up the new items of clothing. Also, Inverse Kinematics if on, will make shoes impossible to fit. You can clean up much of this later, but the IK will cause you much grief, so its best to start with a clean file if you can.

Note: most 'developers kits' for a figure have some sort of donor rig in them

If you do not have either of the programs mentioned in this chapter you can do most of the necessary work directly in Poser, or with another comparable utility program..

IMPORTANT

Zero IK.

Remove all Morph groups.

Remove all Morph Data.

Remove all Deformer channels and objects.

Remove all Contoller Channels in the Body object.

Teksuit for Victoria4

By Lyrra Madril

Most of the visual appeal of this outfit comes from the shaders applied to the two layers of tight suit as well as the translucent tubing. What you don't see, are the more than 300 morphs to fit it to Victoria's various morph packages as well as joint correction morphs.

1   First load the figure you intend
to make into a Base Conformer.

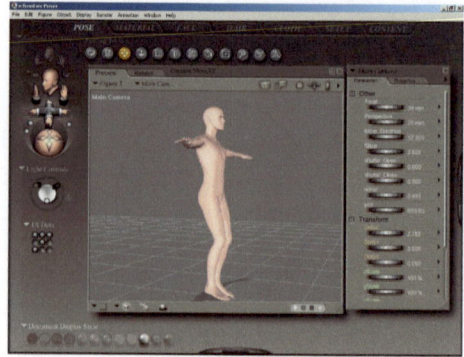

2   Turn off Inverse Kinematics for
all parts that have it.

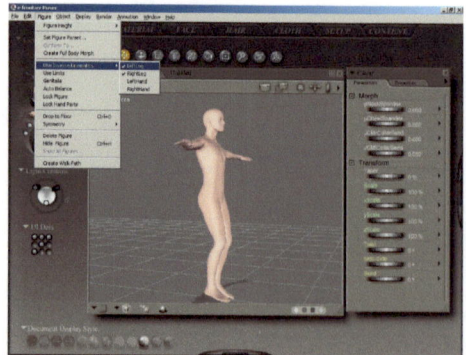

3   Use the Joint Editor window
to Zero Figure. Also make sure there is
zero trans or scale on Hip or Body.

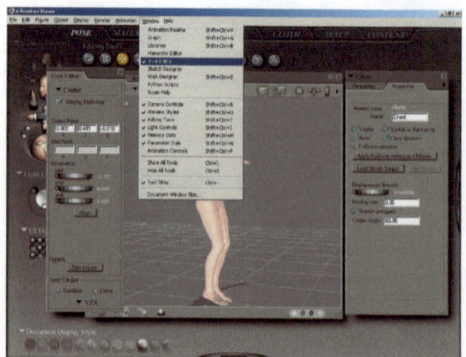

4   As you can see the figure is now zeroed. Now save this into your Poser content library as a new figure. I always use the figure's name and BC so I know this is my donor. I keep mine in a certain folder since I have one for every figure I've ever made conforming clothes for.

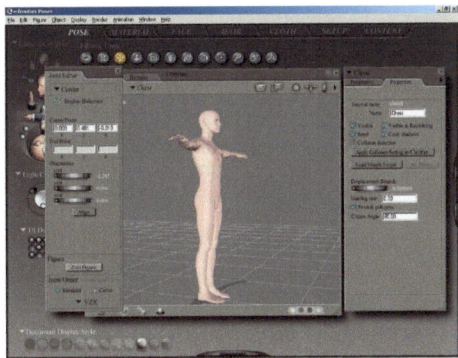

5   The Next step is stripping out the Morphs, deformers if any, Body FBM dials, Morph Groups, and Materials.

I use Poser File Editor which has advanced filtering to help you do all of that very quickly. Here is a side beside after I've cleaned out the morphs from one part.

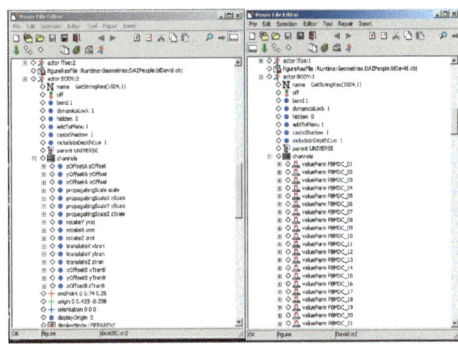

This is also a good time to make sure all your parts have x y and z scale option dials visible (hidden 0). Some figures have these hidden, but they are very handy for the end user to fitting and adjusting clothing later.

The Materials are in the Figure section all the way at the bottom of the cr2, in case you need to check them.

At this time you can also remove bodyparts such as hands and head if you will never use them. I tend to leave that for after the rigging, since adding them back in is much more annoying than deleting them.

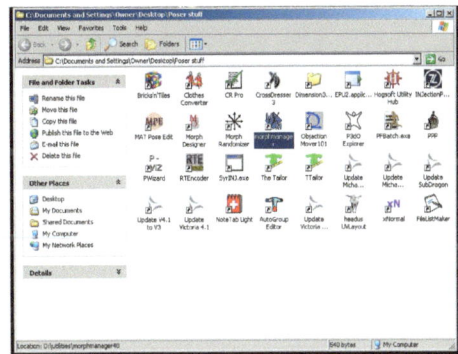

6   An other method to remove morphs from your donor is to use a very old utility called Morph Manager. At the time of writing this is still available out there.

Chapter 3 –   Making a Base Conformer

7   Load your figure in and on each bodypart, right click and select Delete all morphs. Then when you are done save the file.

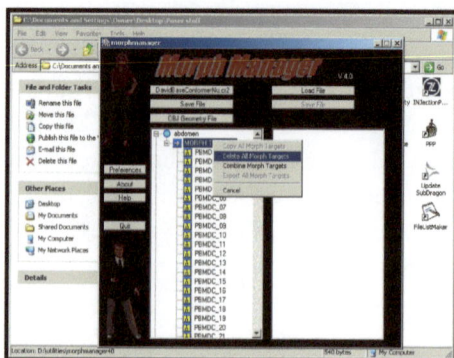

The Birthday Gift

Render by Seeker

Ballet Suit Mimi by BAT for the BallJoint Doll

Textures by Seeker

Chapter 3 –   Making a Base Conformer

Chapter 4 –   Grouping

This chapter covers grouping the model into bodypart areas, which are necessary for Poser's rigging methods. This chapter uses a program called Auto Group Editor, there is a second chapter using Poser's own grouping tools.

Now we start the process of making the clothing movable in Poser, otherwise known as rigging.

In most other 3d programs, the figure exists as a mesh and a skeleton, which are attached to each other by means of weightmaps and so forth. Poser does not do this.

Poser looks at each figure as a collection of bodyparts, defined by groups, and welded together on the fly. The rigging therefor is an hierarchy of bones having the same name as the groups. Various weld and bend statements help the whole thing move and flex. Poser does have weightmaps in more recent versions, but they are added on top of the existing legacy Poser rigging system and do not replace it.

As you can see this is a strange idea if you come from the background of mesh and skeleton as separate entities. There is absolutely no difference in Poser between human skeletons, clothings, animals, or even furniture. Poser sees it merely as an articulated bunch of parts, so what it is shaped like is fairly irrelevant as long as the basic rules of Poser rigging are followed.

Now this book is specifically focused on Poser clothing which by and large are "conformers". That is to say they are a special group of rigged figures which can be slaved to a base figure so that when the figure bends, the clothing bends. In order to do this the clothing must have exactly the same rigging as the figure as far as part names and structure goes. For this reason each clothing item must be made to match the figure it will be used on, both in shape and in rigging. In converting clothing to a new figure the shape, the groups and the rigging must all be adjusted to the new figure.

So our first step in making a conformer is to match the groups of the item to the figure so the donated skeleton will match up. In order to do this we need to assign all the polys into bodypart groups. These groups need to match the general location of the figure they will overlay and must have the EXACT same name as the figures groups.

Poser has some rules that must be followed in order for everything to move and bend as they are meant to. These are not guidelines, they are constraints of the program and if you ignore them your model will not work properly.

Rule 1 : Names matter

In Poser capital letters are considered different from lower case so that lFoot is not the same as Lfoot.

Poser has a Symmetry function, and you can use this to mirror not just poses but joint parameter settings. However if you do use this the names must follow Poser's naming conventions. One letter prefix l or r and then the name of the part. So, lFoot and rFoot is good but NOT leftfoot or rightfoot. Poser looks at that first letter and treats the rest as the bodypart name. Since eftfoot is not the same as ightfoot they will not mirror, and really the less work you have to repeat the happier you will be.

Conformers MUST have the same bodypart names as the donor figure or the conforming process will not work correctly. In general the donor will be named properly already.

Rule 2: Children cannot touch

Poser is based on a hierarchy. One bodypart coming from another is a Child part. If a Parent bodypart has two or more children the children parts CANNOT touch or the mesh will break there. This means specifically in the case of trousers, that the rThigh and lThigh cannot touch. You must ALWAYS have a strip of Hip polygons between them. This is true for any parent with several child parts, but trousers are the most common issue.

There are a few utilities that can group Poser items, and many creators use their modeling program. I usually use a utility program called AutoGroup Editor, but you can group mesh directly in Poser or UVmapper and in many modeling programs.

Grouping With Auto Group Editor

Although you make the model as all one surface, when a rigged figure is loaded into Poser each part is handled as a separate mesh that is welded (via statements in the cr2) to its neighboring parts. For this reason every conforming clothing item must be grouped to reflect its parent figure so its bodyparts can follow along with the figures bodyparts.

The match need not be exact, and indeed, with experience you will gain a feel for how much you can stray from the base figure grouping.

In general though, do try to match body part seams. I often prefer to keep part edges as straight lines, since being able to simply turn off a part and have a short rather than long sleeved shirt for example can be helpful.

1   Well the first step in Auto
Group Editor is to load the source
figure. In our case that is David. And
here he is in lovely multicolored glory.
Each group comes in a different color so
generally its easy to tell whats what.

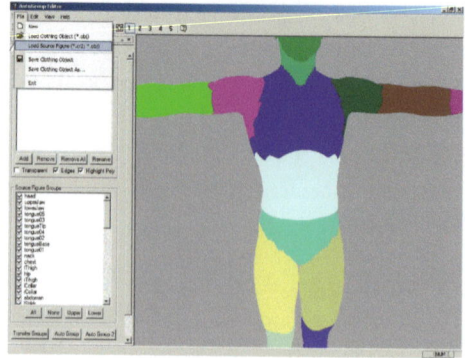

2   And now I've loaded the first
clothing object, the shirt. As you can see
the parts came in as different groups but
that doesn't really matter.

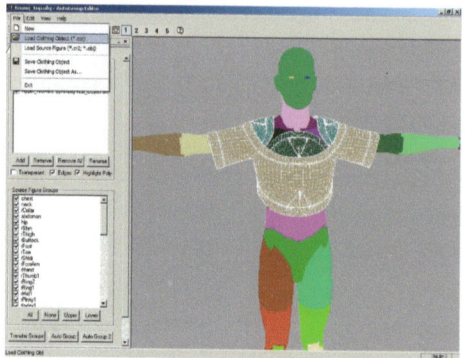

3   Next step is turning off all the
parts of David I don't need. AGE works
by checking each clothing poly against
the closest figure poly. So to keep things
simple, and cut down the possibility of
the program getting confused, you turn
off the parts you don't need.

In this case I need the chest, collars and
shoulders.

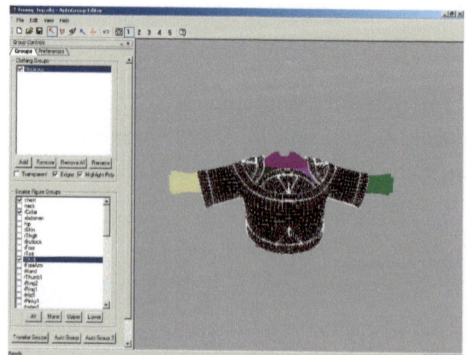

Chapter 4 –   Grouping

4   Now I hit Auto Group 2 down at the bottom of the screen and wait for a minute.

AutoGroup one makes 'softer' groups and 2 makes 'harder' groups based more closely on each poly.

Now if your mesh is denser than mine you will find that this stage and the next few is an amazing nuisance, but unavoidable.

Remember how I said way back when that too many polys is as bad as too few? This is part of why.

5   I have found that you get cleaner morphs and movement if you have clean bodypart cuts. I prefer a straight line or a simple stair-step angle. You need to follow the shape of the bodypart group underneath, but there is some leeway.

So I'm going to clear up the end of the purple and green rCollar and lCollar and make sure there is plenty of Chest group separating the two collars, which are child parts. Child parts cannot touch, they will not weld.

6   And the final grouping on the shirt.

After I rig I may find I have to come back and regroup. I may even decide to go all the way back to the mesh, which as you can see is a terrible nuisance, but sometimes there is no other way to solve a problem.

Never be afraid to rework your mesh to work better, in the long run it is worth the work.

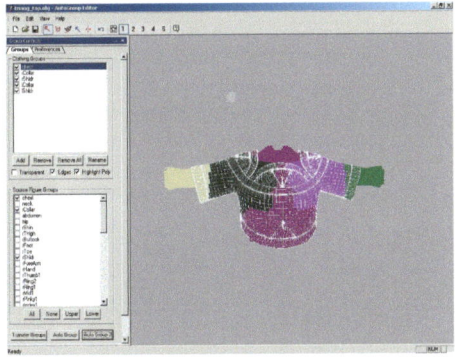

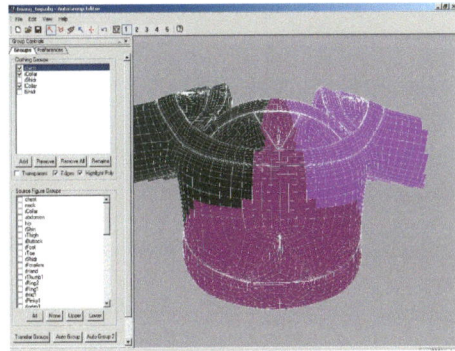

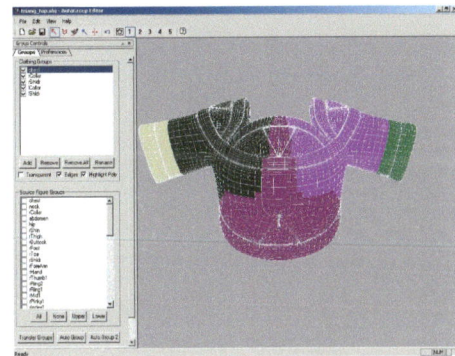

7   So now for the pants. Its pretty much the same as the shirt, but that sash will need special handling.

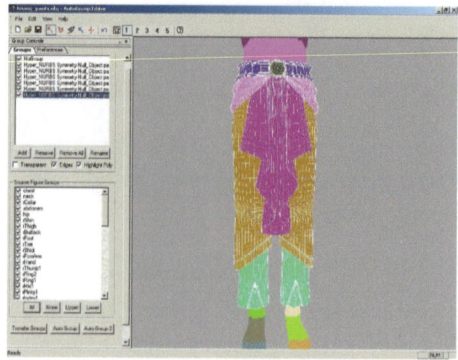

8   Turn off the parts of David not directly near the clothing. And I use Remove all to strip out the current groups from the pants item.

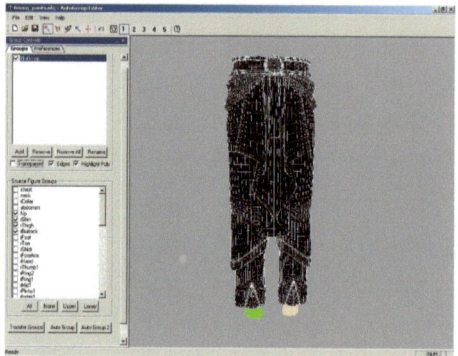

9   Now Autogroup2. You can see the sash gets divided up just like the rest of the mesh.

Now I save the clothing obj .....

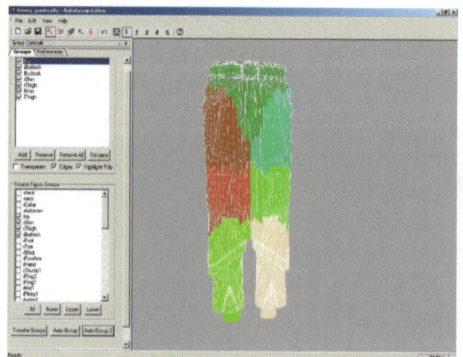

10   And open that saved obj in UVmapper. I select the sash and create a new group 'sash' and save again.

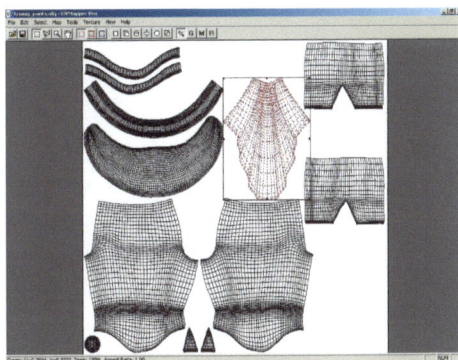

11   Back in AGE, I load the clothing mesh again and you can see the sash has its own group. Now I can turn it off and tidy up the rest of the mesh

Yes I could have done that in AGE. But why? UV Mapper was so much faster than trying to grab each sash poly by hand in AGE. Sometimes a whole different program has one tool that will make your life easier. And really nobody is grading you on how you do this, just the end result. So do what works.

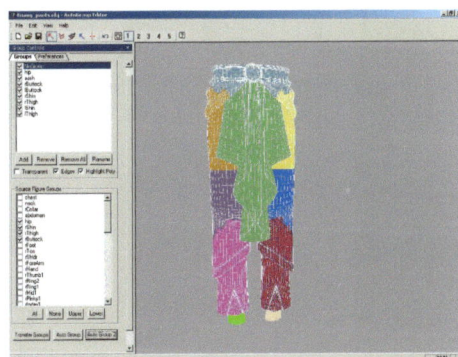

12   This is the most important part. Getting that slice of Hip separating the l and r buttock parts. I find its easiest to turn off one side so I can see the groin mesh easier.

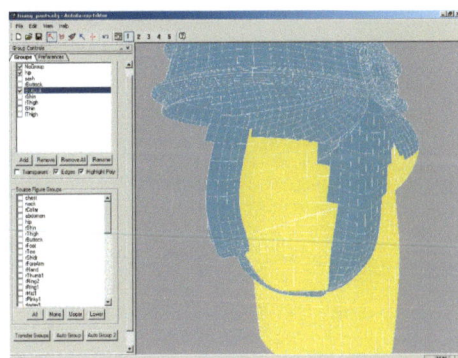

13   And here the pants mesh is all grouped and I straightened up the shin groups as well.

One of the ways a user can modify clothing for fit or style is by turning off parts, so that's another good reason to keep nice straight edges when you can.

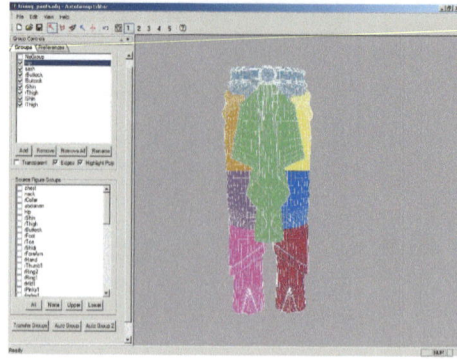

Hakama and Kimono for Victoria 4

By Lyrra Madril

The kimono sets proved to be very difficult to rig. The skirt was handled using several skirt handles and some additional morphs for kneeling and drape adjustments. The sleeves needed to be very carefully grouped, and have additional bones and morphs for movement and fixes. The hakama layers over the kimono, and also has the same complex rigging handles as well as movement morphs. I'm still not entirely satisfied with the motion on this set, but working within the limits of conforming clothing it was the best I could do at the time.

Chapter 4A – Grouping in Poser

It is possible to group mesh in Poser, as well as use its

automatic grouping

Well what if you don't have Auto Group Editor?

Well you can use Poser's grouping, but I recommend a mix of it and UVmapper. Frankly Posers grouping tool is like picking up greased marbles with chopsticks. You can, but you soon wish you hadn't. UVmapper will make the screamingly impossible bits a little easier and leave most of your hair intact.

You might be able to group your mesh directly in your modeling program as well.

Wild Hunt: Wildenlander for Michael 3

By Luthbel

Inspired by game design as well as costume design from films like Lord of The Rings, this outfit for Michael 3 was created with great attention to detail. The hood, cloak and sword-belt all have custom rigging for movement and adjustment.

Chapter 4A –   Grouping in Poser

1   To group in Poser first you will need to load your base, or donor, figure. Poser will be using this as a reference for creating the groups.

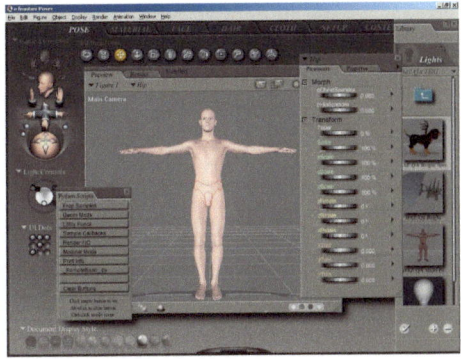

2   However, most figures load in with IK (inverse kinematics on) and not in exactly its zero or geometry, position. This is not helpful for you.

So the first step is to turn off IK on arms and legs.

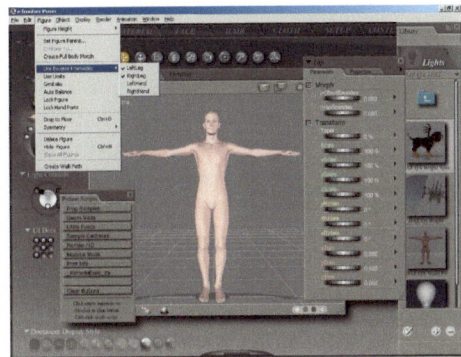

3   As you can see from a side view David is kind of scrunched down with his legs bent. And as we know from the first section (remember that? The fun part?) his legs are straight.

So turn on the Joint Editor, select any part of the figure and use the Zero Figure button.

Also, check Body to make sure there is no Y translation, and Hip.

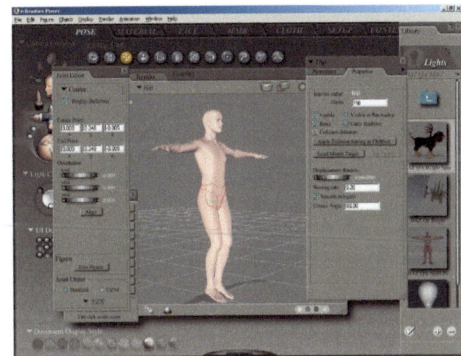

4   and here he is properly zeroed
out with no trans or anything. Now is
a good time to Memorize figure if you
want to. You could also save this is a
zero pose file to use again later on this
figure.

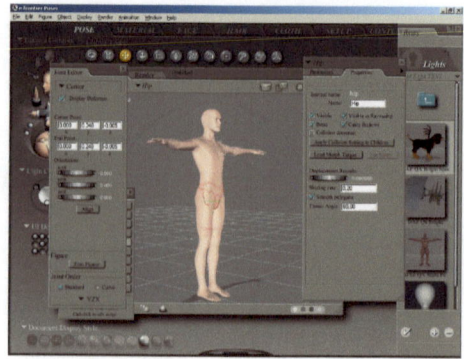

5   Import your clothing mesh as
a static prop. You want to turn off all
the checkboxes. This will make sure it
doesn't get moved, resized, renamed or
anything odd.

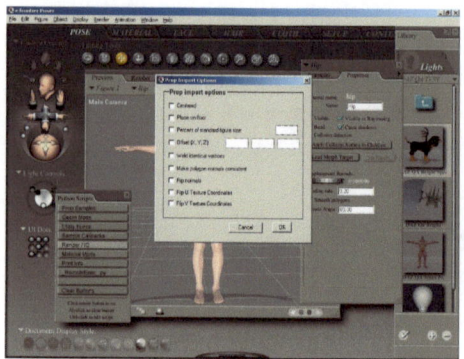

6   After your object has been loaded you want to...

**Wait FIRST save. The Poser setup
room isn't the most stable of things.
For one thing Undo doesn't work
well if at all.**

Ok NOW enter the Setup room and say
OK to this box.

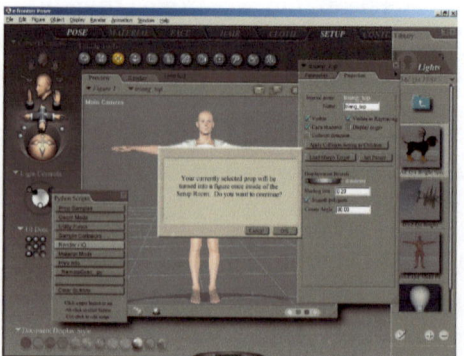

7   You will first see the shirt hanging in space.

Now go to your donor figure in the Library to pick up the rigging. No really, we need to add rigging to get to the next part. Its ok.

You can see on the side I selected my DavidBC (base Conformer) file that I made a while ago.

You can use the base figure as donor, but generally its a bad idea. Please read the section on Making a Base Conformer starting page 64.

8   Now turn on the Poser Group tool. Thats the square box with the dot in the middle. It will pop up a new interface window.

The selected group is bright red. Anything unselected will be dark gray.

Now to let Poser define the groups automatically, click the AutoGroup button at the bottom of the group interface,

9   As you can see now the groups list has expanded and the groups have been defined. And they are a mess generally.

But this is all we want Poser to do. You can try manually editing the groups with the selection tool but I find it much much easier to tidy this up in UVmapper, as well as fix a small problem this method introduces (that apparently causes serious issues in DAZ studio with smoothing).

Chapter 4A –   Grouping in Poser

10   Now to export the mesh to
fiddle it in UV Mapper. Use File Export,
as Wavefront OBJ format.

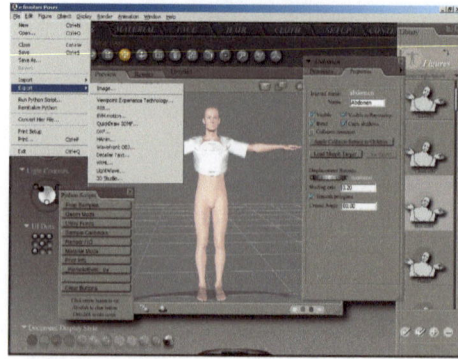

11   In the Hierarchy window
deselect everything and select just the
clothing item (and all its parts).

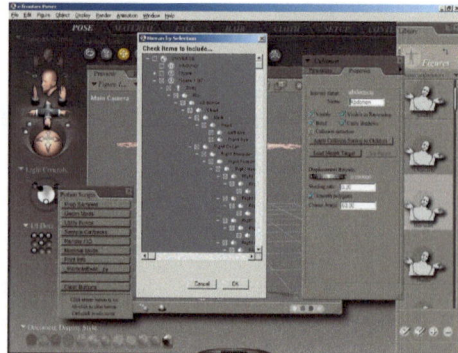

12   Now here you want JUST the
Include existing groups box ticked.

You can click Weld bodypart seams,
though I chose not, so I could show you
in UV Mapper the issue it causes.

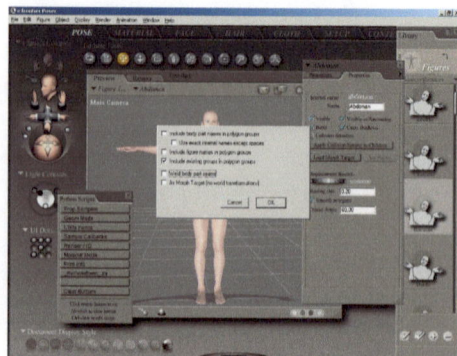

13   And here I've opened it in UV-mapper. As you can see its very ragged and messy.

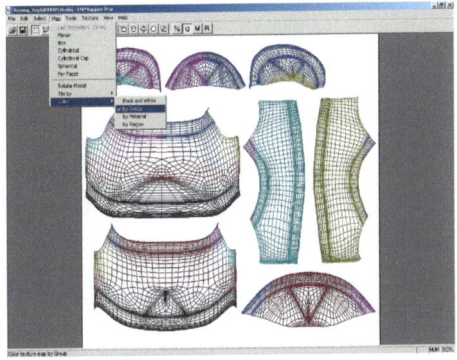

14   Also, when Poser autogroups an item and during various other Poser operations, the bodypart seams come unwelded. Poser doesn't much care, but OBJ for morphs are affected and apparently it also causes mesh tearing and ragged smoothing issues in DAZ Studio.

So its generally a good idea to weld BodyPart seams when exporting from Poser.

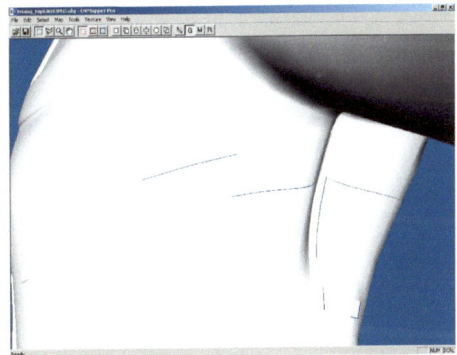

UV Mapper has a Weld Vertice option which also fixes this. If you use this after making morphs, all your morphs will be broken.

15   Here is the end result after I have cleaned up the bodypart groupings. I used the ones Poser created as a guide, but UV Mapper's selection tools are much simpler to use than Poser's group tool.

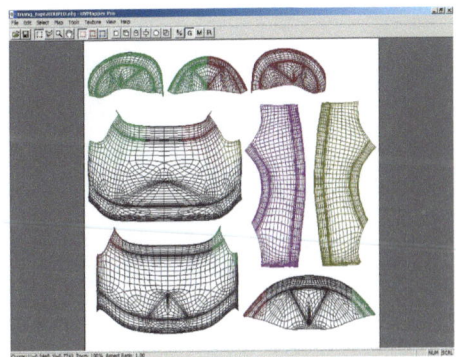

16   Here I've re imported the mesh. See those red lines? Thats where Poser broke the mesh apart on the previous bodypart seams.

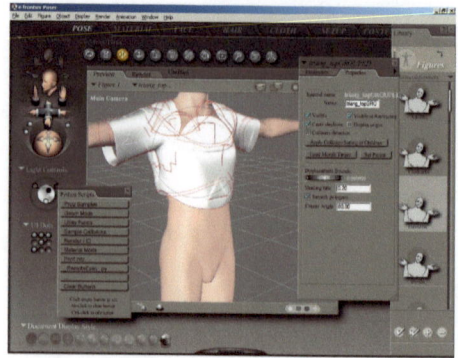

Thankfully the fix is simple.

17   Select and export the shirt again ....

18   .... but this time with the seams welded. And that's that for the Poser grouping.

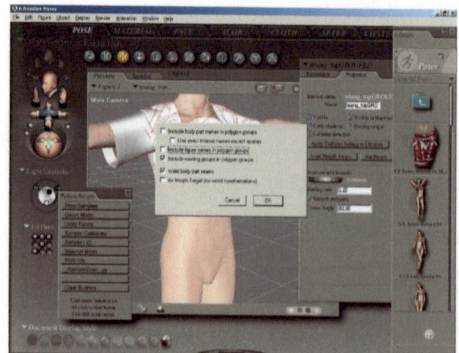

Chapter 5 – Setting Materials in UVM

Material zones dictate which surface settings get applied

to which areas of the mesh

When you apply surface settings or shaders to any item in Poser you are limited by your material zones. Each zone can be given a different shader or set of attributes. For this reason it can be a good idea to carefully plan your material zones ahead of time.

A well made body suit with carefully thought out material zones can be used for a multitude of clothing items.

I show how to use UVmapper to set Material zones, but most modeling programs can set material zones as well.

RULES

Each polygon must belong to at least one material zone.

Each polygon can ONLY belong to one material zone.

Use simple and obvious names , using only the regular English (roman) ASCII character set. Special characters and other language characters may confuse Poser and your end users.

Pumpkin Avenue for Victoria 4

By Mada, Sarsa and Thorne

This whimsical set for Victoria 4 includes several thematic props. Shown here is the Base prop with one of the included textures sets. Adding props to a clothing set can help continue the mood or story of the design. However since props are saved in a different library category in Poser, very often they are overlooked.

1   Material zones allow you to apply different material settings to each zone. This means that special effects can be controlled and used on certain sections, and gives the option to use procedural materials in place of image maps.

Materials also give the option to change the look of a garment by making some sections transparent, such as turning a pair of pants into shorts by turning off the lower legs.

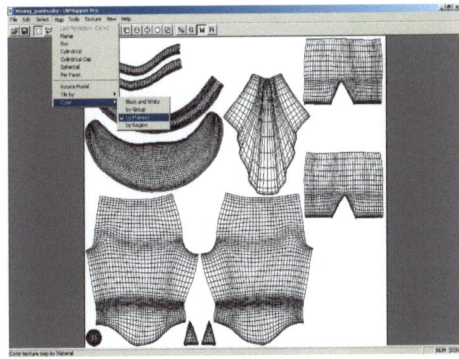

2   I've used UVmapper to assign materials for the pants. Here each part is colored differently by UVmapper so I can see what is assigned to which Material zone.

Try to use short but informative names like Belt, Fabric, Sash, Pants, Leather and so forth.

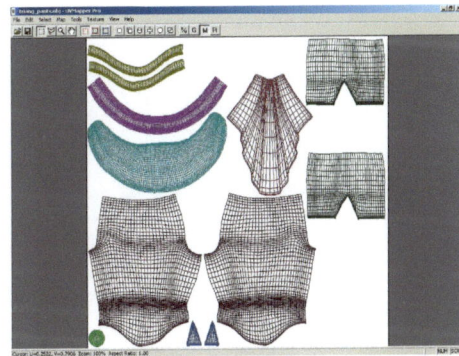

3   And for the shirt. I've given the insets, tabs, main shirt and trim sections different materials so several different materials could be used more easily.

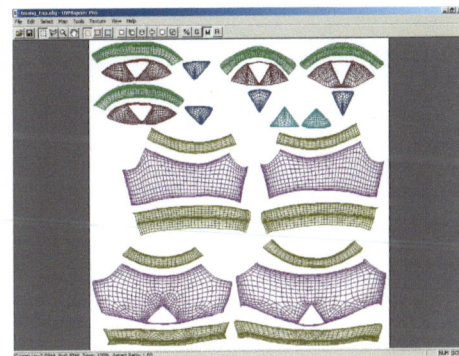

Chapter 6 –   Poser Setup

Setting up a clothing item to be rigged, rigging it, adjusting the rig and creating a project runtime folder

Poser mesh based files fall into two varieties: those with moving parts and those without. Poser does not distinguish between a humanoid, an animal, a shirt, a car or a desk with drawers. It either has rigging, or not. That is it. Conforming clothing specifically has rigging mimicking its donor so when conformed to the figure the clothing moves with the figure.

To create anything with moving parts you need to first define those parts by setting your mesh into groups, or bodyparts, which we have already done. This chapter handles the next major step, that of adding the donor rigging to the set up clothing item.

Poser clothing files consist of two or more files all with specific discrete locations. When creating a project for distribution you must take care to track those files and include all the parts in your project runtime for the end user.

After the main part of this chapter I go over the old school geometry substitution method and cover a little bit about joint deformers.

Poser cr2 Parts

Mesh - the OBJ file, which can be in the Library folder, but most stores prefer be in Geometries.

Cr2 - the rigged character file, which contains morph, rigging and some other information. Usually in the Characters folder, but can also be saved in the Props folder with the .pp2 suffix.

Textures - Any imagemaps used to texture the item usually located in Textures : YourSubfolder : YourProject.

Dragon Lord for Michael4

By Lyrra Madril

This complex armour set includes a fully articulated armored back-piece as well as ERC controlled wings which fold with one control. The loincloth and the arm drapes have custom rigging, controlled with EZpose dials.

The textures use both imagemaps and shaders to create the look of chainmail, leather, metal, enameling and feathers.

1	The very first step is creating a Runtime structure in your working project folder. When items are final in your main Poser runtime, you can then copy them into this structure and have everything nice and tidy for packing.

As you can see I've created folders and sub-folders for all the parts of the product.

Poser format files have lots of pieces, each one of which has to go in a specific place in the Runtime folder hierarchy. Since the final cr2 has these locations written in the file, this is why moving things like texturemaps and obj files isn't a great idea, since Poser will not know where to look to load them.

2	But right now you are making a cr2 so you get to decide where your parts go.

The first thing that gets a home is the obj. I've made a folder under Geometries with my name. I find putting all my stuff under my name makes it easier for me and end users to find them again later.

So under my name is a folder with the product name. I'll use the same name for all the parts of the product to make it easier for the user to find.

3	Now I copy my product runtime into my main Poser runtime. I always build in main, it makes it much simpler to get all the file paths correct. Also some python utilities that you might need can be confused by exterior runtimes.

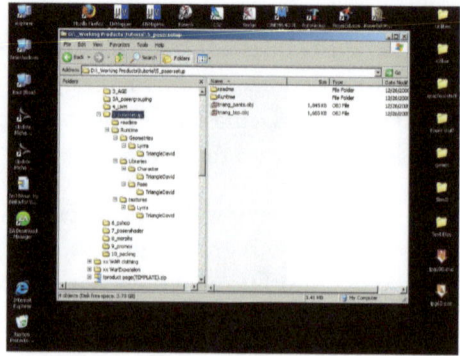

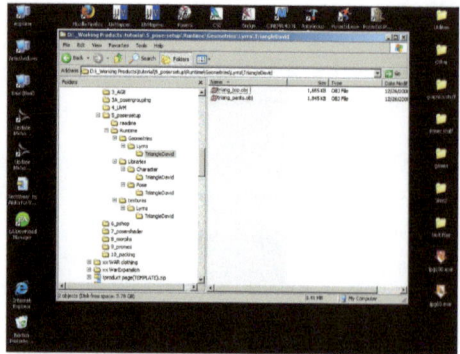

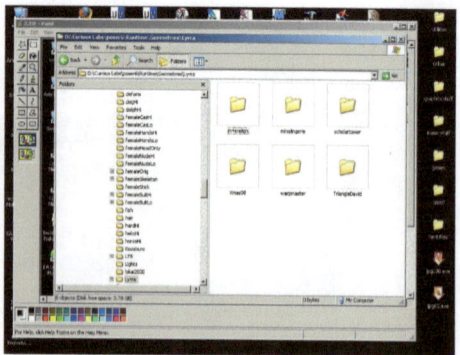

Chapter 6 –	Poser Setup

4   I've started a new Poser scene, loaded and zeroed David. My default Poser lights are set to a set of testing lights and are very neutral and bright so I can see issues more easily.

Here I am importing the shirt obj file using File Import. Make sure to turn off all the boxes here, since I already know I have it the right size with the normals the right way round.

5   As you can see the shirt obj lines up with the zeroed figure, just as I modeled it. This is a good time to check for any pokethrough on tight clothing. Since Poser smooths polygons differently than your modeler, sometimes tight clothing gets new pokes at this stage.

So if you have pokes, go back to your modeler, adjust the mesh out, and go back through mapping and grouping. Yes I know its annoying. But believe me, better than fighting with it later on.

In UVmapper you can copy mapping and grouping as long as the mesh info hasn't changed.

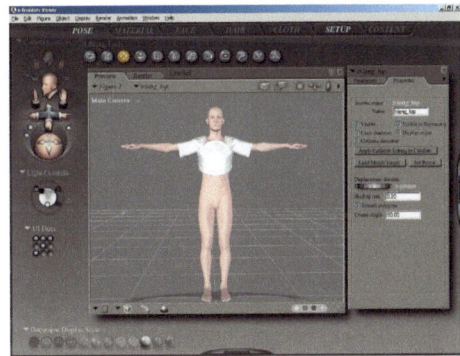

6   You should be careful with the Poser setup room. It can do some very stupid things, and is fairly crashy. So save before you open it and after you leave it. Also, you cant save during the process if you are doing something complicated. Make backups of your working file.

Select the clothing obj, and then select the Setup tab. Say yes to the dialog. You can use the Setup room to copy an existing figured rigging into yours. Here I have select my David Base Conformer that I already prepared and copied its bones.

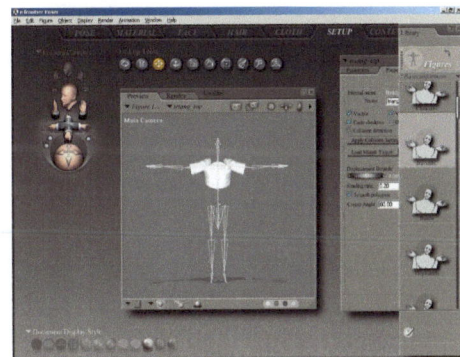

Chapter 6 –   Poser Setup

7   Back in the Pose room and SAVE as a new copy. Now your new cr2 is saved in the pz3 of the scene. You can save a copy of the shirt cr2 to the library now if you want, but it will be a mess. I always rough test all the bends right now, just to make sure I haven't done something silly (like reversing the left right of bodypart names) or made groups that just plain wont work.

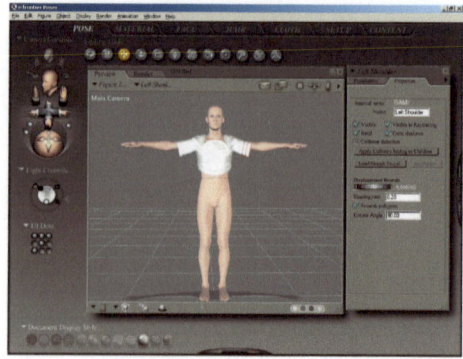

8   I have conformed the shirt to the figure and nothing jumped. That is a good sign. If it jumps, that means you have a problem someplace like IK on your donor, a non zeroed donor, or you moved the rig and or obj by accident.

If it jumped, you should stop right now. Go and check your donor file to make sure its zeroed and has IK turned off, and repeat the process until things behave.

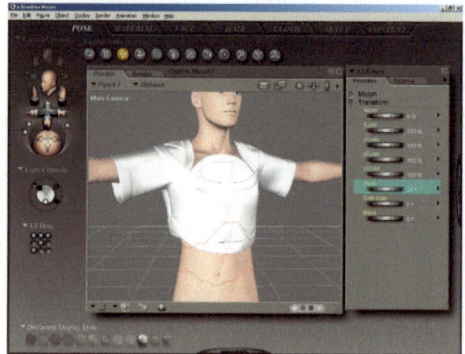

9   Now I'm going to go to each body part, starting at the top of the hierarchy and working my way along. Since this doesn't have Hip mesh, I start with Abdomen and then Chest. Test all 3 bend directions both positive and negative. If the figure has Limits set on bends test it both off and on.

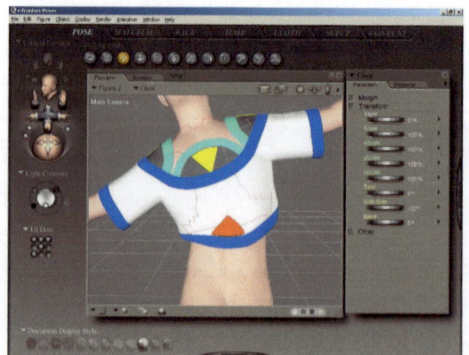

10   Loose clothing often needs more adjustment of the inclusion arms so it bends smoothly. Those are the lil green sticks you can just see in the screen cap. Anything inside the green sticks always bends. Outside the red sticks never bends. The area between the red stick and the green stick is the transition zone.

There are also zone spheres, but not all bodyparts have or need to have them enabled. This one doesn't but I'm sure we'll find some soon.

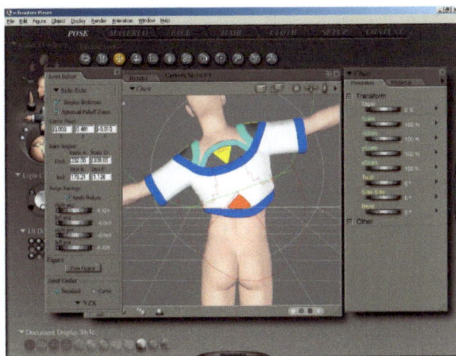

11   See that tight pinch on the left side? I don't like it.

This distortion is being caused by making a large amount of bend with a small transition area. Sometimes this is okay but usually it looks strange.

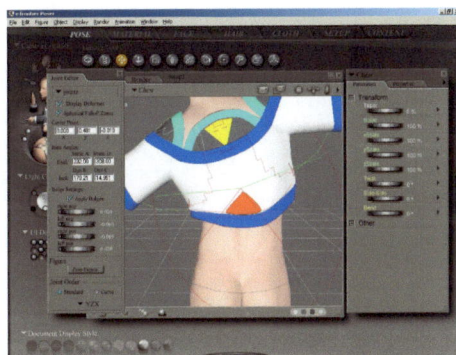

12   Here to ease that pinch I have moved the green stick up to give a larger transition area and smooth out that bend. Now the band doesn't distort as much. Make sure to adjust both side of the green sticks equally.

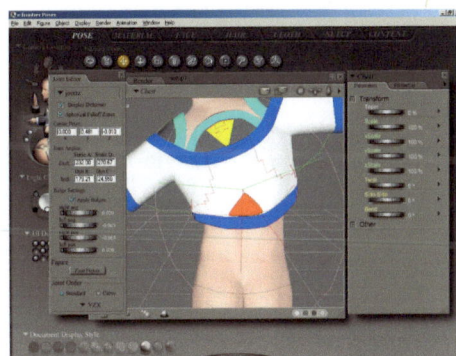

13   Checking the adjustment on the other side.

I also check the other two movement directions but find no issues.

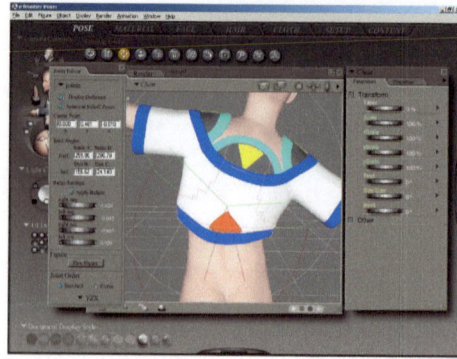

14   After Chest comes Neck. You might think that since there is no neck mesh that you can skip it but you have to remember, Child bodyparts always affect their parents, this is good for ghost bones and cloth handles but can be annoying.

As you can see there is a weird blip in the front if the neck is bent back

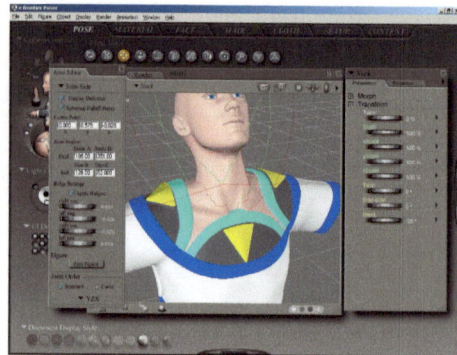

15   Its easiest to see these handles from the side. So I adjust my sticks until that blip smooths out.

See the red and green circle? Those are the joint zone spheres. Just like the sticks, the green ball contains mesh that always bends. The mesh between the red and green circle is the transition and the part outside the red zone doesn't bend.

With the circles and the sticks its possible to get some very fine tuned joints on complicated shapes.

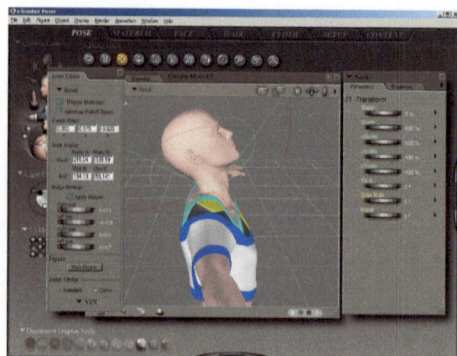

Chapter 6 –   Poser Setup

16   A front view of the adjustment to make sure I got it. Make sure to check your adjustments in all angles.

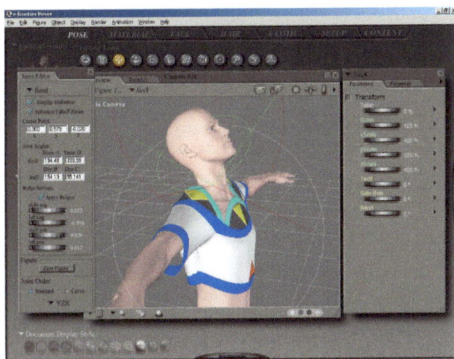

17   Now I've moved on to the Collar. Once you hit the limbs only adjust one side. You can then use Symmetry to copy the adjustments over. (Presuming your clothing and figure are symmetrical.)

I've found an issue on the back bend of the collar. See that jog at the joint seam to the Shoulder of the shirt? Just above the blue cuff zone.

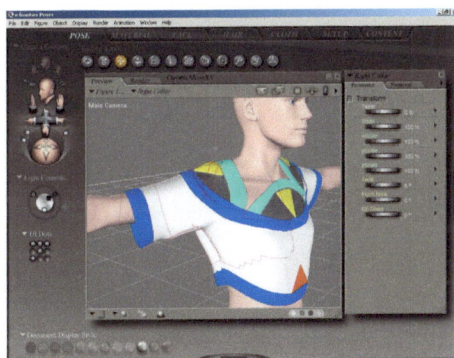

18   Here I select the shirt Collar with the joint Editor on Bend and I can see the problem clearly.

Parts of the collar are not inside the green ball, so they are not being moved when they should be.

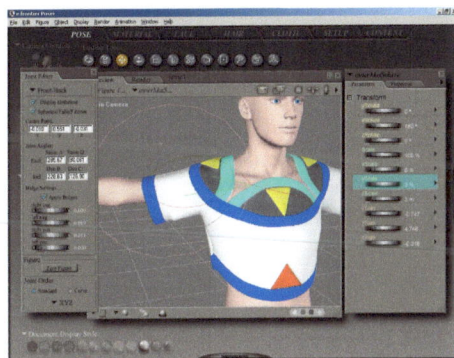

19   I scale the green "Inner-MatSphere" ball taller on Y until it covers the mesh and I see the bump smooth out.

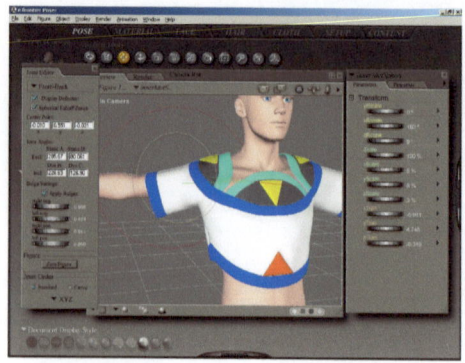

20   Now checking the back bend I see a rumple I don't much like.

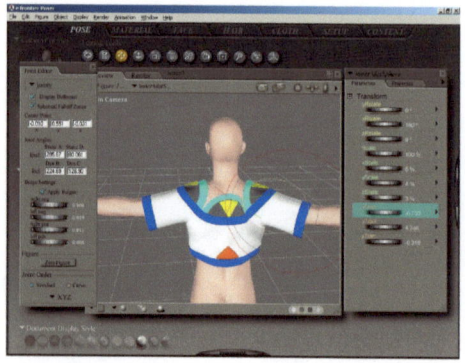

21   Adjusting the green zone on Z (depth) has smoothed out that rumple.

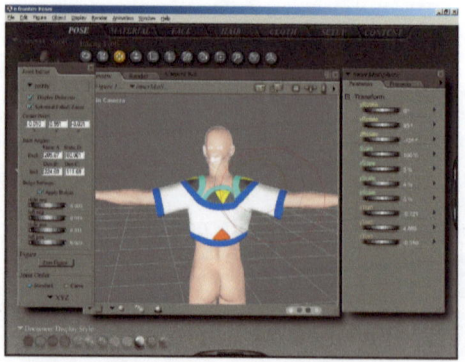

22   Time to move down to the Shoulder bodypart. This has one of the widest ranges of motion and therefor one of the most likely to have distortion problems.

I'm sure you've seen the infamous football shoulders on some figures. Well now you get to deal with that issue yourself.

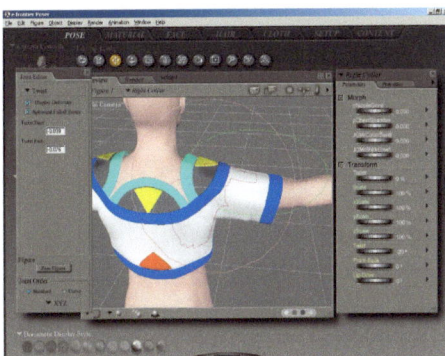

23   On the down bend I see a very obvious break. If you look at the sticks and circles you can guess what the problem and solution are.

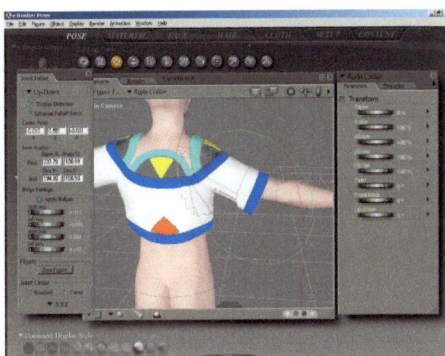

24   Moving the green stick down has fixed the break, but be careful, the sharp angle of the armpit means this area needs careful adjustments or you will break something new by clipping into the torso area.

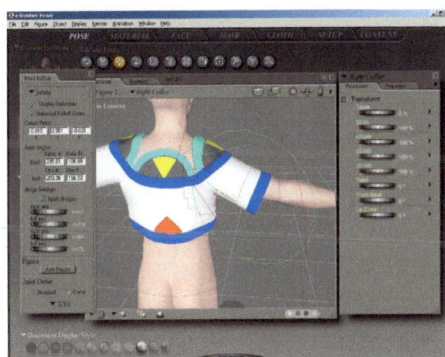

25   On the up bend we get the most classic problem. On the female models it is generally worse. I prefer to handle this issue with joint adjustment, but it is possible to create a Joint Controlled Morph (JCM) to handle this sort of adjustment. Many figures have these JCM's built in (whether or not you can see them) so sometimes we have no choice but to make them in clothing.

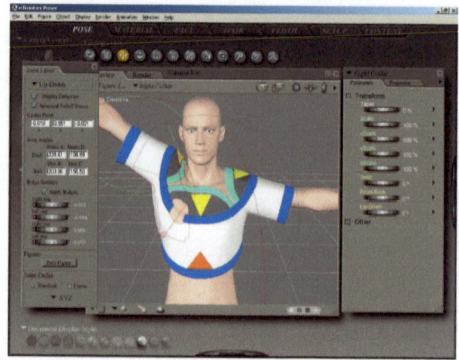

26   Looking at the sticks and spheres I think that my issue is not enough transition zone. Since the shirt is loose I don't think that will cause any trouble to change that a bit.

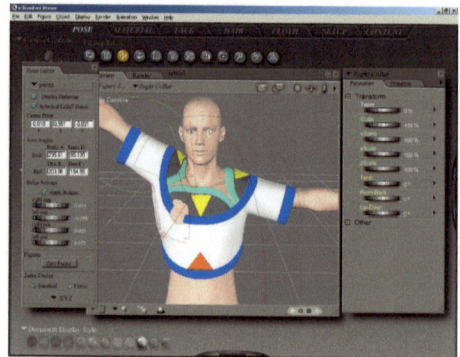

27   Here I've changed the lower red stick and as you can see the larger transition area has made the mesh fit better over the pectorals. It has also made the shirt swing further from the sides. So this would not be a good solution for something tight.

28   Now the up bend on the shoulder. Again we have a poke issue.

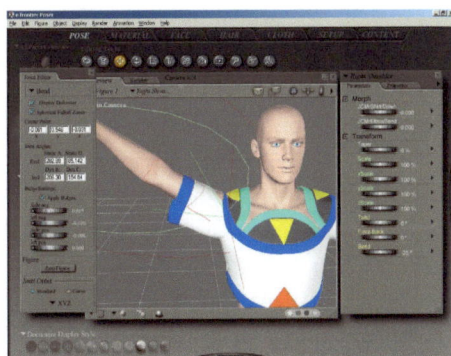

29   Moving both the green inclusion stick and the red transition stick has smoothed out the upper bend on the shoulder.

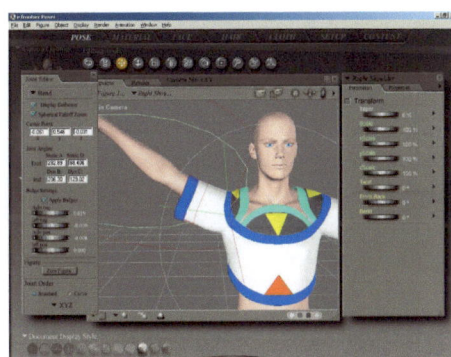

30   Those are all the bends on the parts of the shirt rough checked. But wait! Now for the fun or possibly annoying part. Compound bends, also known as posing.

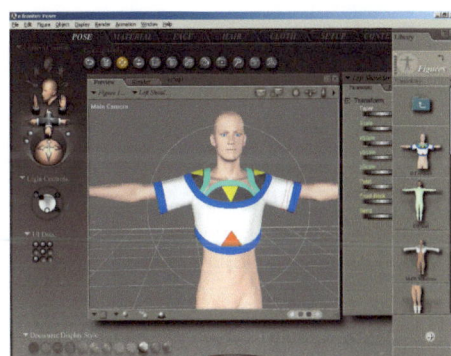

31   Here I start running through a set of basic poses to check what happens with multiple bends together. You can get very weird effects with clashing bend zones. Most stores have a set of poses to check each figure in. This is the Millennium 3 test pose set used by many of the testers at DAZ for the Mil3 generation of figures including David.

As you can see I'm getting a bunch of pokes on the arm as I run through the poses.

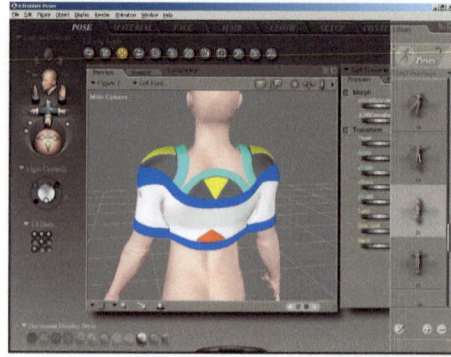

32   These are all very normal bends and positions. As I try each pose I am adjusting the joints a little bit. With luck once I've run through the sequence a couple times I will have either fixed all the issues, or definitely found places where I will need morph correction.

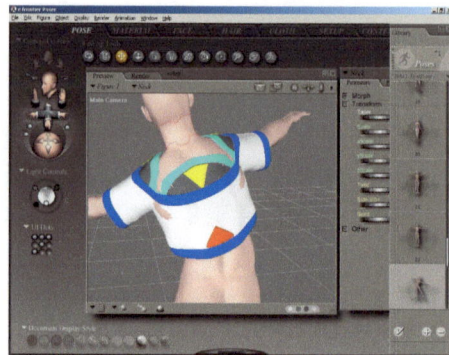

33   You may have to run through the poses 2 or 3 times to isolate all the bend issues. This is not a fast process, and some clothing just this step can take days. Remember to save fairly often, and possibly even multiple save copies in a numbered sequence in case you find out Wednesday you made a serious mistake Monday.

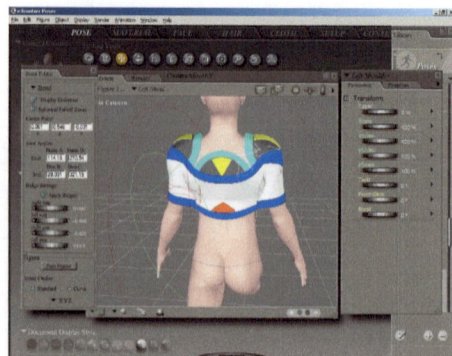

Chapter 6 –   Poser Setup

34   You can see the difference in the left and right sides since they are not symmetrical.

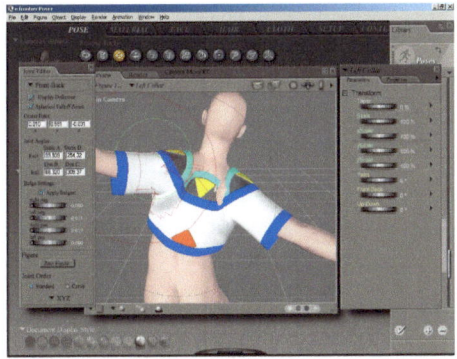

35   This is a slow process back and forth until you reach a balance of the various parameters.

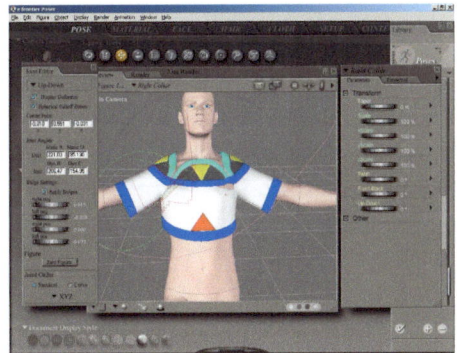

36   This last pose is almost always the one that needs a fix morph of some sort.

** See after note for discussion on Joint Magnets.

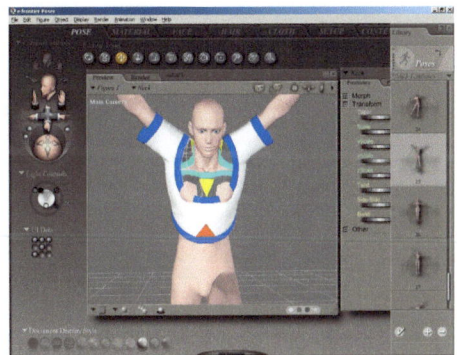

37   This whole time I've been working on just the one sleeve of the shirt.
Now is probably a good time to copy the
joint edits over.

Under Figure : Symmetry I choose Mirror Left arm to Right and say yes to the
dialog about copying joint parameters.
Ever wondered why that was there? Now
you know.

If your figure does not have left and
right parts named in a way Poser under-
stands, then you get the joy of manually
copying all your settings.

This is as good as I'm getting for the
moment, so now I save this to the library
and remove it from the scene to start
rough work on the pants.

38   Shirt has been cleared away and
now I have imported the pants. Everything seems to line up on import.

39   In the setup room I copy the
Figures bones to the pants. If you
remember, I set the sash part as its own
unique group. Now before I leave the
setup room I need to create a bone for
it, or Poser will error.

First I select the bone to which I want
the sash bone to attach in the hierarchy.
In this case, the Hip bone.

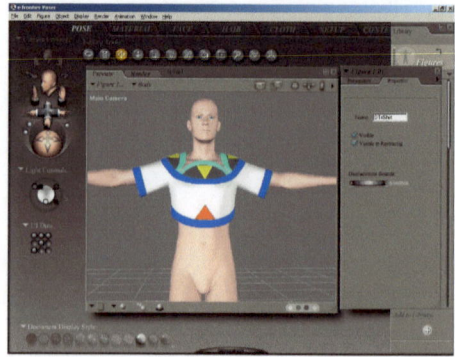

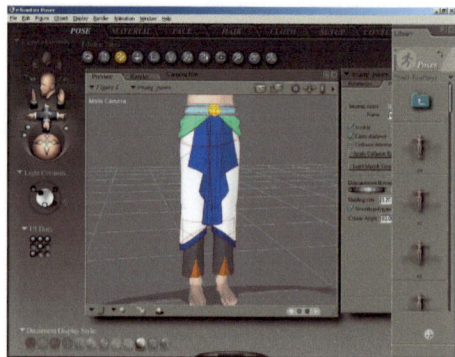

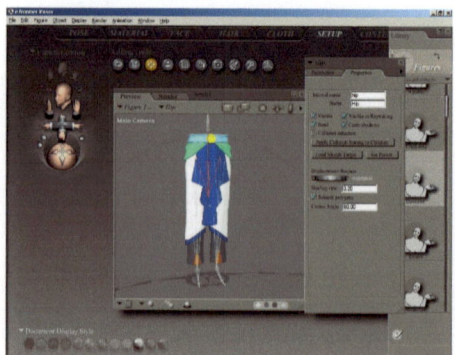

40   Then I draw the Sash bone in something like the right place (don't worry about that, you can change it later) And NAME it right now. If you don't name it properly now you'll be chasing off after errors for ages. Make sure you change both names, internal and external.

41   Now back in Pose room I check the hierarchy to make sure my sash bone has landed in the right place.

In theory you can move it if you made a mistake, but that tends to cause more issues than anything. So if I mess up, I delete it and try again.

Now is a good time to save your scene.

42   As you can see the bone for the sash is a mess. But that is okay, because all of these things can be fixed.

43   The first thing to fix are the centers. In the joint editor I switch it to Center and I can see the crosshairs for the centers. The green one is the center of the joint for the sash bone. Since this bone has no child it has an end center as well, not that it matters terribly much for our purposes.

The center needs to be aligned properly with the mesh for the bone and the resulting bends to line up.

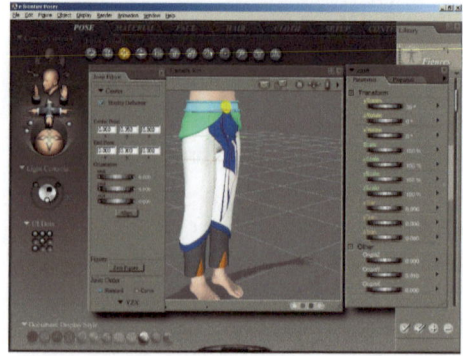

44   Here I've slid the green center to where the top of the sash would go and made sure it is zeroed on X (side to side) so its right in the middle of the part since I know it was modeled symmetrically.

I've also made sure that the rotations on both centers are set to 0. These affect the twist.

All the way at the bottom of the dialog you see YZX. This is the rotation order and dictates which of the rotations is the twist. Since this part is vertical, twist should be on Y (up down), so Y is first.

45   See the stick with the green end and red end? That is my twist bar. Just like the other joint editor controls, anything past the green end always twists, anything past the red end never twists and everything inside the bar is the transition zone.

Right now when I twist the bar the parent part Hip explodes a bit. I need to focus the bend to just the sash part.

Chapter 6 –   Poser Setup

46   I turned on the spherical falloff zones, right away you can see the difference. However now the sash isn't bending very much since the default zone position is all the way on the ground.

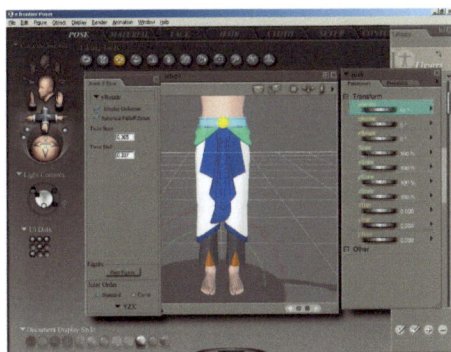

47   I start with the green inclusion zone, moving it up and scaling to cover the sash. The scale on Z is very thin, so it just touches the front of the hip.

Then I copy the settings to the red sphere, and make it a bit larger.

48   Now when I twist the sash nothing explodes, and there is a minimal and natural movement of the hip mesh where the sash touches.

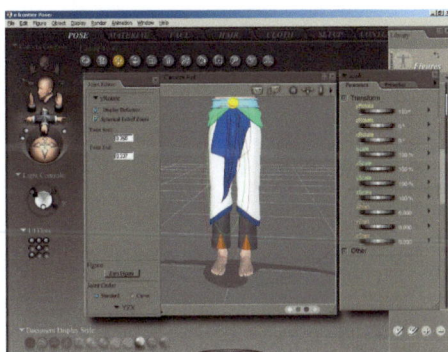

49   I extend the twist bar to make sure the bend transition has all of the sash, which should make for some nice fluid motions. You can also see some clipping on the thing, so I've made a note to make some movement morphs when I get that far.

I keep a text file of notes in each product folder, so I can keep track of little things like this I need to do later, and also what stage I'm up to.

50   Now to check the rest of the bends. The side-side bend has ripped the hip off.

Looking at this I figure I need two things, to add spherical zones to isolate the bend to the sash and to adjust the inclusion arms.

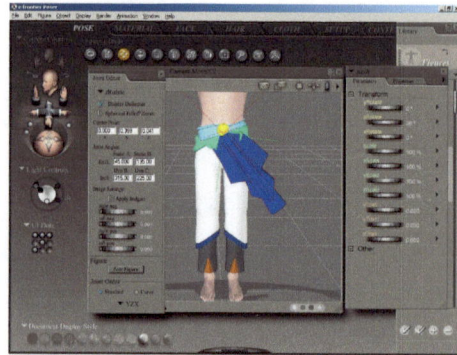

51   Thankfully once you turn on the sphere zones you can copy paste the settings from the Twist to the Side bend. You can see it helping already.

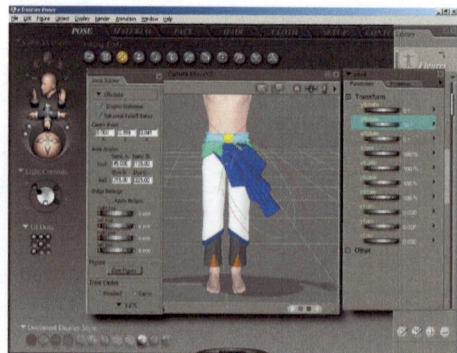

Chapter 6 –   Poser Setup

52   And here with the inclusion arms adjusted the side bend is behaving much better.

Sometimes the setup room likes to make new bones with the inclusion arms set pointing the wrong way. So you might have to bump things all the way round before they start working.

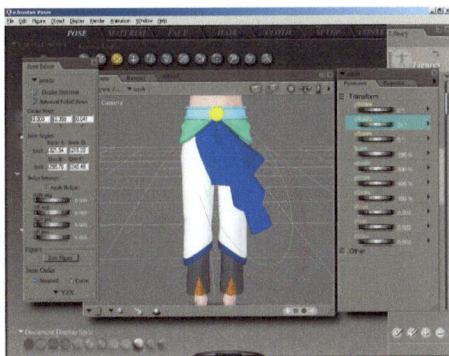

53   And the last rotation to check is Bend. It needs the same routine with the sphere zones and sticks.

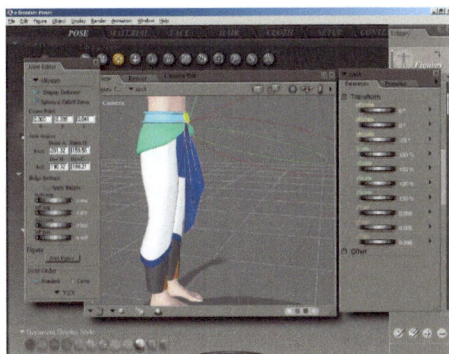

54   Now the custom part is out of the way, we can check the rest of the bends on the pants.

The thighs and hip all checked out fine, but the shin has 2 problems. Small adjustments to the sticks and zones fix that poke through and the dent in the back of the knee.

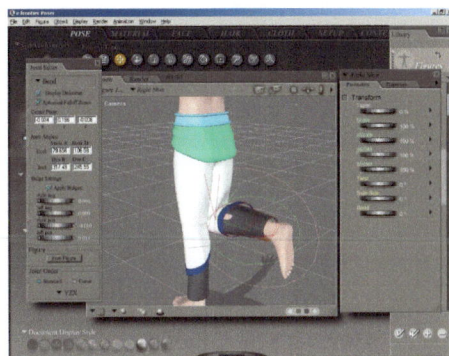

Okay you have now rigged and rough tested the clothing item. Hopefully you didn't run into any major mesh issues. If you did, you are now cussing yourself and going back to the mesh where you get to start the whole export, map, group, etc process again. You definitely want to get this step as clean as possible before moving on to morphs.

This is why I usually do the rough rigging before texturing and all. Its very frustrating to have to re texture everything for new maps.

Another Method - the Old Skool cr2 Donor Method

This method does not work with weightmapped figures

1. Make a copy of the donor cr2 and rename it. Find the file path for your obj file.

2. Open the cr2 with notepad and find the TWO lines that look like this.

```
figureResFile :Runtime:Geometries:DAZPeople:blM-
ilWom_v4b.obj
```

This is the geometry reference line which tells the program which obj file to load for this figure. This one happens to be Victoria's geom reference line.

3. Now change the file path to point to your new object like so. This is the method used before the Poser setup room was created (circa Poser 4 pro).

```
figureResFile :Runtime:Geometries:Lyrra:Triangle-
David:triang_pants.obj
```

Capital letters count. AVOID spaces and weird ASCII characters in names such as < > and { }, since Poser doesn't handle them well. Also avoid any non latin character such as Japanese.

4. Save the file. Load in Poser and continue with the process of joint checking.

About Joint Magnets

Joint magnets are a special application of Poser's magnet deformer. These are built into certain figures at the joints as a way to fix certain joint bend issues, without the use of morphs. This is not always successful.

The most well known figure with Joint magnets is of course, Victoria 4, but the G2 series at Content Paradise also has them. Clothing will move differently with and without them applied.

In Poser you must use a Magnetize Pose to apply the figures joint magnets to the conformed clothing item. (DAZ Studio does this automatically.)

In general, when making clothing for a figure which uses joint deformer magnets like v4, you should first make the clothing bend as well as possible without the magnets. Then you get to choose whether to use Joint Controlled Morphs, Fix morphs to be dialed manually, or require the user to magnetize the clothing (most of them do not want to, or don't understand why they should).

DAZ prefers clothing be usable with the magnets on, since of course, their program DAZ Studio does it automatically and that can clash with JCMs.

Also take into account that users may or may not know to use the joint magnets and certainly don't read the readme where you carefully state to use them or not. So its generally a good idea to make the clothing work without the joint magnets as much as possible.

And just because a figure has joint deformers does not preclude the likeliness of JCM's on the figure as well. So make sure to look for those. Victoria has many, none of which are visible on load in Poser but can be seen in the cr2 if you rummage around for a bit.

Chapter 7 –
Texturing in Photoshop

A brief overview of basic color theory, some thoughts

on textile and costume design and then a step by step

walk-through of creating all the textures needed

Color Design and Balance

Before you dive into your image editing program now is a good time to sit down and think about some things concerning your textures. Anyone who has had any kind of classical art or design training already knows most of this but it bears repeating. Feel free to skip my rambling and jump to the fun part.

Principles of Color Design

Color Wheel

The Color Wheel is commonly used to illustrate the color pallet and interrelationships of physical color. Physical color is any color seen in physical objects such as paints, dyes and so forth. Optical color behaves by quite different rules.

In the color wheel you have the three primary colors, Red, Yellow and Blue shown here in very clear bright tints. When you start mixing these colors together you find the secondary colors between them. For example the point where the color stops being more red and starts being more blue is its own color – purple. Orange, Purple and Green are the three secondary colors and as such are related to the primary colors that mix to make them.

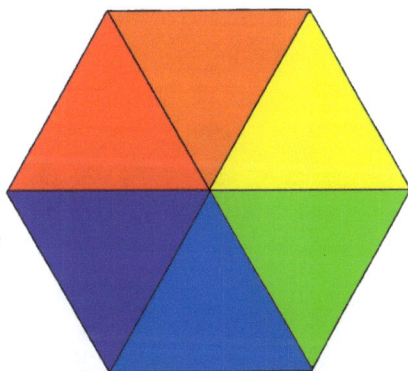

Gray gradient   **Brown gradient**   **Complementary Color gradients**

Stepping away from the strong hues, we have the grayscale continuum from Black to White with shades of gray between, and the browns. Browns are a neutral, and in physical color mixing are often creating by mixing a complementary colors together such as blue and orange.

The one thing that separates digital from real design is never use a black darker than 90% gray or a white lighter than 10% gray, in digital media you need to leave some 'space' for highlights and shadows to appear.

This interplay of the six color hues and the three neutrals can create a complex visual interest if handled well. If handled poorly, you can make almost anything unpleasant to look at.

Some of the most common areas important to consider while choosing colors for textures are discussed below.

Contrast

Contrast can be an important tool in emphasizing certain parts of a clothing item or assembly. A pure white shirt stands out very strongly with pants and jacket of a dark color. Too many high contrast areas too close together can be visually confusing, such as black and white stripes, as well as cause render issues.

Lack of contrast can also be a problem and is often caused by colors too close in hue or value. Colors close in hue are light green, green and forest green. That is an awful lot of green all at once, and nothing to break it up so the green quickly can become monotonous. Which literally means 'monotone' – all one color. Value refers to darkness and lightness, so if you have an outfit that is all pastel colors, or all very dark colors such as forest green, burgundy and navy, it will also become monotonous.

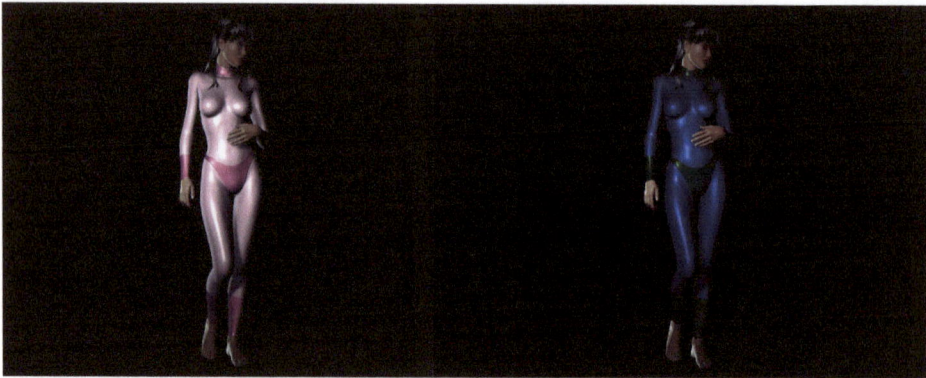

Low Contrast - Hue   **Low Contrast - Value**

There are times to use heavy contrast, no contrast, tone-on-tone or very subdued coloring for special effects. Black and white stripes are often associated with madness, pastels with innocence and dark rich colors with luxury. Tone-on-tone can be very striking if handled well, such as pure white, all black or any hue but there the visual interest will come from clever use of materials and surfaces to break the visual monotony with subtle surface variation.

Complementary colors

Complementary colors are shown opposite on the color wheel. In physical color mixing, you add the complementary color to the color to mute the brightness of the hue. To make a pure blue more subdued, you add orange.

In visual design the complementary color makes a very strong contrast to the main color and so is very good to use in accents, decoration and trim. For example a dark blue dress will be considerably enlivened by an orange belt and accessories.

Complementary Colors   **High Contrast**

Emotional Language of Color

Many colors are associated with specific emotions. However, bear in mind these associations are largely cultural. In the western countries white is the color of innocence, black of death and red of passion. In many eastern traditions, white is the color of death, and red the color for joy and celebration. Keep this in mind if you are texturing a clothing item from or for a specific culture. Other cultural baggage lends emotional weight to other colors or combinations. Red, Green and White for winter holidays, Red White and Blue for patriotism, Purple and Gold for royalty, so forth and so on. This is of course different for various cultures. You can evoke certain emotional responses to an outfit by choosing specific colors, such as selecting navy blue and white for clothing of a sailor, or red, navy blue and gold to evoke classical military dress uniforms from Europe.

Tints, Shades and Tones

Tints, shades and tones are the fancy way of describing colors mixed with black, white or gray. Pure black in small values added to a pure hue leads to 'jewel tone' colors. White leads to pastels. Grays lead to more muted or subdued tones such as mustard, tans, and slate blues. Starting with one hue and creating tints, shades and tones form it can give you a range of related colors with enough variation to be visually interesting.

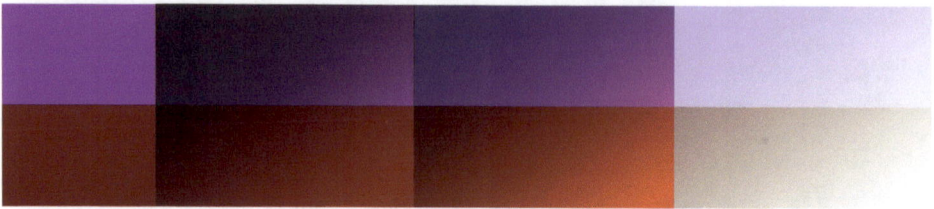

Hue   **Shade**   **Tone**   **Tint**

Hot and Cold

Many artists describe colors as being hot – red, orange, yellow or cold – blue, green, purple. This is mostly an emotional reaction. Many natural things that are hot are reddish, and cold things bluish. Many people prefer one or the other. If you are doing several textures for an outfit, it is a good idea to do at least one hot and one cold to please both camps. Also, pay attention to your grays – a reddish gray often feels dirtier and a bluish gray more forbidding.

Neutrals

In design a neutral color is a good break from stronger hues – black, white and grays are used as neutrals and of course every tint, shade and tone of brown, ranging from very pale cream to dark dirt browns. Many metals are some color of brown – excepting yellowy gold and whitish silver. For many centuries brown was the color of poor people who could not afford expensive dyes, so it is only relatively recently that neutral color schemes became popular. Brown also evokes nature, and humble origins in many cultures.

Use neutrals to break up and dilute the impact of strong hues

Principles of Color Layout

Visual Balance

In general if you are working on one item or a set of items that will be used together you will probably want to balance the colors out. Avoid putting too much of one color all in one place, or having only one isolated spot of your accent color.

Unbalanced   **Balanced**

Design Elements

If you are using decorative elements, consider how their colors will break up your spaces. You may need to make a design motif more subdued and less distracting by embossing it, or coloring tone on tone rather than having a distracting colored element.

Breaking Up Space

Large areas may need to be broken up by bands of trim, decorative motifs, or other design elements to help balance the colors and avoid awkward visual clustering of other design elements at hems and cuffs. This is often used on large sections like skirt or cloaks.

Overlays

Using an overlay such as lace, netting, translucent fabric or allover decorative motifs can help blend a large awkward visual spot in better. You can also create the impression of toned colors by layering black or white laces over a solid color. Black lace over red satin is commonly found in classic Spanish styled designs, and a good way to mute a very strong bright red.

Selecting Materials

Most of these points to consider often do not hold true for most fantasy or science fiction design. However, by paying attention to the look and feel of certain eras you can evoke those eras in your texture designs simply by the use of color and material.

Use

Always consider what your clothing item is used for when selecting materials for it. Using a heavy denim on a light peasant style blouse will look odd. Armor is likely to be metal, or leather treated in various ways. If you choose a material that is implausible, you break the illusion and make it harder for the viewer to accept the clothing as real. Some materials have always been more costly than others, or didn't exist in certain times. Satins and velvets have always been expensive when available, while coarse weaves and leathers were very common. Fine woven modern cloth did not become common for middle class people until the height of the Industrial Revolution.

Era

Different eras and cultures throughout history have had access to different dye materials. This effects not only the range of colors possible at a certain time, but the materials the dyes were used on and the price of them. So if you are texturing any-thing that has any kind of historical basis of it, you should check into what colors were possible and fashionable at the time.

Until the advent of inexpensive coal based aniline dyes in the late 1800's most strong bright colors were very expensive to make. So until a certain point in time, bright red, blue or purples were exclusively for certain very wealthy peoples. If you make a texture for a poor medieval peasant in bright red, it will look implausible. However a more muted blue-red, like a burgundy, is easy to achieve with beetroot or red onionskin dyes and thus a likely color for a peasant.

Some eras in culture can almost be defined by their color combination. A small amount of research on your part, can lead you to vast areas of inspiration.

Patterns

Prints are another area where use is often heavily dependent on era. For modern or fantasy clothes it is less of a worry, but for anything historical check your mate-rials to make sure you don't make yourself look very silly. Most four color or full color prints are relatively modern, though embroidered designs have been around for thousands of years.

An interesting print, often called a 'hero print' in costume design, can be the focal point of a good texture design if used sparingly. Try to avoid prints with prints in most cases, as it makes for a very busy outfit. Some prints are nearly solids – such as tone on tone, calicos with very small patterns, checkers and stripes and mix well with other 'hero' prints.

Brocade and jacquards are specific designs created by the interweaving of dif-ferent colored warp and weft in the fabric. These patterns have been found as late back as the 900's but until the invention of the computerized loom were too expensive for most people. Interestingly enough the early jacquard looms used a punched card to hold the pattern, and gave inventors the idea for the punch-card system used in the first computers.

Trouble Shooting Textures

Too bright and cartoonlike

No matter what you do, your clothing looks too bright and cartoonlike. Well a common culprit for this is using colors that are too pure and saturated. Except when brand new, most dyed clothing has some fade. So you may want to try muting down your hues, either by desaturation or mixing the complementary color in. Also, adding details such as stitching, wrinkles and stains may help.

Nothing Stands out

You used some beautiful fabrics and nice color .. but the whole outfit is just one undistinguished blob. You most likely need to add some contrast. Try switching one color for a high contrast or complementary color or value. You can also add trim or decorative elements in a high contrast color.

Too Busy

It's too much to look at. You may want to step back on the number of colors or fabrics used. If you have used more than one print it can look very busy, or if you have a small patterned allover design in a large area it can be overwhelming.

Try swapping in some solid colored areas, or replacing vivid colors with neutrals or more subdued tones. Bands of solid colored trims may also help.

It Looks ... Wrong

There are times when you look at an outfit and think 'this is wrong' but can't quite put your finger on why. Here are some things you can ask yourself:

Do I have good color and value balance?

Do the fabrics and colors match the purpose of the clothing?

Did I get the fabric pattern scale right on the clothing across all the pieces?

Do those fabrics really go together when I render it on a full figure?

Would this look better if I made all of one fabric black or white?

Do I have an interesting balance of textures?

Does this textile really look like plausible realistic fabric?

Ask a (bluntly honest) friend of yours what they think about it.

Briana Culaith

By Danie and Maforno

This outfit packs a lot of detail into ten items that still don't cover a great deal. This is a classic barbarian heroine outfit and still very popular. The jewelry is based on classic Celtic designs and works very well with other sets.

Choosing My Colors

With many clothing items it is often relatively easy to color the various material zones in your rendering program to get a quick rough draft of possible color schemes and balance across the outfit. Here I've recolored the outfit six different ways in Poser to get an idea of some color sets to explore, and what will make for a good visual balance.

As you can see I played with a couple different color schemes, and various tonal combinations. On all of them I have balanced the color throughout the outfit, using the different trim and panel areas to distribute the color. This outfit was designed with plenty of color panels, in many outfits you will need to add them yourself on the template.

Another method is to render a black and white image of your outfit and color it in a few different ways in Photoshop to try different designs.

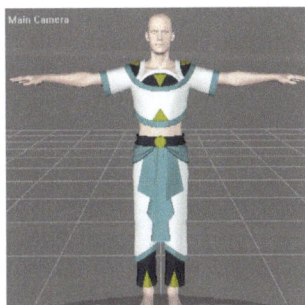

Three tints of the same hue of green, plus an accent of a complementary yellow.

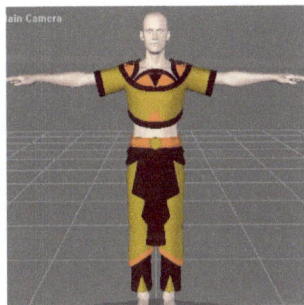

Very hot colors in red, yellow and orange. Evokes the sun, especially with the triangle motif.

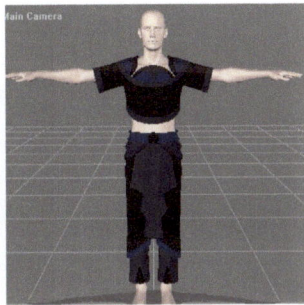

Very dark toned, with 2 values of gray and a dark blue. Makes me think of police.

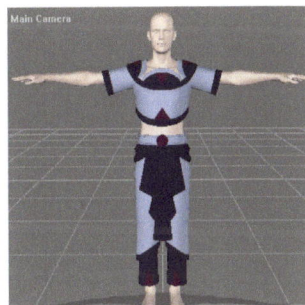

Two tones of a purple hue, with some accents in a reddish purple. Possibly a bit too saturated.

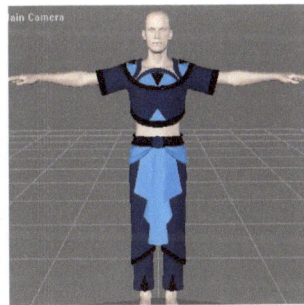

Black and 2 shades of blue. A bit too jarring – the light blue is too light.

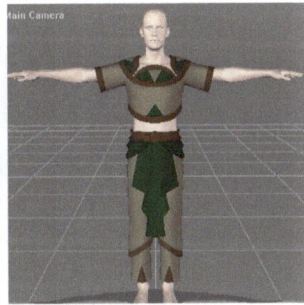

A very foresty combination of two browns and a green.

Chapter 7 –   Texturing in Photoshop   119

Photoshop
(and a brief stop in UV Mapper)

1   My first step is to create map templates. So I find the obj files for my clothing. You can see my project folder set up with a folder for Templates (which will be in the final product zip) and Texturing, where I will put all my texturing related files while I'm working on them.

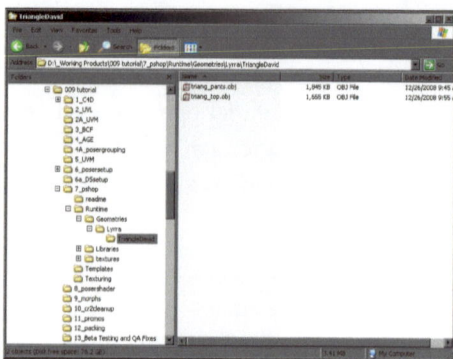

2   Here I have opened the pants object in UV Mapper. You can use Pro or the free Classic for this.

3   This is the export template options dialog box. I have to chosen to exclude hidden (not that there are any) and to include labels. This is a good hab- it to get into. I have also chosen a nice large, but not too large, template size.

Small items like rings and shoes can have smaller maps – 512 or 1024. I find 2048 a decent size for larger clothing items and some things that need very sharp detail or are very big should be 4052. (But not larger since many pro- grams have trouble handling them.)

Why the weird numbers? I could give you a long explanation involving 8 bit computer machine language and the slow evolution of digital graphics. But to cut a long story short – try to use image sizes in multiples of 16. Many imaging programs handle that better.

Should you make everything 4000 px sq? Oh please no. Each map adds more file size, and textures use from 3 to 6 maps for a single item. Try to keep it down, your render times will thank you.

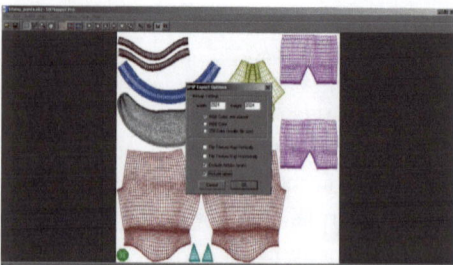

4   Here is the folder with my two new templates. Move them down into the templates folder for the product packing, and then copy them into your Texturing folder to work with them now.

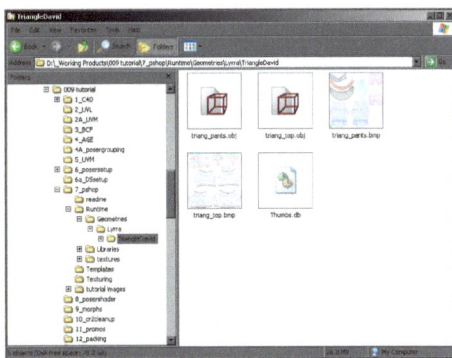

5   Here I have opened Photoshop and my two templates. The very first step is preparing the templates for work.

This is not the only method for preparing a template, but I find it is the most flexible and leads to tidier work flow.

Expect to make a lot of layers in your image. Always save in PSD format.

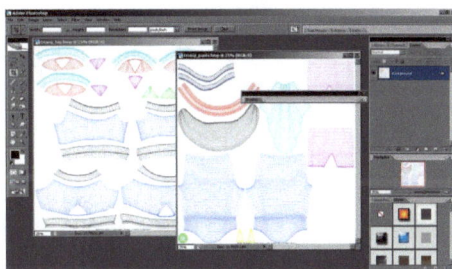

6   Use the Magic Wand tool (default tolerance of 20) and click in the white space outside the template areas.

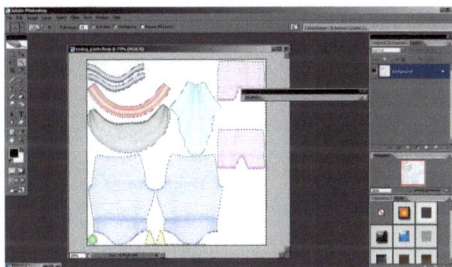

7   Invert your selection (ctrl-Shift-I). You now have just the template areas selected.

But since graphics programs (including UV Mapper) are not perfect, its best to leave a seam allowance around the parts, just as in sewing patterns. If you do not, bets are you will see a thin white line on seams when rendered. Some programs do better with this than others, but its best to be safe than sorry.

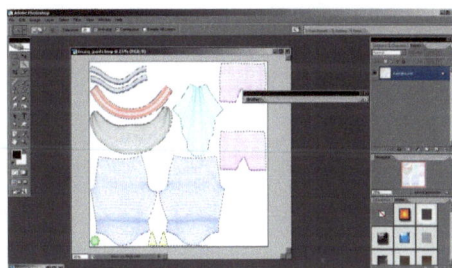

8   So now expand your selection by 12 pixels. Smaller maps can use smaller seam allowances down to 8 pixels. As you can see you now have space around the edges of each template part.

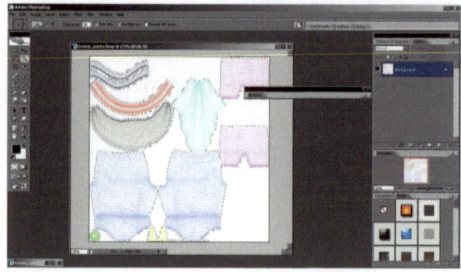

9   Create a new layer and fill it. Use any color you like, since this is a temporary layer.

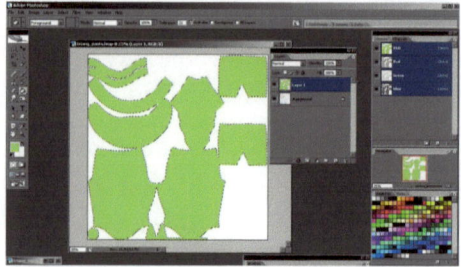

10   I have double clicked the Background template layer and turned it into a regular layer. The background layer as default cannot have its layer order changed.

11   Layer Modes are different modes that layers can use to interact with layers below them. Photoshop uses various mathematical methods and the pixel information to Add, Subtract and etc the layers together. The best way to understand layer modes is to try them all with various layers and see what happens.

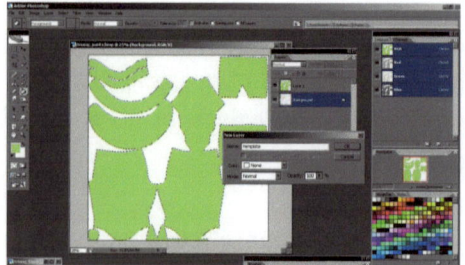

In this case set the template layer to multiply, this will make the lines appear darker over any layer under them.

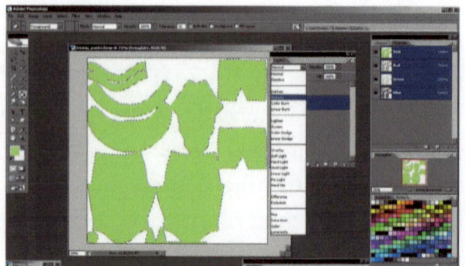

12   Once I move the template over the blank parts layer you can now see through the template to the layers underneath. With the Multiply mode dark colors, like my lines, will multiply with the colors below, but white will essentially disappear. Save your file!

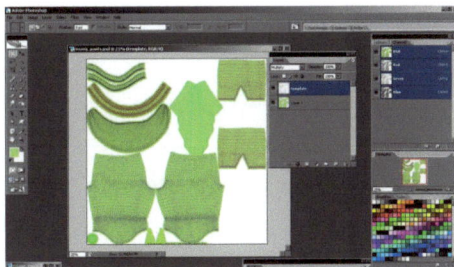

Always save in PSD format while working. Some other file formats support layers or transparency information, but PSD is the most robust.

NEVER work in a jpg file. JPG format uses lossy compression, which is to say it actually throws out some data every time its saved. That is the last thing we want. Use jpg only as your last step.

13   Now I'm going to make a layer for each section in the garment using the material colors UV Mapper saved as a guide.

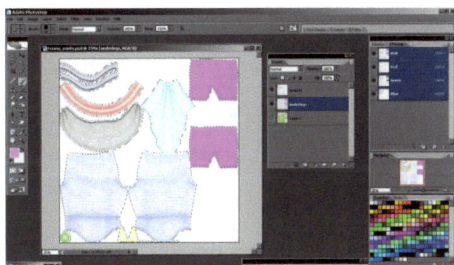

Hold down Ctrl and click on the lil thumbnail of your parts layer. You will now get a selection of just what is on that layer. For each part, paint inside your selection.

TIP – name your layers as you go or you will very quickly get confused. You may also want to color code some layers such as stitching or metals so you can see at a glance what they are.

14   All parts have been created onto layers and the temporary parts layer removed.

Now I can quickly fill sections of the map with patterns or layer styles to rough out the areas of the texture.

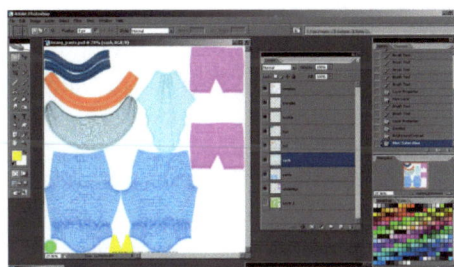

Chapter 7 –   Texturing in Photoshop

15   The top template has been prepared in the same way.

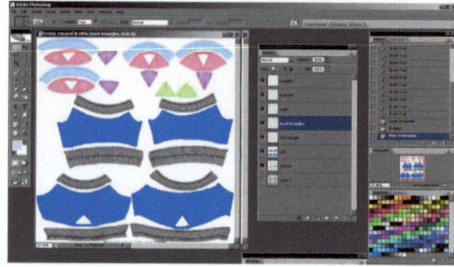

16   Looking at the six possible
color-ways I created earlier, I decide on
the woodsy green brown one and on the
dark black and navy one.

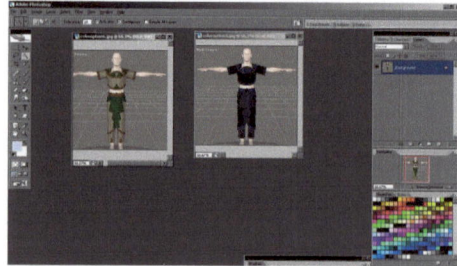

17   I've gone through my various
fabric textures and picked out some that
may work for this color set. However, as
you can see the colors don't match what
I had.

18   There are many methods of
adjusting colors in Photoshop The
method I use the most for simple changes is non destructive – that is to say the
texture tile itself doesn't get changed, I
simply use various layer style options to
tint or tone it.

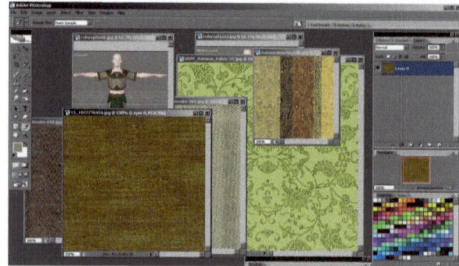

Here I have chosen Color Overlay, set
the Mode to Color and used the eye-
dropper to pick the medium brown from
my mockup. As you can see the textile
image is now tinted to match that color.

This method works best if just changing hue, to make the color lighter or
darker you need a different method.

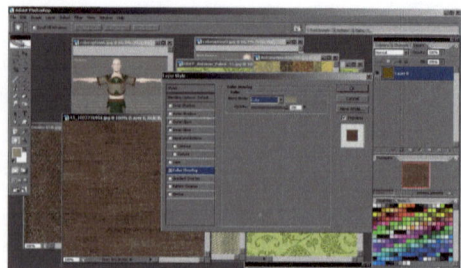

19   The two plain brown fabrics are now tinted to match my design. The fancier fabric still has to be tinted green to be used on the sash.

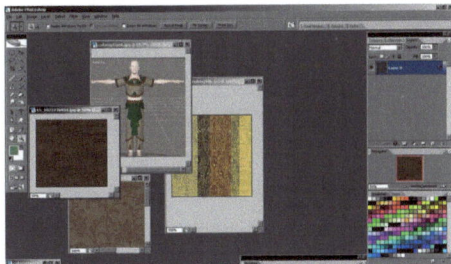

20   For most leathers I have a selection of grayscale patterns already saved – smooth leather, patent leather, suede, alligator and so forth. When I need them in a design I simply tint and choose the right grayscale leather for the darkness I need. Since so many textures need leathers and plain fabrics I keep a grayscale variety set loaded in Photoshop most of the time.

21   I tend to use Photoshop layer styles for metal most of the time. When I get to the breakdown of the image maps into specular, bump, etc I break down the layer style as well.

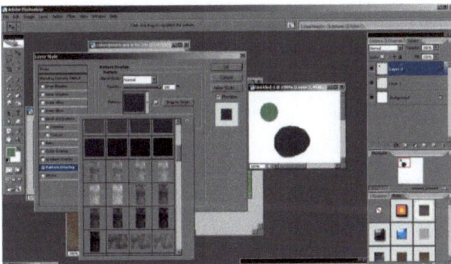

There are thousands of Photoshop layer styles out there. Over the years I've combined my favorites into one file.

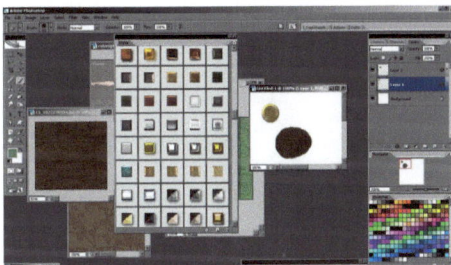

22   So after some editing, picking and choosing here are my two texture matrices. Each blob is a layer with a layer style. So now I can choose each one and save the layer style into my Style palette for fast application. Please note – each fabric has been made with horizontal and vertical options. If you don't do this now its very annoying to go back and redo. If your template has sections on the diagonal this is generally where you curse the person who uvmapped it, or at least I do. Those will have to be matched by hand.

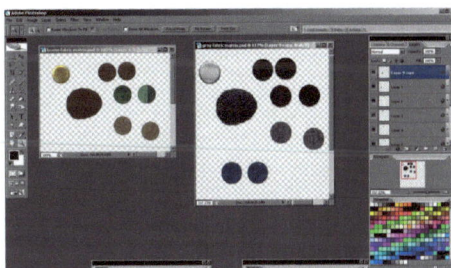

23   Here are the styles saved into the palette I also save this into a folder in my Resources folders named Projects with the name of this project so that I can always come back to it later. This is very handy if you have to do updates, or want to match a certain texture to make several clothing sets that match.

24   Now for the fun part! Coloring in the pieces.

I open my clothing template, which is already broken down into layers by material. Using the layer styles I apply my textures to the sections using my mockup as a guide.

This is not the final product, just a fast first stage. There is a lot more work to go, trust me.

25   Right now on first application the pattern is blurry and kind of out of size. When a layer style is saved Photoshop saves the pattern scale relative to the size of the image you saved it in. If you then apply it in an image with a different size, the image may scale weirdly.

ALWAYS use an pattern fill layer style at a multiple of 5%, or preferably 25%. So use 100% or 50% but never 32. Why? The scaling algorithm makes the image blurry at anything not a 5% ratio.

26   Here I have resized the pattern to 50% and it is now nice and crisp as well as a pleasing size on the material.

REMEMBER – make sure to use the same pattern the same size across all clothing items in the set or it will look weird and seem less realistic. This is not necessarily the same size in Photoshop. Check on the models and adjust as needed.

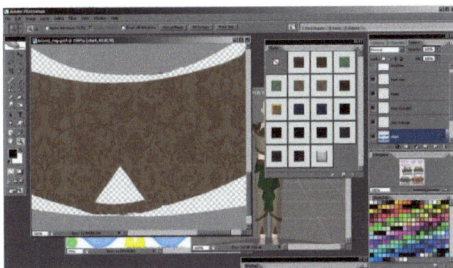

27   The top of the clothing with the layers dropped onto it quickly. The colors work well together and the patterns are subtle enough not to clash.

Save as a jpg so I can quick preview it on the object in UVmapper.

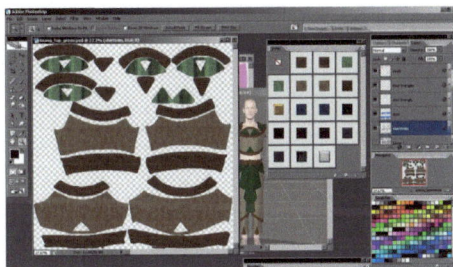

28   And here are the pants, again with the texture quickly applied via layer styles. I'm sure this texture will need some editing. I don't think that curved sash section is going to look very good.

Save as a jpg so I can quick preview it on the object in UVmapper.

29   In UVmapper Pro I load the object and load the texture. Here I can quickly see how the colors and patterns work on the mesh. The top is pretty good already.

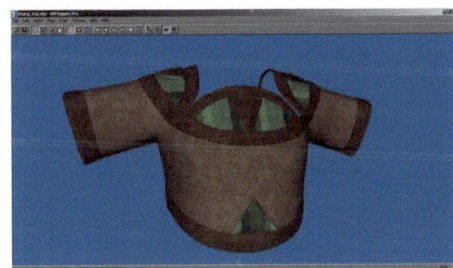

30   As I guessed the pants are going to need some work. Those fancy stripes on the sash are coming out very oddly. This is one argument for solid fabrics, but sometimes a fancy pattern like this is worth the fight to get it to look right.

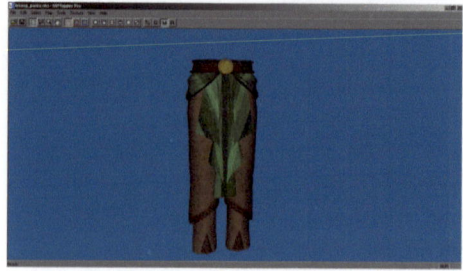

31   And the back of the pants so you can see how the stripes on the sash are fighting the mesh. Not attractive or realistic.

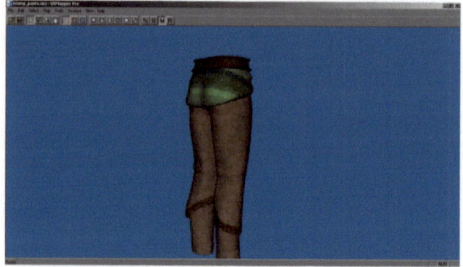

32   Closeup of the front of the sash. The patterns definitely need to be aligned to flow with the mesh folds. Also the metal looks out of scale on the belt buckle. That however is a very easy fix.

33   Back in Photoshop I choose the belt buckle layer, right click on it and choose Scale Effects. I can now adjust the slider to adjust the whole layer style at once to suit. You can also go into the layer style and change each section manually, but this is faster. Remember to go in and check your Pattern fill so the scale percentage is still a multiple of 5%.

34   I'm going to have to do some fancy distortion to get the pattern laying right on the mesh. So first I need a large swatch of the fabric.

I create a layer with a big rectangle, and apply the layer style with the green fabric.

Now to turn it back into pixels that I can edit, I make a blank layer, select both and merge.

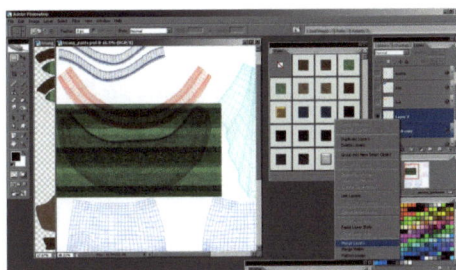

35   Photoshop's warp tool is very powerful and very useful. Previously I would use the Liquefy tool, but it can distort the pixels, and will need to be gently sharpened afterwards. Warp tends to have a cleaner effect, but may still need some sharpening.

When you start Warp you get a grid , with handles at the corners to control the curvature. It is easiest to use on rectangles.

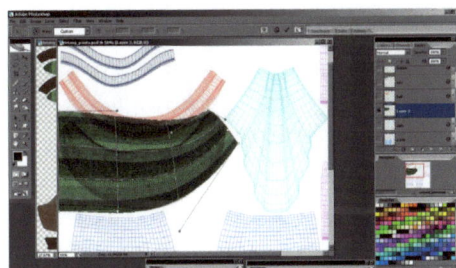

As you can see I'm warping my fabric so the stripes line up with the lines of the mesh. At this stage being able to see the mesh is invaluable.

36   The back of the sash warped into place following the mesh.

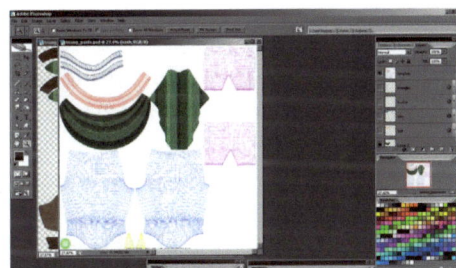

37   I repeat the process for the front part of the sash. It takes much less warping.

38   And checking the sash in UV-mapper it looks much better. Now that the basics are laid down I can go back and start adding all the little details that make a texture more realistic – stitching, seams, wrinkles and so forth.

If you have a complex set with four or five pieces, now is a good time to do a quick check in Poser with everything together. Just to make sure the combined effect works.

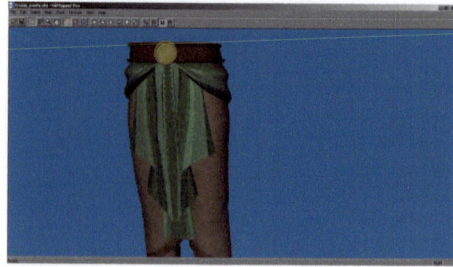

39   Photoshop's brush tools are very powerful, with a lot of options. By using spacing we can make a stitching brush that follows the lines you draw very easily.

I start with a simple circle brush, squish it down and add spacing. Under Shape Dynamics set it to follow the angle of the line. This will line the length of the stitch up with the line as you draw it.

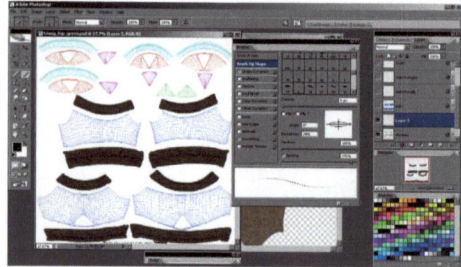

You can use brush dynamics with all shapes of brushes, so you may want to experiments with X shapes and zigzags for fancy stitches.

40   I start the stitches on a new layer, and so I can see what I'm doing I use a bright red color over layer style. Once I have the stitches laid in how I like them I'll change this. No point straining my eyes until I have to.

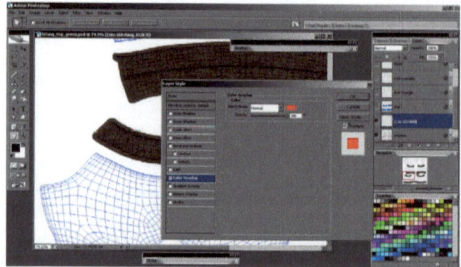

41   A quick row of stitches so I can check how it looks in UVmapper.

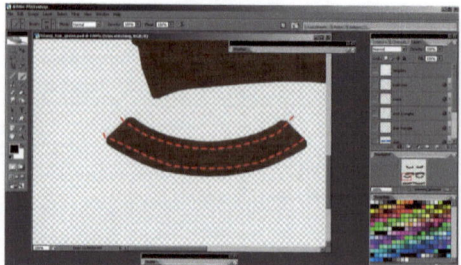

42   Oh these are much too big. Perhaps if this was being used in a video game at a distance I might leave it, but for closeup work this will look very odd. Its always important to pay attention to scale.

If you are making a more cartoony set than larger stitches, if any, might work for you.

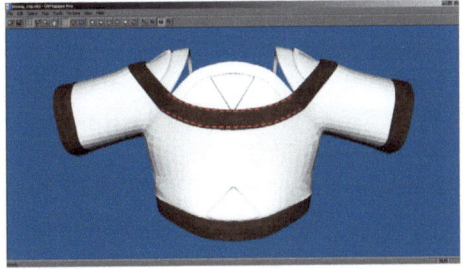

43   I adjust my brush to be much smaller and try again. You can see the flow of the stitches is much smoother now with smaller stitches.

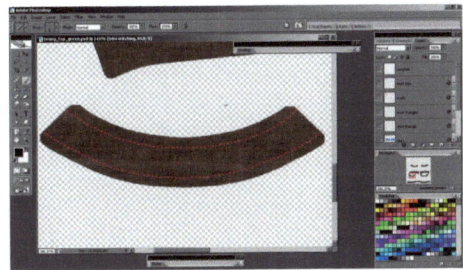

44   And in UVmapper the size looks much better.

IMPORTANT – pay attention to where stitching is visible on clothing. On most cloth-to-cloth seams the stitching is on the inside, where it cannot be seen. On appliqués like this, or on hems you are more likely to see stitching. Where two fabrics are turned in to join as in most side seams, you will very rarely see any stitching.

Some cultures use decorative stitching, but on modern clothing its fairly uncommon.

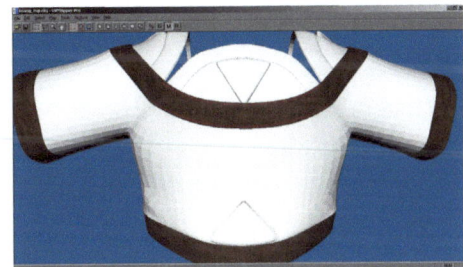

45   Here is my basic stitch layer style. I've turned off the pattern underneath so you can see it. Using layer styles I've matched the thread to the brown of the cloth, added a tiny bevel and emboss so the stitch pop out a little and importantly added an Outer Glow set to multiply with plain black.

Stitches almost always compress the fabric around them creating a slight depression. When the layers are broken down for the image maps, this shadow will be used to create a slight downwards displacement so the stitches pop out a little bit.

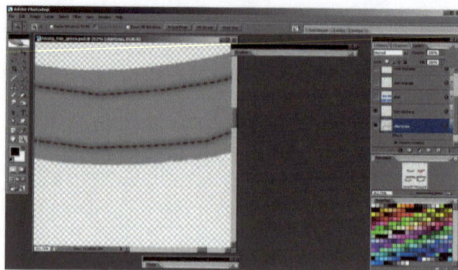

46   A test of the final stitching in UVmapper and its looking pretty good.

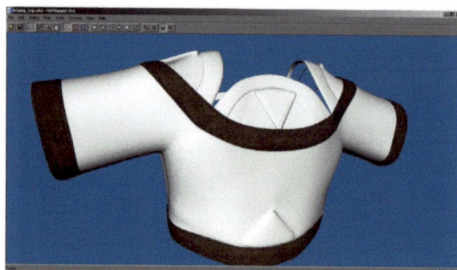

47   And all the layers turned back on. With the construction of this garment, the bands of trim and the triangle appliqués are the only places it would be likely to use a top stitch.

Don't know anything about sewing? Look at similar garments or find someone who can sew and ask their opinion.

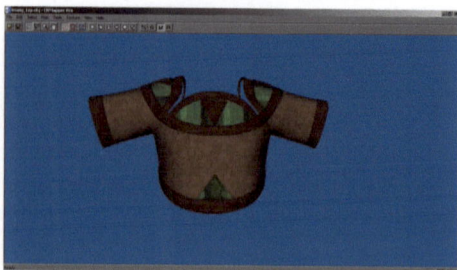

Chapter 7 –   Texturing in Photoshop

48   Now that you have the basic fabric down, as well as some simple detailing now for the fun part. Adding wrinkles without driving yourself crazy.

Make a new layer filled with 50% gray

This wrinkle layer will also be used when making the bump and displacement, so don't be tempted to work directly on the fabric. You will hate yourself later.

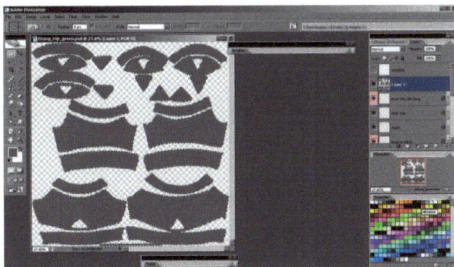

49   Set your gray wrinkle layer to hard light. It will now effectively disappear. If you used any gray shade other than 50% your texture will be lightened or darkened.

Use a large soft brush and the Dodge/Burn tool at no more than 25%. The DB tool got its name from the old fashioned photographic technique for darkening and lightening areas of film.

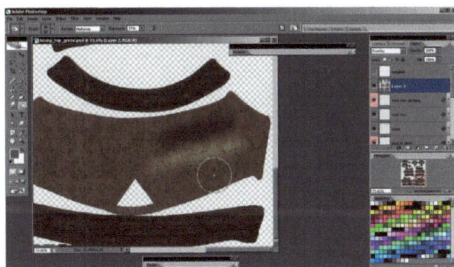

Now we can just paint it in. Used on this layer as you can see, you will get light and dark areas. Turn the layer mode to normal if you want to see your wrinkles in their grayscale glory.

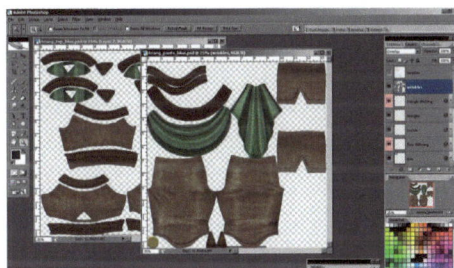

50   Here you can see the completed diffuse (color) textures, with wrinkle layers.

Now I 'Save As' to start the second set of textures.

51   Most of the of the work has already been done. Stitching is laid in, wrinkles are done. So a quick change of fabrics and these textures are just about done, but I'll get back to them later.

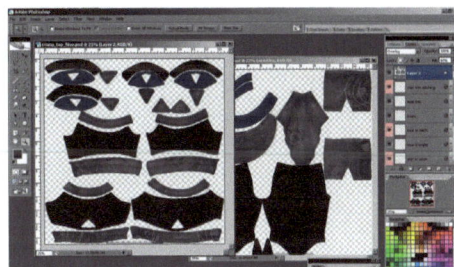

52   Now its time to start breaking down the texture into all the maps needed. I group the layers together and name the set 'Diffuse'.

53   I've added a plain black layer under everything and duplicated the groups for the maps I will need.

The Bump map should carry the surface bump information – rough, smooth, etc.

The Displacement map carries surface disturbance information. Wrinkles, stitching, any place where parts of the surface are raised or lowered

This texture does not need Specular maps – the only piece of metal already has its own material zone. And no Transparency map is needed either.

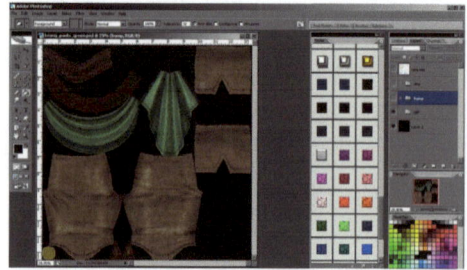

54   I start with the bump map. First I turn off the other groups, than all the layers but the bottom one. Since the bump maps uses only grayscale information, I add a Hue-Saturation Adjustment layer, with saturation set all the way down.

This will make any layer under it grayscale.

I prefer adjustment layers when possible, since they are non-destructive edits. They change appearance, without actually changing the pixels. This makes edits or going back to the original much easier.

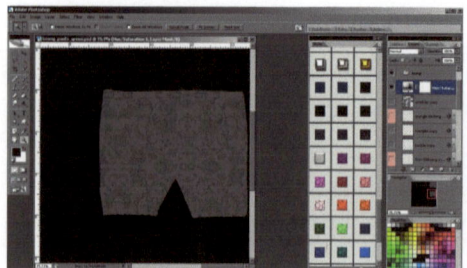

55   Starting with the lowest layer, the pants inset fabric I consider the material. It has a dark pattern on a solid lighter background. If I turned that into a bump map the light area would be raised and the dark lowered. This is the opposite of the raised embroidered effect I want.

So I add an Invert Adjustment layer. For tidiness sake, I right click on the layer to select just the area on the layer, and add a layer mask so just the section of the fabric is affected.

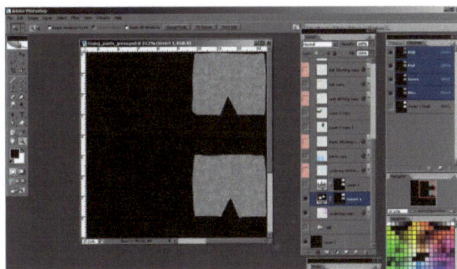

56   With the inversion the fabric is very light. So, one more adjustment layer is needed. This time a Levels Adjustment and I drop the values down to about 90% gray.

Different programs prefer black as 0 or 50% gray as zero for bump and displacement maps. So that lighter is up and darker is down. DS prefers gray, so if you plan to use the same maps for both you may want to start there.

57   The next layer up is the stitching.

Remember this is the bump map. So I add a slight black outer shadow to smooth the surface near the tension of the stitching and a solid gray for the stitching.

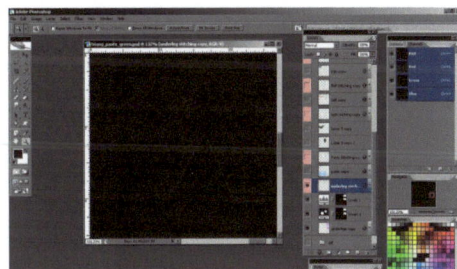

58   Remember how I color coded all the stitch layers? Select your edited layer, copy the layer style. Now select all the other marked stitch layers and copy the style to them. Nice and simple.

Why have them on separate layers? Well in the diffuse map they end up on all different colors of fabric and need different thread colors.

You could, if you really felt like it, combine all the layers and then add the style effects.

59   Next layer up is the pants legs. They have the same fabric as the lower leg inserts. So I move the layer down below the adjustment layers and add the selection to the masks. This will add the effects to the pants legs, and everything will match nicely.

60   I've jumped to the belt. The surface here is pretty good for a bump already, it just needs to be a little darker. I use a layer style Color Overlay, set to darken with black to darken the layer. Again, a nice nondestructive editing method.

61   This is the buckle before adjusting it. It has a number of layer styles applied, which are great for the diffuse but for the bump we need to simplify things.

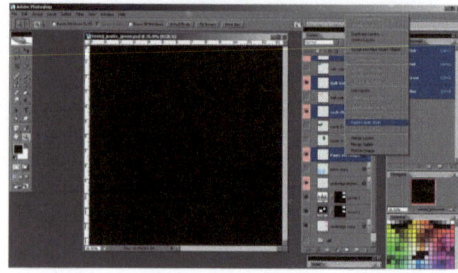

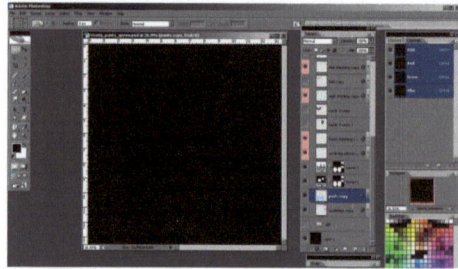

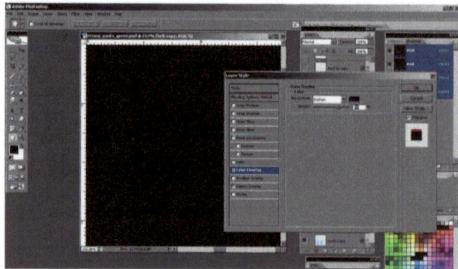

62   Here I have taken out almost everything but the underlying pattern overlay. This will leave a nice rough surface. Since the buckle has its own material zone I can adjust its settings individually, or I can adjust the map again if this image makes too harsh a bump.

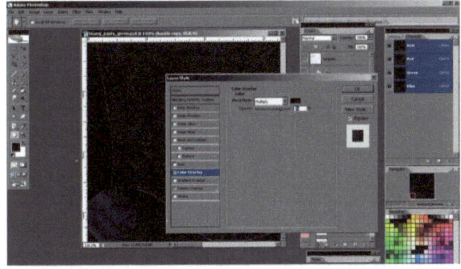

63   The colored stripes on the sash will make a weird bump as is. So I create a hand painted layer of black, set to darken, to fade them to match the rest of the sash.

Possibly a better way to have handled this section would be to hand paint the entire fabric on the template, so the texture and colors are separate and easier to split up for a bump.

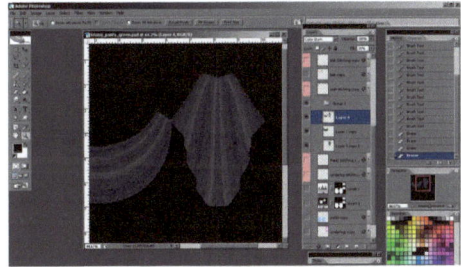

64   This is the final bump map for the green pants. As you can see for the most part is very low contrast. By adjusting the values in your shader you can make this a very strong bump or a very subtle bump and it should do tolerably well in other programs as well that have more limitations on shader settings.

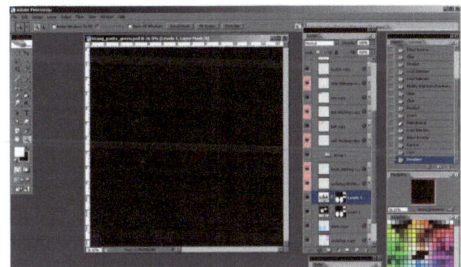

65   Now the same treatment for the Displacement map group. I turn off each layer, and set the background to 50% gray as preferred by DAZ studio. In this case this gives me the option of displacement positively and negatively, whereas if I started at Poser's preferred black its all uphill. You can use Poser math nodes to darken this, or use as is with smaller settings.

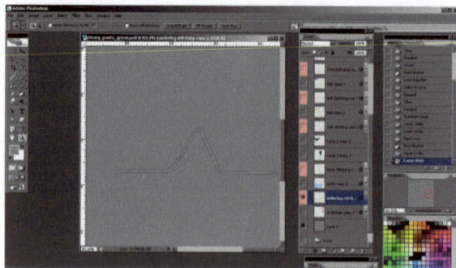

I only need displacement for the stitching and the wrinkles. The surface texture is covered by the bump map.

So the fabrics are skipped and I jump right to the stitching. The stitches are set to white with a black outer glow to create the stitch ditch.

66   I have now deleted all the un-needed layers in the Displacement group. The stitching has been clumped together and the wrinkle layer slid down to be below the stitches.

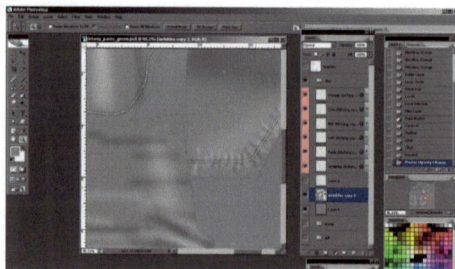

I have used the Levels command to gently adjust the Wrinkle layer so the base color is 50% gray and fades into the background.

67   This is a little complicated. I have created an edge fade so the wrinkles (displacement) does not cross the seams.

I made this by right clicking the wrinkle layer to load the selection. Then I expanded the selection by 4 pixels, created a new layer and filled it with 50% gray. Then I contracted the selection by 16 pixels. Then feathered the selection by 6 pixels, which makes a soft edge to the selection. Then deleted hit delete which has left a soft edged rim around the edges of the uv shapes.

68   Here the edge fader is highlighted in red so you can see it.

You can also hand paint this if you really wanted to, but it can be a tedious process.

And that is the last of the breakdown for this texture.

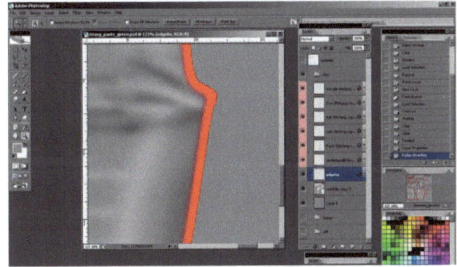

69   Here is the final version of the Blue Pants texture. As you can see I went back in and added some decorative bands of trim, an embossed shape on the buckle and a transparent edge treatment on the sash.

I find it easiest to make transparencies with actual cut outs when possible. That makes the break out stage much easier, especially with fiddly stuff like lace.

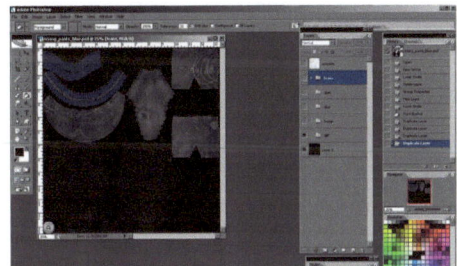

Chapter 7 –   Texturing in Photoshop

70   This texture has some issues not covered in the previous texture. I've worked up through the layers of the bump map until I reach a section with a printed pattern. The actual surface of such a fabric would be a plain weave.

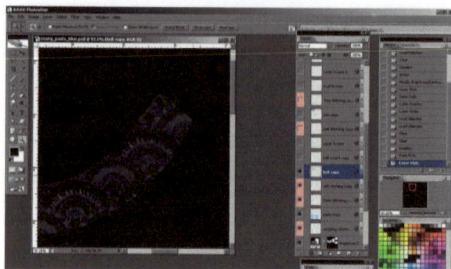

71   So here I substitute a new pattern – one of my plain grayscale twill fabrics. This layer style gets copied to all the other fabric layers with this pattern.

Most prints are simple ink on the cloth surface, so the actual bump attributes can be supplied by a plain woven cloth of some sort. Using the print itself would create raised patterns of the print which is generally not realistic.

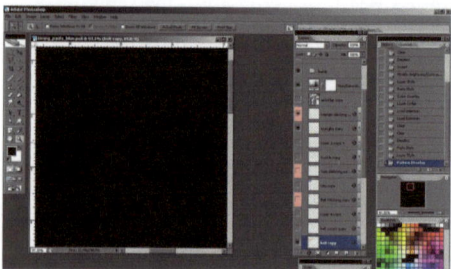

72   this is a nice piece of raised metal trim on the belt. I want it to look like piping when I'm done. The surface of the metal is smooth – the raised effect will be handled later in the displacement. So on the bump layer the metal style is removed and the layer is given a plain gray.

73   The displacement map for the blue pants needs stitching, wrinkles, trim effects and the embossing for the belt buckle.

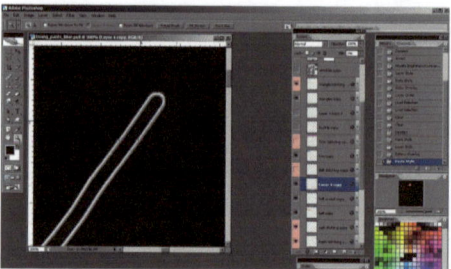

Here on the belt the metal layer has been given a white layer style with a 50% grey inner shadow so that is slopes smoothly up to the center.

The center trim is slightly lighter than the base gray to raise it up and the stitches are base gray, with a dark outer shadow to create the stitch ditch.

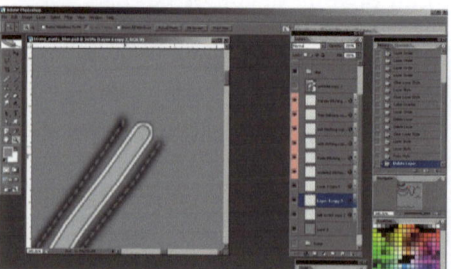

74   When metal is embossed, you get a low edge, then usually the edge at the same height as the base, and often a raised center

The shape was given a layer style with a color of 50% gray, a black outer glow and a white inner glow set to Center, so the middle of the shape is lighter fading to the base color at the edge.

This is an interesting thing to experiment with for various repousee and emboss styles on metals, leather and wood.

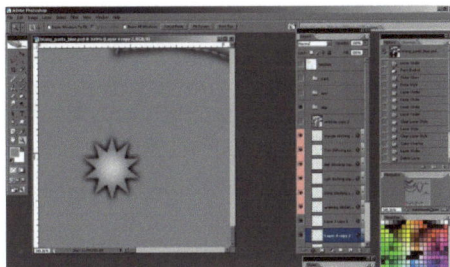

75   The specular map needs white areas for shiny sections and black for non shiny. If you need to shade from shiny to non shiny use a shades of gray.

I remove all the unneeded layers – so everything but the metal areas and the black background.

In this texture the only shiny spots are the metal trim on the belt and the belt buckle.

If it was just the belt buckle, which has its own material zone, I would not need a map.

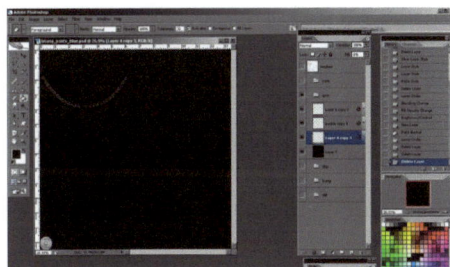

76   But in order to control the specularity on the belt, I have made a map to restrict the shine to the metal trim.

The metal trim is plain white.

When you emboss metal, the lower part often collects dirt or is deliberately darkened. It is often less shiny than the rest of the metal. I have added a gray outer shadow to the metal shape to create a slightly less shiny area around it.

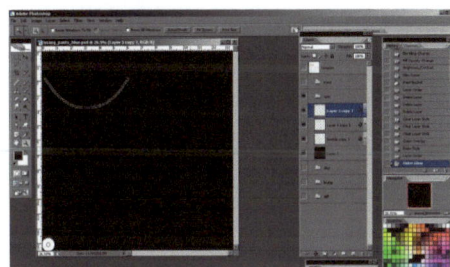

Chapter 7 –   Texturing in Photoshop

77   If you set up your layers cleanly making a transmap is a snap. All the visible areas should be white, the clear areas and black and gray for in between.

You can see the scalloped edge cutout on the sash shows up nicely with the white layer style.

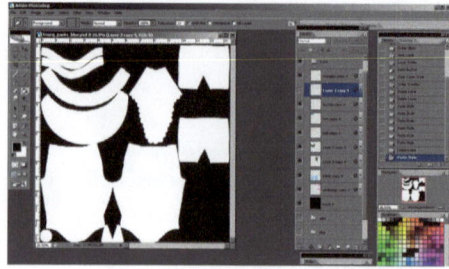

78   One quick edit left. On the diffuse map the metal trim still has an emboss effect. Since that is now being handled by the displacement map I can remove it here by editing the layer style

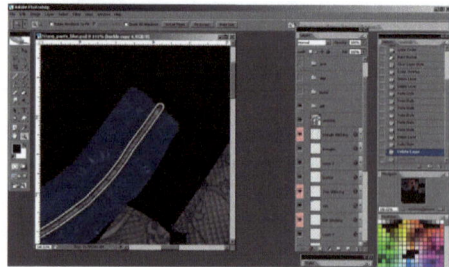

79   And the metal trim with inner glow, outer glow and emboss all turned off. That leaves the pattern, gradient and satin which effect only the color.

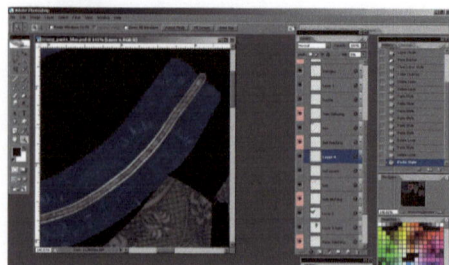

80   Now that all the textures, and breakdowns for each one have been made I save each as a TIF file. To make it easier I use a simple naming convention. Color_map_maptype. So that gives me Blue_pants, blue_pants_B, Green shirt_D and so forth.

Diffuse I never mark, displacement gets a D. Then S for specular, B for bump, T for transparency, S for specular and on rare occasion SC for specular color.

Different artists use different naming methods, but in general you want to avoid spaces, weird characters, and very long names. Not all programs can handle spaces and strange ASCII characters, so its best to keep it simple.

81   And finally, I use ImageReady to convert the TIF files to JPG. NEVER work in a jpg file. It uses a lossy compression format, so every time it is re-saved you lose more detail.

I use ImageReady's jpg conversion, or the Save For Web option in Photoshop since it uses a better algorithm than Photoshop's plain save as jpg does, and you will get crisper results.

Copy all the jpgs into the Textures folder of your working Runtime structure and now you are ready to set up in Poser.

Now unless you got lucky, or have been doing this for a long time, you will probably have to come back and adjust your textures. Expect this at some point, either in the next stage setting up shaders or after QA has found the 1 pixel mismatch you overlooked. (And they will.)

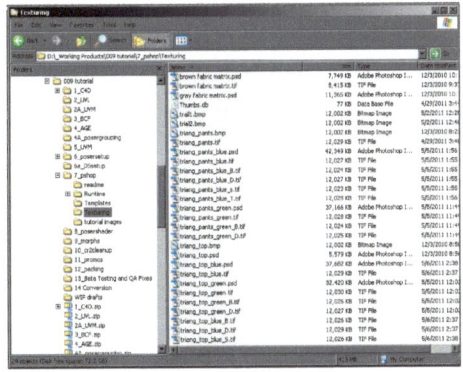

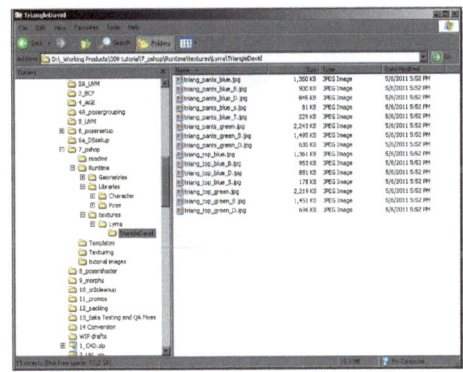

Chapter 8 – Poser Texture Setup

Loading your imagemaps into Poser, setting up shaders and saving your files

1   In order to set up textures you need to have the clothing items loaded. Since you are going to need to render several times to check its a good idea to use lights that don't take too long to render and no textures on the figure.

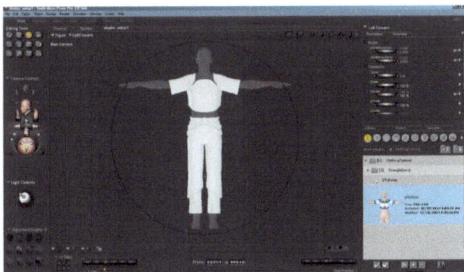

2   When you first open the material room its starts in simple mode. For very basic shaders you can use this interface, but the real power is under the hood.

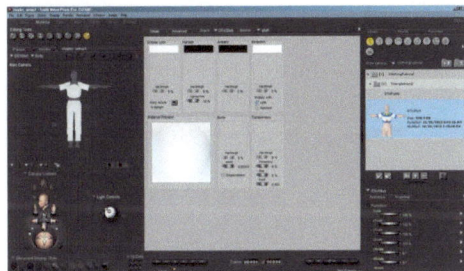

3   This is the advanced material room interface. As you can see every material zone on the figure and clothing item has a Default Poser surface.

This is the basic set of options for every single material in Poser. Various effects are created by adjusting these settings, or plugging procedural nodes or texture-maps into the inputs.

For most basic texture all the inputs you will use are Diffuse, Bump, Displacement, Specular and transparency.

4   I have created 3 Image Map nodes and loaded the maps for the shirt into them. You can see that each node contains various options and will give you a preview of the effect or image loaded.

The main surface will also show you a preview image once nodes are connected.

Chapter 8 –   Poser Texture Setup

5　　It's easiest to check bump and displacement without the diffuse map distracting the eye. I attach the output of the displacement to the input of the displacement. This is the default value.

6　　After rendering you can see that the displacement is too high. You could adjust the maps, but its generally easiest to adjust the displacement values.

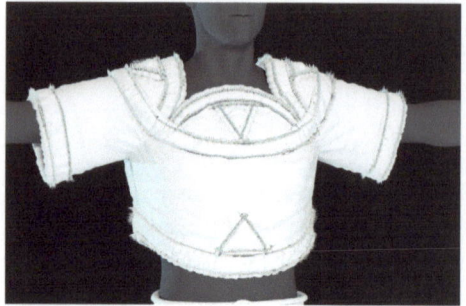

7　　I've reduced the value of the displacement.

8　　And here I can see most of it is fine, but the stitching itself is too high. So I will need to edit the imagemap, to make the stitching darker.

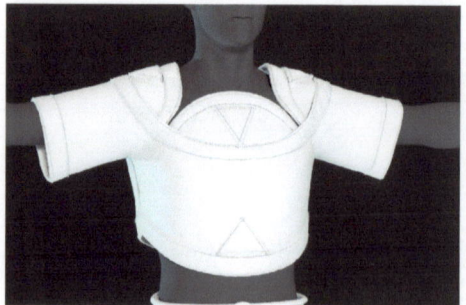

9   Rather than go back and forth between the programs, I'm just going to start a todo list for later so I can make all the edits at once. This is also a good idea in case you get interrupted or forget things.

10   So now I detach the displacement and test the bump map by itself.

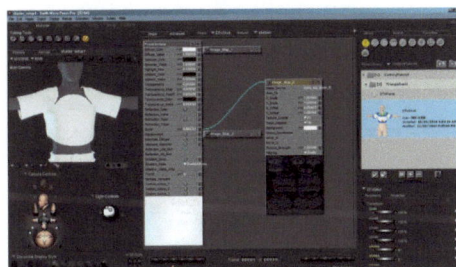

11   The bump map renders fine, I don't think any adjustments will be needed.

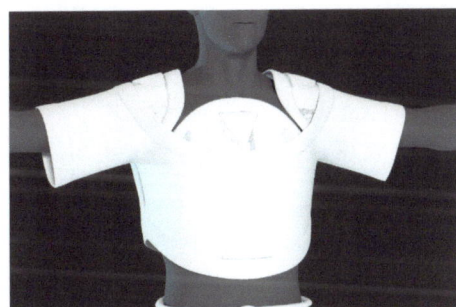

12   Here I have connected all the image maps, and rolled them up to keep the view tidy. I 'Select All' and copy and then 'Paste it to All Surfaces'.

13   Please note that when you copy to all surfaces, any nodes that were there already remain but are detached. Detached nodes still call on image files, and still take up space when the material setting is saved. So its best to go through each material and clear out the node buildup.

14   Thankfully Poser ships with a macro that will remove Unattached nodes for you.

15   I have set up the materials for the pants, using the same strength settings as the shirt.

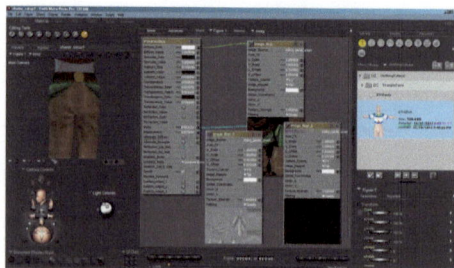

16   As you can see the pants render fine.

17   But there's one little thing. The belt buckle is metal, and most metal is shiny. A brass or copper buckle like this usually has a red or orangeish specular highlight, whereas gold usually shines yellow where lit strikes it.

So I plug the image map into the specular color for the buckle, this will use the metal itself to generate the specular color.

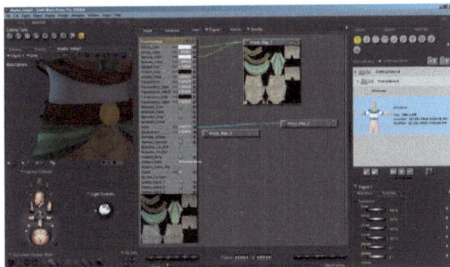

18   And here is a closeup of the buckle with its metallic color. Its fairly subtle but you can see the highlights are an orangeish color.

Many creators use completely procedural textures for the metal bits on clothing. This is a perfectly acceptable method, but it does mean that if the user uses the clothing in say DAZ Studio or Vue, they will need new metal shaders for those bits.

For that reason I prefer to have an imagemap for at least the diffuse channel to give a starting point.

19   Now to start the setup for the blue textures. I 'Save As' the green texture pz3 and start loading up the textured for the blue top.

20   The blue displacement map with the adjusted settings from the green one renders up ok. You can clearly see the bands of trim and stitching.

21   I've loaded all the textures up. The Specular map has been plugged into the specular channel, itself set to full value (white). As you can see the medallions and trim have nice shiny highlights.

The transmap for the sash was plugged into the transparency channel with a full value of 1 (100%). you can see the scalloped edges of the sash came out nice and crisp.

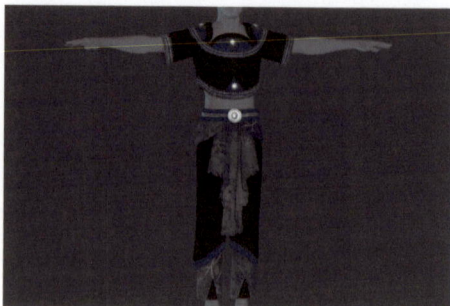

However this test has shown me a new problem … look at the black fabric on the shirt and pants. The sizes of the patterns do not match.

22   I add another item to my todo list. I will have to go and scale the black fabric pattern down on the pants.

23

Here is a render of the green shirt with the displacement on the stitching adjusted. No need to adjust the material setting or MAT files since I simply changed the maps they refer to.

24   Now that you have all the materials created, its time to save them to the Library. Give each one a logical name. I try to keep outfit parts together so I put the color-ways name first and then the item so Green_pants and Green_top.

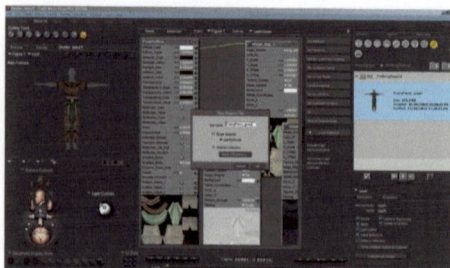

Remember to save as a Material collection (mc6).

25   When you save a material a png preview image, the mc6 and an xmp file. The xmp file contains author metadata for the expanded Library palette.

I generally delete the png and xmp, they will be replaced later.

26   Now most users are used to pz2 format MAT presets. So to make them we will copy the mc6 files you just made into a Pose folder.

Change the file suffix from mc6 to pz2, ignore windows panicking.

If you do not have file suffixes visible, now is a good time to turn it on in your preferences.

27   Now you will need to open each setting file in Notepad and make one edit. This will tell Poser what to apply the pose to.

Change

`mtlcollection`

to

`figure`

28   And here the change has been done. If you have a text editor that can open multiple files at once you can use a search and replace function to make this task go faster.

Do NOT use Word or any text editor that changes the file by adding in any extra information or hidden characters, that will mess up the files internal syntax and Poser will no longer read it correctly.

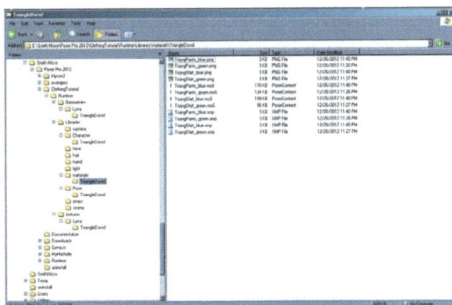

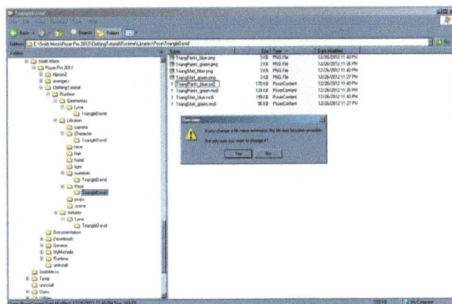

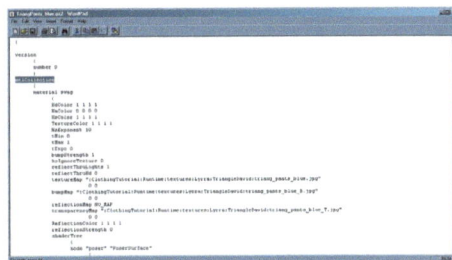

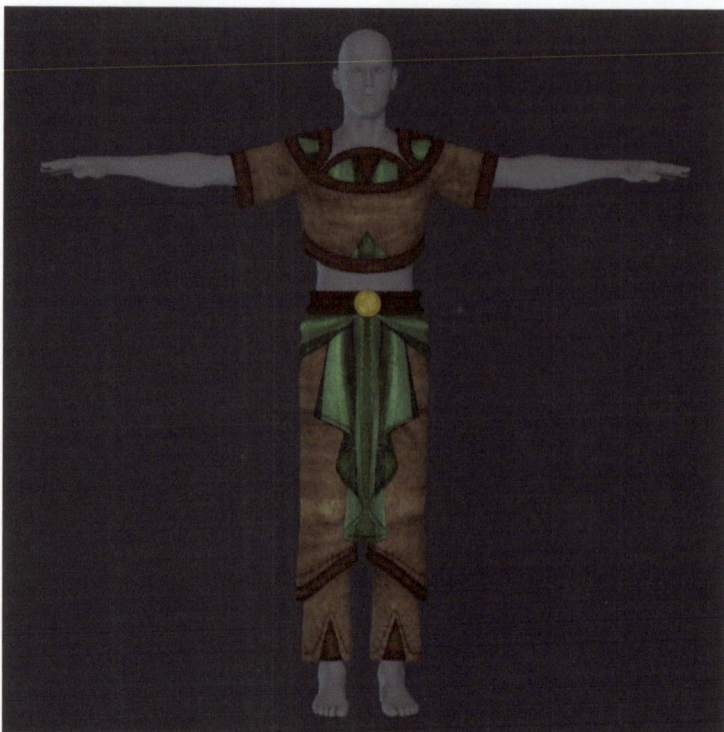

The Final Green and Blue Textures

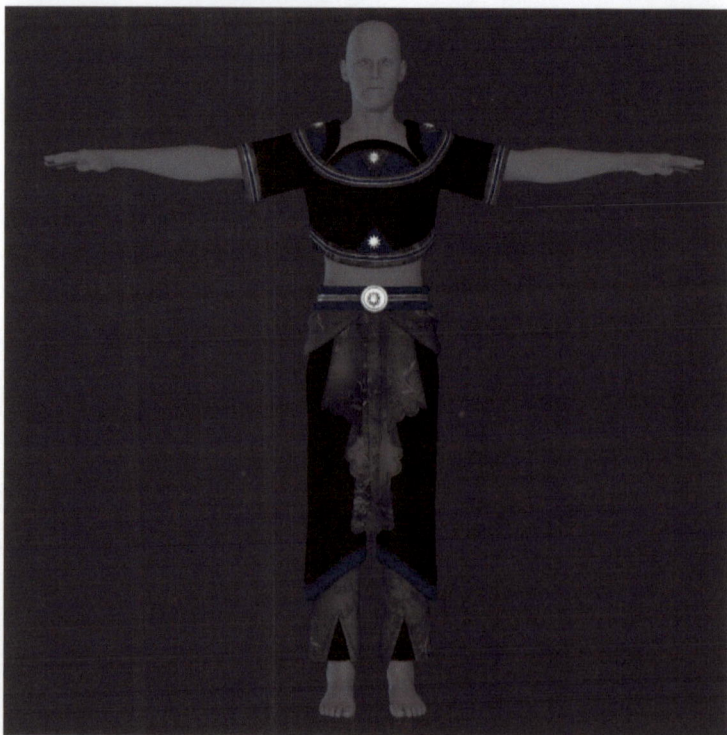

Chapter 9 –   Morphs

Theory on morph targets and morph channels. Several different methods for creating morphs, including with magnets, in your modeler, and via Poser's own morph brush tool

After the clothing fits the default shape, and moves properly when the figure moves the next large step is adding the morphs for the clothing.

What are morphs? To your average user a morph is a dial in the figure (body or bodypart) which changes the shape of the figure. The content creator must discern between dials that contain morph geometry and those that do not. There are dials that do not contain morph data such as scale dials, rotation dials, and specially programmed dials that do strange things like controlling many rotation or scale dials at once. The LegsLengthen dial is a scale handling dial common to many DAZ figures. It contains no morph data whatsoever, and can confuse the inexperienced creator.

Under the hood, morphs are a little more complicated. A morph is a secondary object, based on duplicate mesh of the figure, with some alteration in shape, or 'difference'. This geometry is then loaded into the individual bodyparts of the figure. The program looks at the original mesh data and the changed morph data and saves only the data points which are different. This process creates a dial, for each morph, in each affected bodypart of the figure.

So you can create say a Hips_Larger morph and follow the import process and it will show up in lThi, rThi, Hip and probably Abdomen. It would be a complete nuisance to dial each morph by hand, right? Especially if it is a morph that affects all of the fifty some odd parts in most figures.

Thus enters the BODY (as of Poser 2.)

Poser figures are made of various mesh groups called bodyparts, which is how Poser articulates figures for movement. In addition there is the mysterious BODY. The Body is the part of the cr2 programming which refers to the figure as a whole for the sale of transformations, and for any control dial that controls things across the collection of bodyparts. In order to get all the morphs on thighs, hip and abdomen to dial at once, a simple programming line is inserted in each morph and the control dial is placed in BODY. The end user sees one dial in Body, which they can now use to control the connected morphs throughout the figure.

Common nomenclature is Full Body Morph or FBM for any morph that affects most or all of the body and PBM or Partial Body Morph for a morph that affects only a small are like chest or thighs. This is not standard by any means and often applies only to external morph names – the name you see in Poser on the dial. The internal morph name, the one the program sees and uses, may be wholly different. This mismatch of external and internal names causes many of the issues with superconforming not working, so its something to pay attention to when working. To check the internal morph name you usually need to open up the cr2 file and look there. I find it helpful to make a cheat-sheet of internal morph names for figures I work with often.

Dials in BODY do not always save with poses. Poses with BODY or bodypart dials that affect morphs are called MOR poses. Injection poses are specialized hacked pose file that inject binary morph data contained in special files into already existing channels in a cr2. Victoria3 extensively used INJ technology, and quickly showed the limitations of having a set number of expansion channels. Injection channels can be created for clothing as well as figures, but I've never seen much point. There are many pose files named INJ that are not actually Injection poses, but MOR poses which is easily seen by the internal programming. Exterior morph targets (PMD) can be created for clothing figures, which may help for updating, but in general are not necessary.

Morph target data is saved inside the cr2, except in special cases, or when using the PMD. Please note that it does increase the overall file size by one third of the file weight of the original object approximately. So a clothing item with ten morphs is going to be much bigger than one with no morphs. This file size often affects render times and other calculations. Poly heavy clothing items with a lot of morphs are going to be very unwieldy for many users. This is one of the few times that Injection poses for clothing items becomes a good idea.

In addition some morph dials are master controls that dial other morphs, a prime example are the Generation 4 Muscle morphs. These master controls dial up to 32 other morphs in the figure. To make clothing compatible with morphs like these, you will need to track down and create a morph target for each morph used by the master dial and hope they all add up correctly in the end. (They hardly ever do) Recreating the master dial itself will then not be necessary.

Morphs have some limitations and creating them has to follow certain very simple rules. There are different methods to create them and a number of utilities to help the process of both creation and insertion in the cr2. The three main methods are: Creation in Poser using deformers, Creation in Poser with the Morphpaint tool and Making them in your modeler and importing.

Rules:

A morph object must be identical in vertices and cuts as the target. It must be exactly the same as the original, with the except of being squished or stretched.

A morph cannot alter the length of the bodyparts such as arms or legs, without corresponding rigging changes.

Morphs are linear. The data points move in a straight line from A to B.

Morphs in Clothing

In order for clothing to fit over a morphed figure, the clothing must have corresponding morphs. This can be a troublesome process and not all clothing makers can or will make clothing fits for all morphs in the main figure. In addition to fitting the morphed figure, clothing morphs can also be used to change the shape and style of a garment, fix certain bend issues, and create drape and movement morphs for sleeves and skirts.

As of the latest release in Poser you have the option to 'Copy morphs to clothing'. This will work for some but not all morphs and usually requires a bit of cleanup with the Morph Brush, but is a good place to start.

Why can't I just inject the figures morphs into the clothing? Well reading the first of the morph creation rules will tell you why. The mesh must be identical. Since the figure and the clothing are different mesh, this can never work.

Can I just make the morphs automatically? There are utilities to automatically create the morphs in the clothing to match the figure. In general you will not get the precision and smooth fit that you can achieve with a hand created morph. However, it can be a time saver to use a combination of the various following techniques and auto generated morphs to create morphs in your clothing. Many users will skip over a clothing item if it does not have the morphs they commonly use supported. In general, including fits for the FBMs shipped with the original figure is a good idea. Additional morphs or third party morph fits will add more work, but may make your product more attractive to the end user.

What is a super conforming morph? Exactly the same as an old 'crosstalking' morph or 'autofit' morph. This is simply a morph in the clothing that is programmed to automatically enslave the Body dial for the morph to the Body dial of the figure, so when you adjust the dial on the figure the clothing morph adjusts to match. With Poser's new 'conform morphs' option the programming is only needed for custom bodyparts and for older versions of Poser.

Creating in Poser with Magnets

One of the simplest methods of making morphs in clothing is the Magnet method. Poser has a set of deformers built into it called Magnets. These magnets can be used to deform any mesh in the scene. A great many Magnet Preset or Morph Fit kits are available on the market to make this task easier. Here I will show the process of using a preset magnet kit setting to make a clothing morph target.

1   Load your figure and clothing. Zero the figure, and make sure both Body and hip translations are at 0. Conform the clothing and dial the morph you wish to fit on the figure.

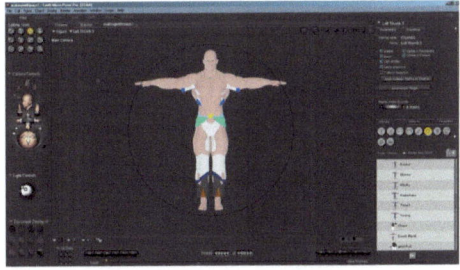

2   Select the clothing and load the magnet set that corresponds to your morph. In this case 'superhero' for David.

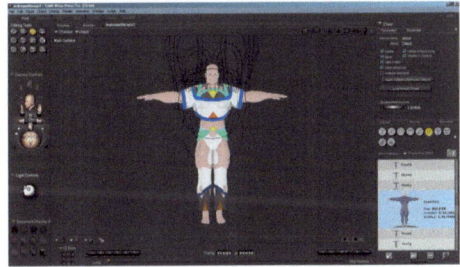

3   Here I am using the Python script by Dimension3d to spawn all the morphs on the bodypart and create the Body dial all at once.

However, if you do not use python scripts, you can sue the old fashioned method.

On each bodypart in the Object menu Spawn a morph. Remove the magnets. Now set each of your new dials to 1. In Figure, you can now create a FullBody-Morph (FBM) which will hook all those morphs to the new dial.

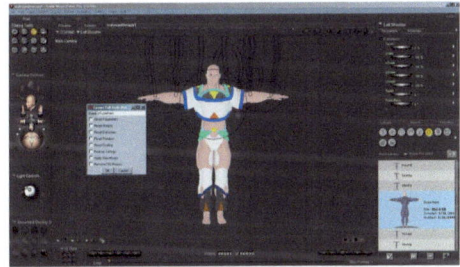

4   I recommend using a magnet deletion script such as DelMags by Ockham to remove them from the scene. You can however delete them manually. Please note, some magnets may jump to the figure so make sure to check there as well.

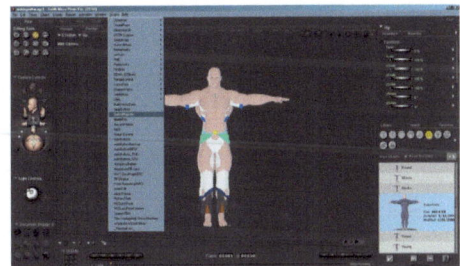

5   In the body properties of the shirt I set the 'Conform morphs' selection box. Now when the clothing item is loaded the morph will automatically follow the figures morphs, no extra programming needed.

NOTE: this only works if both bodypart name and morph name are identical between the figures.

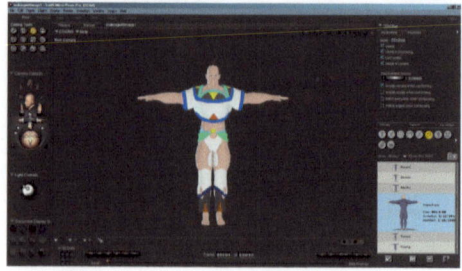

6   Here I have loaded the magnet preset onto the pants. I have turned the sash of for the moment. As you can see there are some issues.

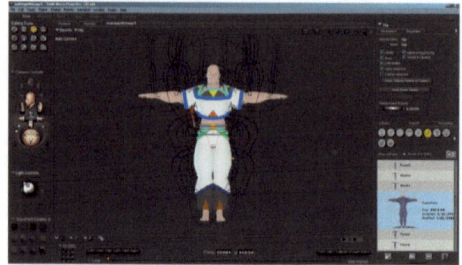

7   Here is a closer view of the issue. As you can see on both sides there is a sharp jag at the knee. When you have a sharp jag like this, generally it means that one bodypart has a magnet zone affecting it that the other part does not.. This makes a mismatched edge.

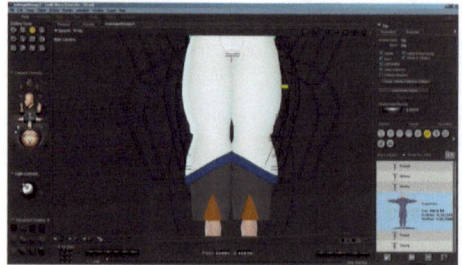

8   So first I look at the Shin part and write down the magnet numbers. Each magnet will have a unique number in the scene.

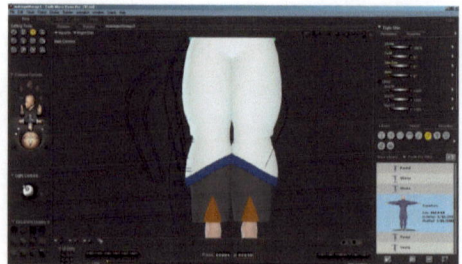

9   Now I look at the magnets on the thigh and check those against the Shin list.

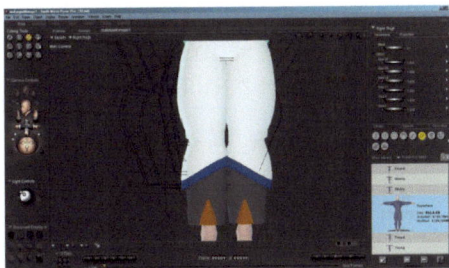

10   Sure enough I have Magnet9 on the thigh but not the shin.

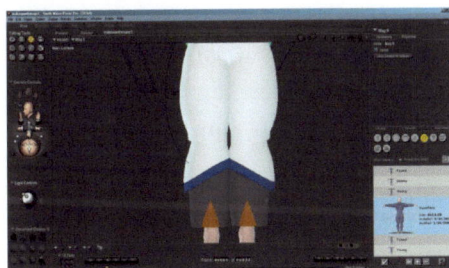

11   I select the magnet and in properties 'Add Element To Deform'. In the hierarchy dropdown I choose the rShin and as you can see the annoying cliff goes away.

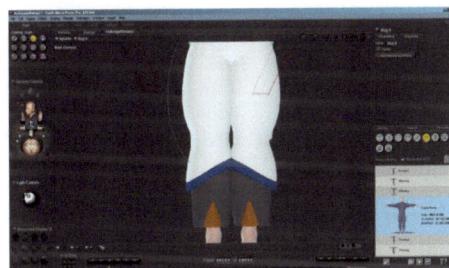

12   Now I turn the sash back on. As you can see, none of the magnets affect it. Why? Its a custom bodypart. So I will need to manually, or with a script, add the magnets affect to the sash.

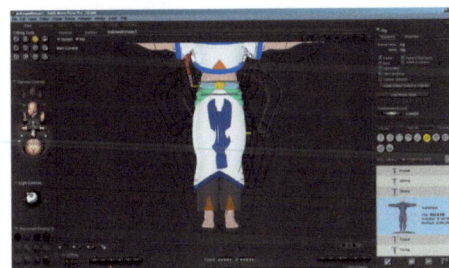

13   Here you can see that I've added some magnets to the sash. The shape is starting to fit over the morph now.

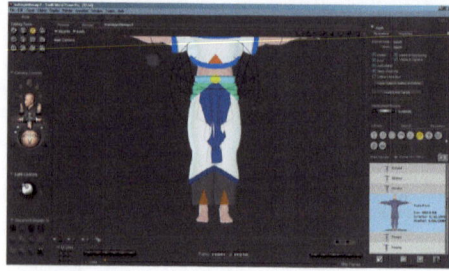

14   I added one custom magnet to pull the lower part of the sash out. Now that everything fits I can spawn my morphs and remove the magnets, just as I did on the shirt.

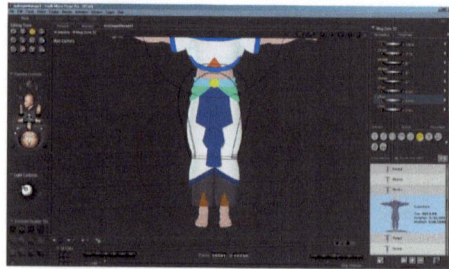

15   I have ticked off 'Conform morphs' on the clothing and you will immediately see that the sash does not follow.

Why? Its a custom part. Since the part name does not exist in the figure Poser completely ignores it. A line of custom code will need to be added to make the sash super conform as well.

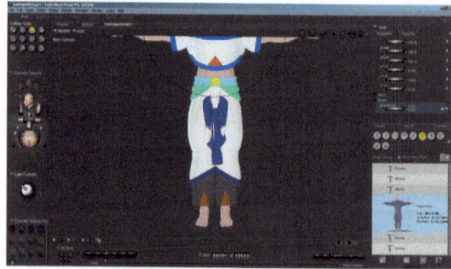

16   Here is the final morph. One down, thirty more to go.

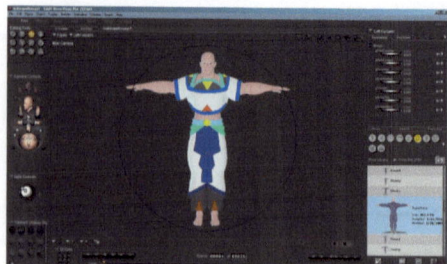

Some morphs are simple enough that no preset is particularly needed. Here is an example of setting up a simple fit adjustment morph using magnets. This morph will narrow the lower hem of the shirt for a tighter fit.

1   Load your figure and zero it. Load and conform the clothing.

Select the clothing you wish to deform. Create a new Magnet.

You can just see the edges of the magnet zone here and the top of the horseshoe shaped magnet.

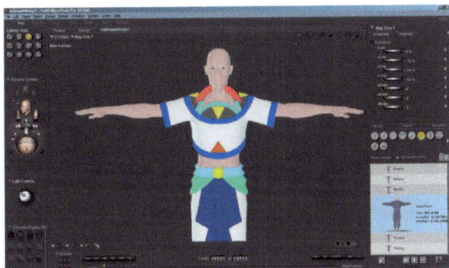

2   Here I have aligned the magnet to the area I wish to deform.

Each magnet has three parts – The magnet area which you see as a circle, but is actually a wireframe view sphere. The Magnet Base, which is a bar that lays across the bodypart and the Magnet itself, which is the horseshoe shaped part. Here I have set the Element view of each part to wireframe, so I can see the figure more clearly.

3   The magnet zone is expanded to fit around the entire area I wish to deform. As you can see it encircles the lower chest region of the shirt.

The Magnet Base lays across the shirt. I have found the size of the magnet effects the strength of it somewhat, so generally I make sure both ends stick out past the object.

The magnet itself is the proxy – if you move, scale or rotate the horseshoe, that change affects the mesh.

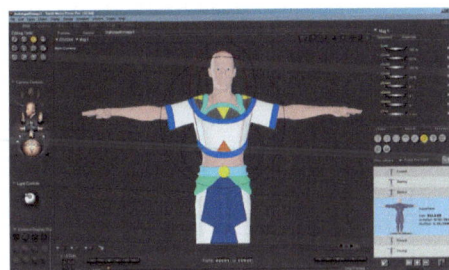

Here I have scaled the Magnet on X. As you can see the shirt has narrowed across the area inside the Zone.

4   I used Dimension3D's 'Create FBM' script to create the morph but you can use the manual method if you prefer.

Then remove the magnet and save the cr2. Remember, the morph is saved in the cr2, so until it is saved to the library it is possible to lose your work.

Creating in your modeler

Creating a morph target in your modeler allows you a great deal of control. Sculpting programs like Zbrush allow the creator a chance to make some very realistic fits for such problem areas such as loose clothing over large chests and tight clothing on heavy figures. This method is also often used for undressing morphs, movement morphs and style morphs.

You will need to get the morphed figure into your modeler – whether with a specific Poser importer or by exporting the figure from Poser with the joints zeroed and the FBM dialed to 1.

The next section shows how to manually break apart and load morph targets into Poser. However, if you are using a dedicated import/export feature for your modeler it may have its own methods. Poser File Editor has an inbuilt tool for importing morphs in batches, and other full-mesh-to-morph creation helper tools exist.

Before the creation of INJ and EXP technology often the only viable way to distribute morphs without violating copyrights was by distributing the actual morph target obj. These special obj were stripped off all but the difference information and thus are not useful as anything but a morph target. You can still find some of these around in older archives, especially for Poser 4 era figures.

Poser morph target separation

1   Make your morph in your modeler and export as a normal obj. If necessary, use UVmapper to transfer grouping information.

Remember, the morph obj and the destination obj must be identical except for morph changes.

Import your obj to Poser.

Chapter 9 –   Morphs

2   Open the Group Editor by switching to the Group tool

As you can see the view of the model changes, now I can see the Hip polygons as selected (red) and the rest unselected (gray).

In this case we will make no group changes or selected – we are simply need to use the Geometry Function for Spawn Props.

When you have clicked on that button, you may see no change in the scene, but Poser has created a prop object of each bodypart.

3   Here you can see the new objects listed in the Hierarchy window. Do NOT move or change anything. In fact even manual selection is not a good idea as that often moves things.

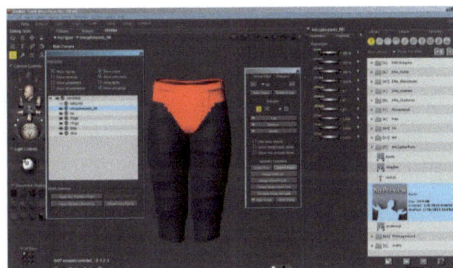

4   Export each new object as a morph target object. In the object export dialog, export only one item at a time and choose only the Export as Morph Target option.

This option will preformat the obj to be a morph target, and hopefully cancel out any changes that may have accidentally been made.

Each part will need to be exported and named, to indicate where it should be loaded.

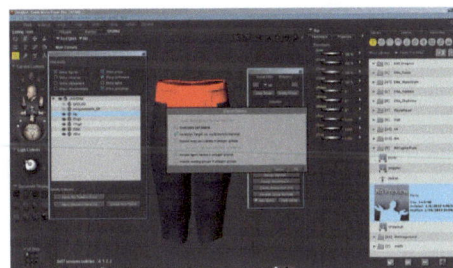

5   Now to load the morphs into the bodyparts of the clothing. Load the clothing figure.

Select a bodypart. In the Object menu choose Load Morph Target. This is the menu option that will allow you to load any matching obj as a morph target.

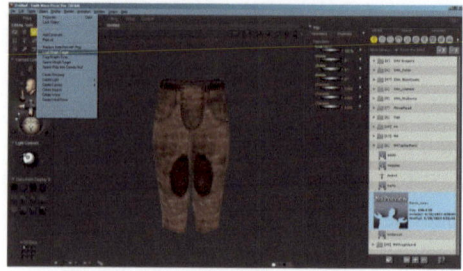

6   In the next dialog window, choose the morph-target obj, in this case Hip, and assign it a name.

7   If all went well, you should have a new dial in the bodypart. If set to 1 the morph should appear in full force on that bodypart.

You will need to load each morph object, for each bodypart.

You can name them anything you like, but if the morph will be auto conformed the name will need to match that of the corresponding morph on the figure.

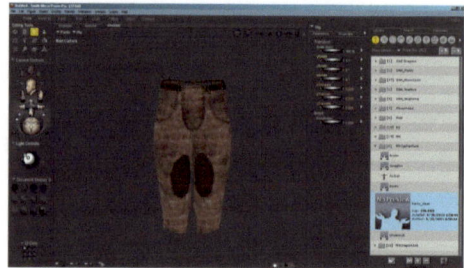

8   The next step is to create the master dial, the FullBodyMorph dial, in the Body of the figure.

Dial each bodypart morph to 1.

In the Figure Menu choose 'Create Full Body Morph".

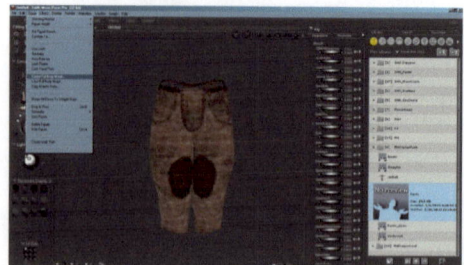

Chapter 9 –   Morphs

9   In the dialog, give your morph a name and say OK.

A new dial should appear in the Body area of the figure.

Zero out all the bodypart morphs and dial the new FBM dial to 1 to check it.

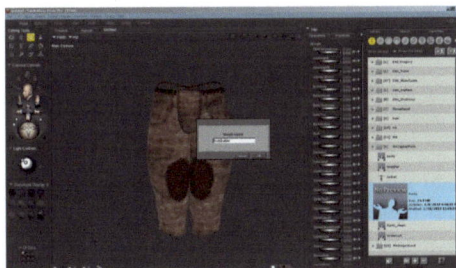

NOTE: if you have any other dials active when you create the FBM Poser will assume you meant those as well and wire them to the FBM. Be careful.

Poser Morph Brush

Another method is to use Posers own morph painting brush directly in Poser. The only tricky part here is getting the morph named properly.

Making a New Morph

1   I have dialed the Trap morph on the figure. You can clearly see where the figure has popped through the short on the back.

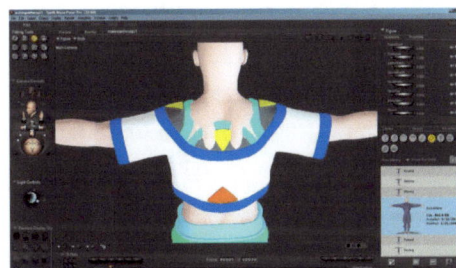

First I copy the name of the morph from the dial on the figure. Just open the dial properties and Copy.

2   I have selected the shirt and started up the Morph painting brush. There are two tabs, Create New and Combine. We need Create New.

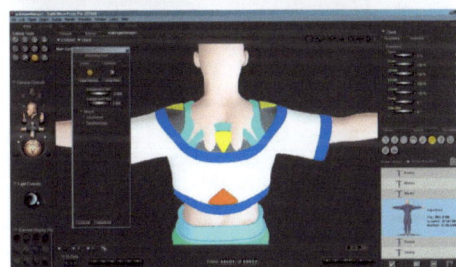

3   On the proper tab, I choose to Create New and in the menu box paste the name of the morph.

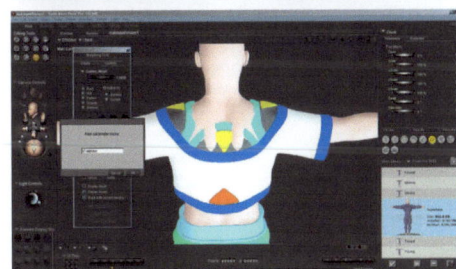

Chapter 9 –   Morphs

4   The morph brush has several settings which alter its behavior.

First – type of change. You will mostly use Push and Pull. Flatten and smooth will help you smooth out bobbles in the mesh. Restore removes the morph entirely in an area, this can be very useful when tidying up auto created morphs.

The second important option is the softness, size and strength of the brush. This is similar to the same settings in Photoshop.

Hover the brush over the mesh to see the vertices it will affect, red the strongest fading into green, the least affected. Paint the morph in. I find short sweeping dabs have the best effect. Use several lesser strokes, as often trying to do it in one pass leads to distortions.

In some areas you will have better results with push/pull than loosen/tighten, so if one doesn't work try the other.

5   Here you can see the finished painted morph. It will automatically create the FBM. Save the cr2 to the library.

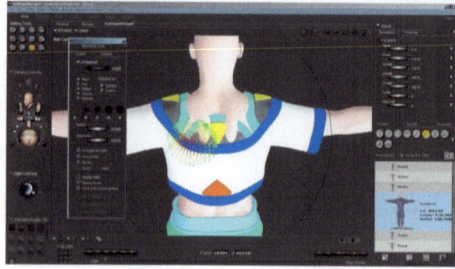

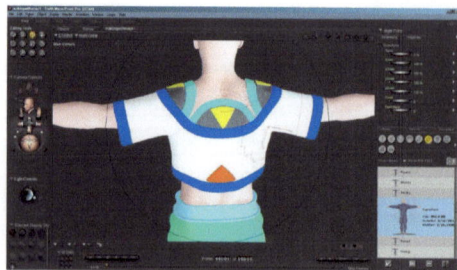

Chapter 10 – Cr2 Cleanup

The final tidying up of the clothing cr2 file, clearing

away junk data and setting the morphs to conform

As you create your clothing item certain things in the programming commonly get broken, created by accident, carried over from an earlier version or misnamed. One of the final steps in making clothing ready for someone else to use is tidying up all the loose ends.

Your item may have some or none of these issues. Use the following checklist to examine your clothing item for issues.

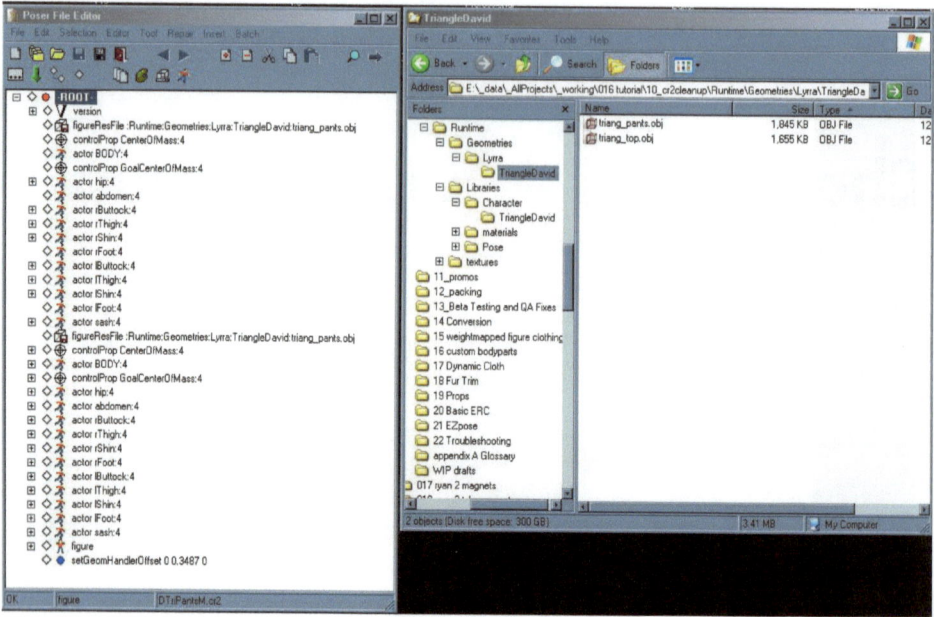

Check the geometry reference file

The geometry reference line appears twice in the cr2.

It will look like this.

```
figureResFile :Runtime:Geometries:Lyrra:TriangleDavid:-
triang_top.obj
```

This is a hard-coded line that tells the program the exact location of the geometry file and its name. If your mesh is not in the place specified, the program will ask for it to be found, or load a ghost cr2. Or sometimes pick some random other .obj with the same name.

All stores require the geometry location call start at :runtime: and preferably be in the Geometries folder. Most vendors use their own name for the next folder, and the project name for the final folder containing all the items. Make sure the geom reference lines are proper.

Remove all excess geometry and actor calls

When using a donor rig it is quite common to have extra bones left over, that are not needed by your clothing item. They generally do no harm, but can inflate file size.

All cr2's should have a string of parts following the hierarchy from Hip to the part the clothing covers. It is possible to make items that do not, but they can have issues such as jumping on conform and most auto conversion processes will have trouble.

Also leave one more bone past the body part. For example this shirt has the geometry part for Chest, rCollar and lCollar. But the skeleton has hip, abdomen, chest, neck, lCollar, lShoulder, rCollar and rShoulder.

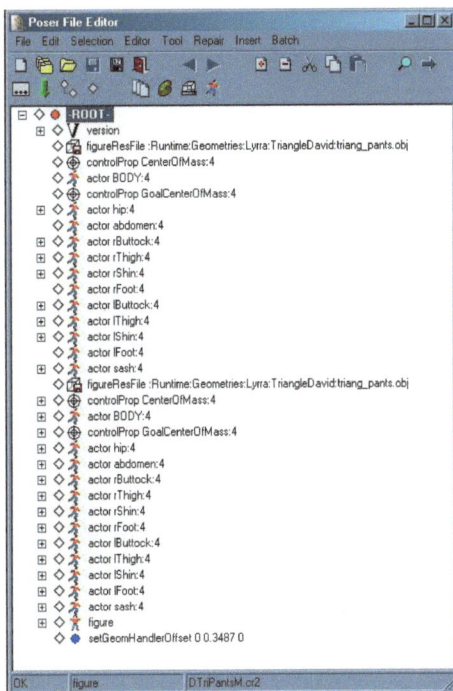

Remove empty or unneeded morph targets from Body and all parts

Some morph creation scripts or methods will leave empty or unwanted morphs in various parts of the figure. Check the Body and all bodypart morph channel sections to make sure that only wanted morphs are included. Check your fit morph names against the internal morphs they are for, to make sure crosstalk (auto-conforming) will work properly.

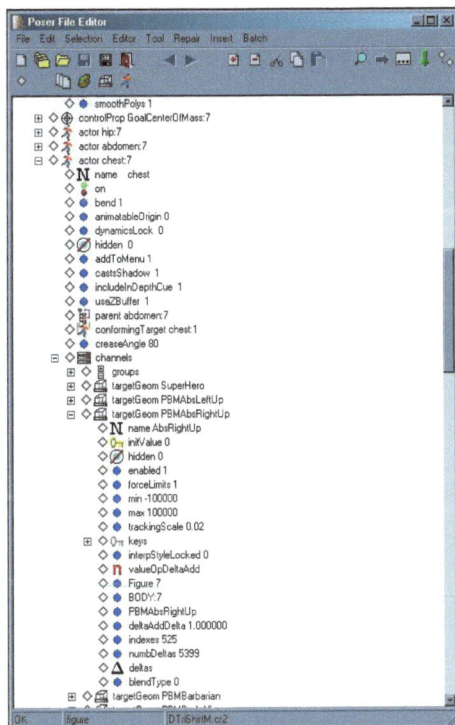

Chapter 10 –   Cr2 Cleanup

Add conforming programming to morphs if needed

In Poser starting at version 8 you can choose an option on conform to 'conform morphs' this will automatically activate morphs in the clothing that match both bodypart and morphname with the figure. The problem however arises, if you have custom bodyparts or use an older version of Poser.

Please note that you must change ONLY the figure # in the channels section of the cr2. If it is changed elsewhere Poser will crash spectacularly on load of the clothing item.

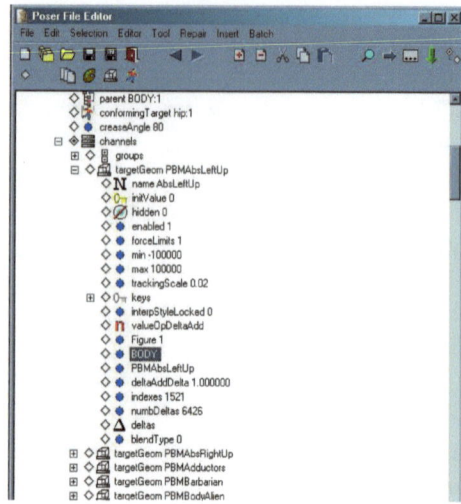

Check used materials

The material names and current settings are saved in the figure section at the end of the cr2. Make sure that the ones loaded are correct, and contain no extra material zones and no incorrect texture references.

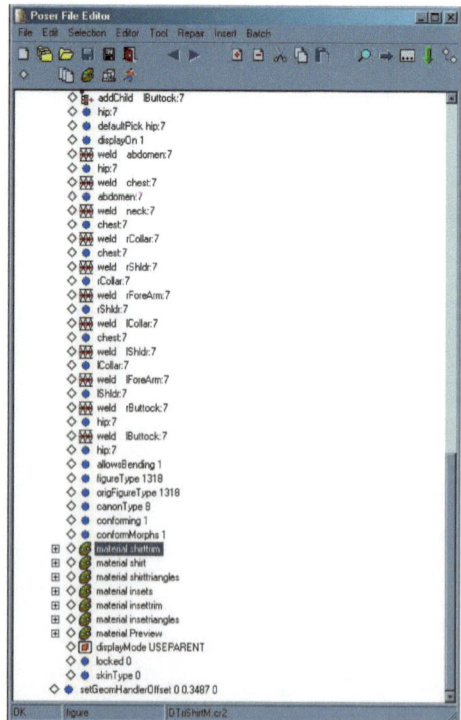

Zero all morph targets

All morph targets on clothing should load at 0. Generally the easiest way to do this is to zero them in Poser and then save the cr2. You can manually change values in Poser File Editor or a text editor if you rather.

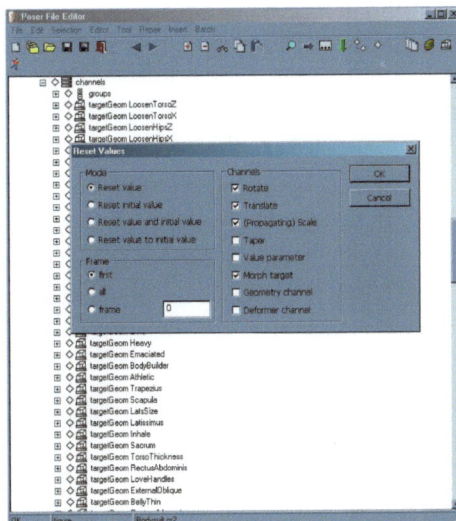

Make sure item has unique internal name

To cut down on internal code error and to make it easier on the end user, make sure each clothing item has a unique name. This line is in the Figure section at the end of the cr2

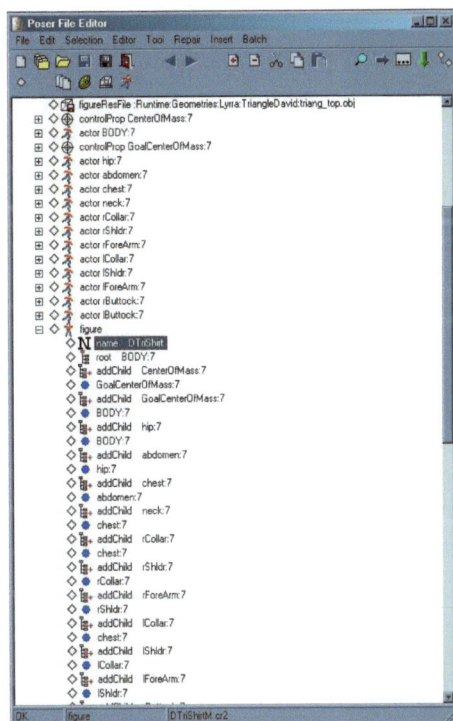

Set all to figure1

As you load several items into Poser each one is internally assigned a different figure number. This means you can see values of up to 54 (my highest to date). In general to cut down on internal morph code issues, its a good idea to make sure to reassign these to 1. Best practice is to search for example ":5" and replace to ":1" You will also need to change "Figure 5" to "Figure 1".

Resolve Binary Morphs (pmd)

If your cr2 references a PMD file you have the option for binary morphs turned on. Since most stores prefer internally stored morphs, you will need to put them back in your cr2. You can do this by either loading in Poser and re-saving with the binary morph option off, or by using the Resolve Binary Morphs option in Poser File Editor.

Chapter 11 –
Promos and Thumbnails

Promotional images are how people see your product. This chapter walks you through some theory and examples and through the process of making promos for the project clothing set

You have finally passed that point where you are probably pretty much done with the creation of your item. However, the real use test of making promos images almost always exposes something that will need to be changed, so expect to have to go back and fiddle some things.

Any time that you are trying to convince someone to acquire your product you will need to make promotional images that show the items being used. You will also need to make the less sexy but still vital png thumbnails for the library, and the various back, front, wireframe and options renders for the store images.

Store Requirements

Every store has different requirements and limitations for promotional images. You will need to find and make yourself familiar with these requirements. Number of images, size of images, types of images, resolution and so on.

Some stores also have rules about nudity, violence, implicit sexuality, in-store items only and so forth. Check your requirements before you start composing images.

Images you Will Need

Store thumbnail image, Main Promo or Beauty shot, Front & back shot per texture, Morph shots, Wireframe or untextured shot front and back, Advertising image (banners, page inserts, etc), Per Part renders, PNG renders for Poser library. Additional images for advertising thread and or gallery promotional posting.

Other Items you Will Need

Since you have made clothing items you will of course need to show them on the figure. So at the very least you will need the following:

The figure and its morphs, hair, skin and or custom characters, poses, lights. Thankfully many of these can be shared by various figures.

Prop (hr2) hair is very versatile and can be used across multiple figures. Cr2 hairs since they are rigged present more complications but can often be adjusted or converted to fit.

Most poses should be usable on figures with similar bodyparts to various degrees of success.

Lights of course should be universal. I suggest investing in at least one good set of clean white lights for promo purposes.

You may also need some props. Simpler is often better, after all its your clothing that should be the star of the show.

Tip: make friends with other content creators who have different specialties. You can often help each other by trading items for promo images. This also gives your work more screen time.

Things to be Aware of

I think we've all seen some promos that make us wonder what the maker was thinking. Remember: you want people to see and want your clothing item. So it should be the most important item in the image. The lighting should be clear and bright, not dim or colored. Any hair or props should not hide the clothing. If you have some very small items like jewelry, you may want to do focus images just for those, or inset shots as part of a larger image.

Avoid postwork. **AVOID POSTWORK**. I don't think I can mention that enough. Small edits like compositing images, and very small level / brightness adjustment tweaks are fine. However heavy postwork that obscures the images and especially anything that alters the shape or fit of the clothing should be avoided.

Another common issue in promos is making the promotional artwork too specialized. If your item is say, a pair of bluejeans, show it in more neutral settings. If you show it only on science fiction aliens, then the casual user will see 'aliens' and skip right past an item they would otherwise buy. Try to make it as obvious as possible what your item is.

Avoid using niche characters to show off your products. I know its cruel to say, but try to use a display figure that is more generic. A more generic model will appeal to a larger range of buyers. Some clothing sets will only appeal to a certain market segment, and for those you can use the goth girl for the goth clothing, the Asian man for kimonos and so forth.

Try to make your item as obvious as possible. If you are making a specialized thematic or seasonal item, choose background items that complement but do not distract. Santa suits rendered over snow, steampunk items with a suitable Victorian era building. Or leave it plain and let the viewer imagine their own scenario. Plain will also save you the time and expense of obtaining and rendering complicated and often distracting background sets.

You need to plan three main kinds of images. The simplest is the part renders and thumbnail pngs. These are simple renders, for each item and in each color to be used for the library thumbnails and to show all the options in the store preview images. These are usually best rendered in clear white lights, over a solid background. They will probably be viewed very small, and it will need to be very clear what item and or color each thumbnail is showing.

The second type of image is the plain fullbody render to show morphs, all color options in front and back and the untextured renders. These again should be rendered in clean white lights, and usually over a solid background. These are very often composited together over another background so I usually render them over black. If you render over a color or light shade you will get a halo around the image that can be distracting, but a dark halo tends to fade in. Halos are often very visible on hair so think about hair colors when building a render that will be composited.

The most complicated sort of image and often the most important is the main or beauty shots. This is the first image the customer is going to see, so it needs to hook their interest. For this render you can use more dramatic lighting, but I usually suggest staying away from any lighting that obscures or tints the item.

You can render with or without background props. This is generally a matter of taste, time and the suitability to your clothing item. You can do perfectly well with very minimum props, and often a simple render of an interesting backdrop texture can do just as well as something more complicated.

Try your best not to confuse your viewer, but at the same time the main beauty shot should be attractive and compelling. Remember when glancing through a storefront most people look at each main image for ten seconds or less. You may not need to show the entire figure either. Often a standing figure does not take much space in an image, so cropping in closer will fill the screen with more of your set, at the expense of the legs.

Here I will be making an example of each sort of commonly needed promo image, as well as the basic postwork and compositing to assemble them. I will also go over some simple image construction rules that may help in putting together a more appealing image.

Should I have multiple renders in Poser versions / DAZ studio / Reality render / LUX render

Generally I say don't bother unless your item has special settings just for that program or version. For some items additional settings are a selling point, but not everything. They should at least be mentioned in the ad copy, but a full beauty image per is in most cases not needed. Leave these for the options images. If your set is say metal or glass that has specialized settings you have made for Lux or Reality or DS, then by all means include insets showing both or a tagline mentioning "DAZ Studio 4 settings included" and so forth.

Remember your average user is probably using the stock render engine and probably normal (no IDL, no AO) lights in Poser. You want your item to look as good as possible in those situations, where it will be used most often. If all your promo renders are in another rendering engine with specialized lighting the casual user will never be able to replicate them and will be discouraged with your work.

Part and preview renders

These are the renders to show all the parts in the set, and that will be used shrunk down to 91 pixels in the Poser library so the user can find things. Each item should be isolated on a plain solid colored background to make them easier to see.

1   Load figure. Use either a very boring skin or a solid medium gray material on the figure. No hair or morphs are needed. Load and conform clothing.

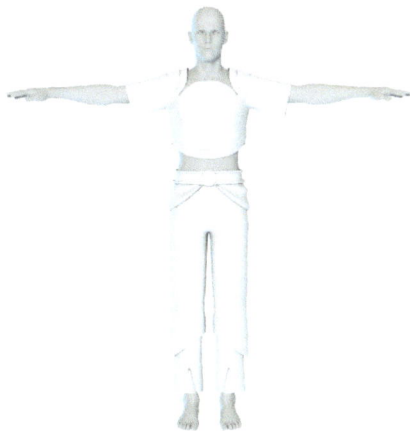

2   Each clothing item should be rendered separately in plain white (or with just displacement.)

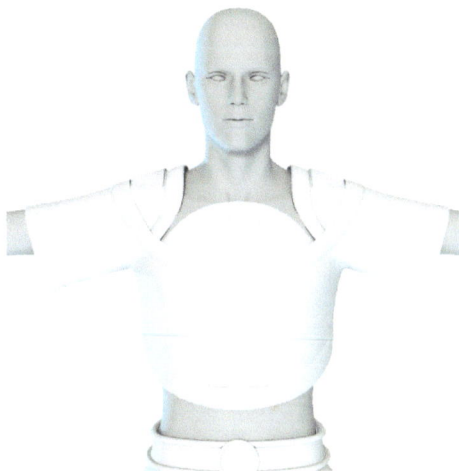

3   And another separate render for
each color included.

4   If your item has multiple
variations like stone and metal colors
for jewelry, set the whole item to a plain
solid gray or white and show each color
change in close up, to make it obvious
what changed. These options can be
added in small insets next to the main
image.

Plain Full Figure

1   Load figure. Load a plain skin and or simple character. (Minimal shape distortion recommended). Choose a simple fast rendering hair that does not obscure the clothing. Choose a simple light set that does not obscure or tint the image. Load and conform clothing.

2   Choose a simple pose that does not distort the clothing. Rotate the figure to find an appealing angle. Render once in plain white, possibly with just displacement maps. Save the scene.

3   Save as, and rotate to get a good back view and render again.

4   Make multiple copies of your Front and Back scenes and render each one with each full color scheme for your outfit.

5   To render a 'wireframe' preview simply load the jpg template map for each item in as a diffuse map over plain white. It should line up perfectly with the mesh. When rendered it will give the appearance of the wireframe being visible. Since my template is colored, it also gives an idea of the material zones.

Not all stores require a wireframe preview, but I have found that most users appreciate it.

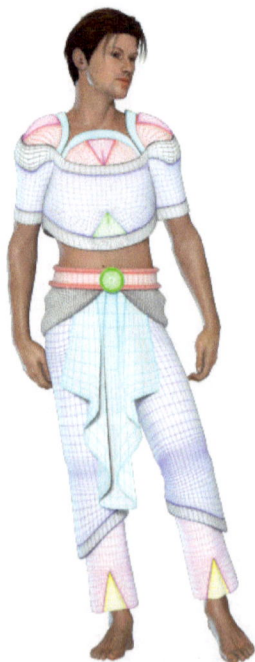

6   Most stores request that the clothing be shown with at least 3 morphs. You probably only need the front render for those.

Save as, and load the morphs onto your figure. Choose 3 distinct morphs and render each separately at full value.

This is Emaciated.

Here are examples of the above renders composited together for various store promos.

Composite 1 –

Front and Back Pseudo Wireframes

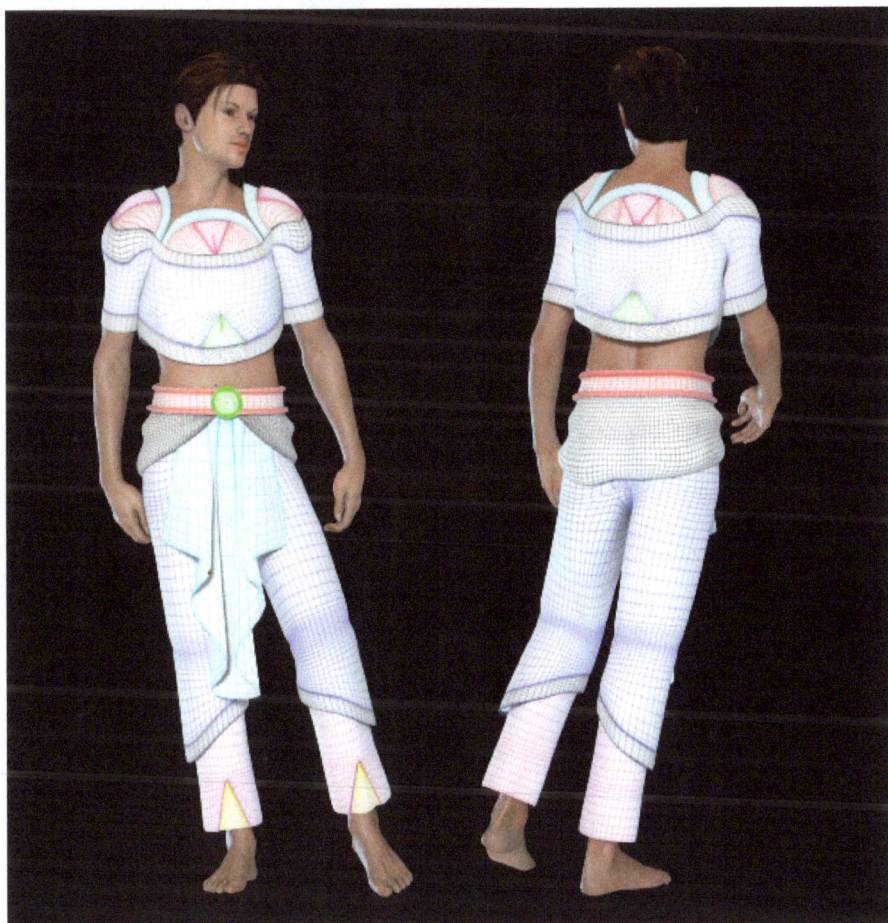

Composite 2 –

Morphs

Composite 3 –

Colors Front and Back

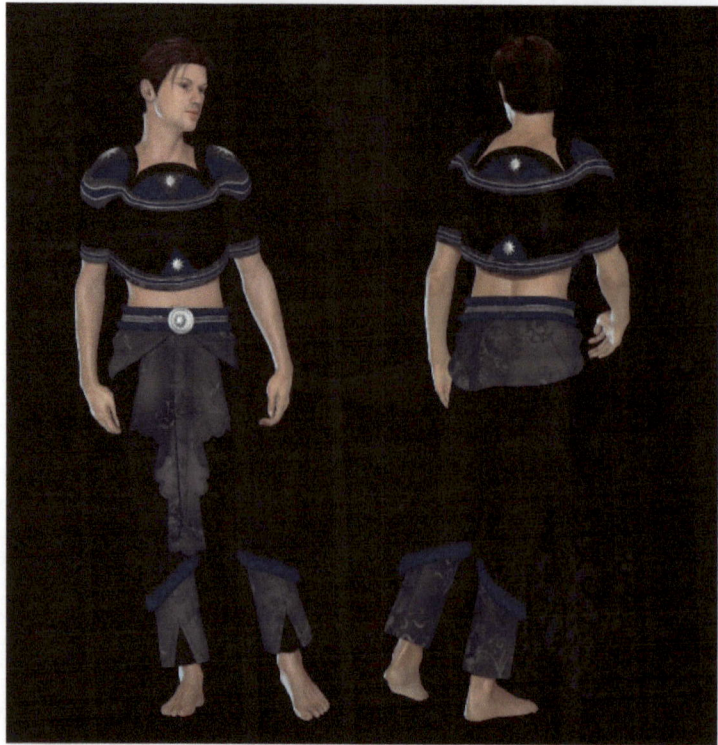

Basic Image Construction Theory

Constructing a compelling image is something that all artists struggle with in various ways. It can be very subjective. For promo images, a form of advertising image you have constraints in addition to the aesthetic. The store you are building your images for will have rules about size: landscape and portrait, and usually also about nudity, and violence.

Then in addition to that you have aesthetic concerns. This is a much fuzzier area and really could take entire books of its own. I do recommend reading some simple references on image composition and design. These are bread and butter images ... they do not need to have great visual drama and an important message. They do not need to be amazing art, just clear, visible and appealing.

Basic things to keep in mind:

Avoid text on the image. Simple things are okay but not anything more complicated. The main reason is that the Poser content market is global and so the chances that a non English speaker is looking at your work are pretty good. A website translator only works on text, not images. So try to keep as much as possible in the written description and as few words as possible in the images. Its also keeps the visual clutter down.

Simplicity – Advertising art like this is necessarily more limited. But there is a lot you can do with a person just wearing a pair of jeans as we have all seen in the very successful ad campaigns for certain notable brands. The success of those ads comes not from the jeans, or the person in them, but in the skill of the photographer and the image designers. Real world clothing ads are one resource for ideas for your own virtual clothing ads. Not certain how to advertise shoes? Have a look how real shoes are advertised both on store shelves and in photos, that should give you plenty of ideas how to approach it.

Jewelry

The necklace is from FinishingTouches by Ryverthorne.

Here I have the main beauty render and then clusters of insets to show all the color material options for the necklace.

This is a bit busy, so I might break it up into several images.

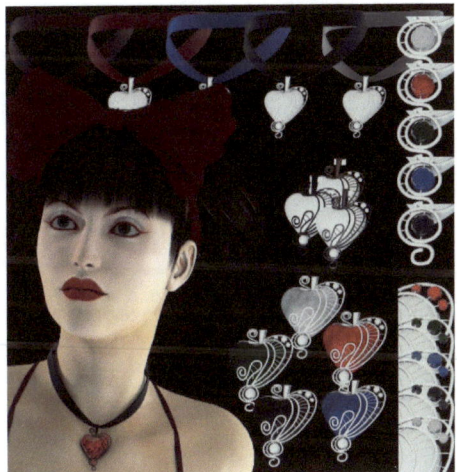

Avoid Action Shots – Keep action shots to 'paused moment' shots when possible. A flying action kick taken in isolation usually makes for a bewildering image. But a man holding his pistol at a jaunty angle at the ready tells a whole story in a single paused moment. Your clothing should be as visible as possible and not scrunched up in a kneeling pose or in awkward angles that make it hard to see details. For these images the figures face is less important, and the details of your clothing the focus. So cover her face up with that big hat, its ok. Hide his profile behind his raised arm ... just as long as we can see that lovely row of buckles on the wrist bracer nice and clearly. Like I said before – make your clothing set the star. Keep supporting items like hair, props and character relevant but not as exciting as your clothing. (Unless of course you are lucky enough to be working in collaboration with a character or hair designer).

Contrast and Value – utilize color and value contrast in your promos as much as you did when making the clothing textures. Try to keep backgrounds muted, and less busy so they do not overtake the figure.

Major Cache for Michael 3

by Uzilite

The Major Cache outfit is a very intricate piece of modeling in the sci-fi armour style. This set has been converted to Michael 4, and is still used in many renders by various artists. The rigging may be fairly simple, but the level of details in mesh and textures makes this set still stand out.

Beauty Renders

This outfit, to me at least, seems somewhat ceremonial. However, several people have mentioned it looks fantasy or science fiction. Since I have two colors I'll make one image for each.

1   Load the figure and conform the clothing. Apply clothing textures.

2   Choose hair, hair texture and character and apply.

3   Choose a light set.

4   Test render in the default pose. Check to make sure the hair and skin work together and with the clothing colors. Adjust or change lighting as needed.

5   Pose the figure. Rotate the figure – do not move the camera – until the angle is appealing.

6   Test render again. Now is the time to adjust any little things on the figure or lighting.

I think the skin looks sort of flat and lifeless. So I'm going to apply the Ezskin2 settings, which add SSS and so forth, and see if that perks it up a bit.

7   Do a full render as is.

8   Save as and set up variations
with different background settings. As
you can see Poser decided to quit on me
at knee level, which is fine for once.

9   And the Second color variation with completely different props.

And the final Beauty renders, mildly touched up in Photoshop with a levels adjustment and cropped to size.

Chapter 12 – Packing

Poser content has many files. Use this procedure and checklist when packing up your product, to make sure you have everything

In order to send your project out into the world, you will need to pack it and all its bits and pieces up. This will require copying all your bits and pieces from your working Poser folder into your project folder, as described in earlier chapters. If you followed along this guide, you will have most of the bits already in your project folder. At any rate, make sure to go through the packing checklist to make certain.

Since Poser files are in so many little pieces scattered through the folder here is a checklist following a basic Runtime structure so you can herd everything together.

After the parts are arranged, then you also need a Readme file, possibly a packing list and most stores requires some sort of boilerplate EULA or license text be included.

Some stores requires a specific location in the Runtime structure for the text files, so make certain to check their requirements.

Packing Checklist By Area

Runtime:

Readme file

The Readme file is a text format document that contains information about the item, the creator, resources used if any, what sort of licensing it has and so forth. Many stores also request a packing list, with a list of all items in the zip file, be contained in the Readme. The readme ideally will also have contact information so the user can contact the creator of the item.

License file

The License file is a separate document, usually supplied by the store, containing a legal agreement detailing exactly what the end user can and can not do with the content. This is also known as a EULA, an End User License Agreement. If you are supplying a free item you can have a EULA or not, its your choice.

Any additional tutorial, guide or help files as needed.

Some items are complicated or unusual enough that creating a guide to go with them is a good idea. Dynamic clothing items for example, are less intimidating to the user if a step by step guide on how to use them is included. Sets that are very complicated, or have different versions for use in Poser or DAZ studio benefit from a guide document explaining what the different files are for. However, in these cases expect that more than half your users will not actually read the supplied documents, so make sure if someone else is handling customer support, that they are aware that explanatory documents are included.

Library folders

Now if you followed the project creation guidelines I advised all the way at the start of the book this next step is fairly easy for you, since everything is pretty much in the right spots already. However, it is always a good idea to go through each section and make sure everything is ship shape. Make sure you have to most recent versions of all files in your project folder.

Naming Your Files – its a good idea to put the figure name and product name on any supporting content folders. So in this case I will have a D3_TriangleSuit folder in Figures, Poses and Materials. Some content makers put their name in content folders, but personally I've never found that to be all that helpful. If I am looking for textures for 'Triangle Pants', then I'm looking for 'Triangle' and not the name of the maker, who I probably don't even remember. Also as enticing as it is to use special characters to influence the folder sorting (like ! Or _ or *) please don't. It just makes it harder to find things. It is of course your choice in the end.

If you make additional textures for a clothing item put the name of the item in the folder name. I have plenty of textures that I have no idea what outfit they go to. Example: Daytime_for_EveryDayWear.

Geometries Folder – all your current mesh files, with the proper uvs and groups.

Characters Folder – the cr2 files for your clothing items. Each cr2 item should have a corresponding png thumbnail image.

Props Folder – any props for the set, with all versions as needed. Again each should have a png preview. All props should have corresponding geometry objects in the geometries folder, no embedded mesh.

Hair Folder – if there is an hr2 format prop, it and its previews will be needed

Pose Folder – a pose file and png for each item in each color. Any additional poses such as Fit poses or special poses, and png images for each.

Materials Folder – a material setting for each item in each color and preview. Possibly additional shaders such as metals or matching materials with pngs.

Textures – all texture images as needed for the shaders, jpg format is recommended. Additional specialty maps such as tiling texture, reflections and so forth.

Additional Files – python scripts, magnet presets, instructional pdfs, injection binaries.

Readme Files for Free Items

Free items can have as many conditions of use as any commercial item, as well as still need to explain how to use the item, and what resources if any were used to make it. So if you are making items for free distribution it is a good idea to supply a comprehensive readme file. Plain txt or pdf format is suggested.

A sample txt readme is supplied, as well as one in my fully packed project runtime. Below I go through the various sections in most Readmes. Remember, you will have non English speaking users so keep this as clear and informational as possible. If you are making an item for free distribution this is a good structure to follow.

Product Name – The name of your product. I find having the models name included makes it easier to identify items such as V4Bikini, M4Pants etc.

Copyright (c) CREATOR NAME DATE – This is your copyright statement, with your name and the date.

End User License – Commercial or non commercial use.

Commercial use allows use in for profit projects.

Non Commercial forbids use in for profit projects, this is common for free items or for fanworks.

Distributable or Non distributable – Distributable items can be redistributed by anyone.

Non Distributable this product or any of its parts can not be distributed.

On occasion there are other use limitations such as merchant resource items which must be edited before redistribution. Make sure you are as clear as possible about how your items can be used.

Description – Describe your product here as clearly and simply as possible.

System Requirements – PC or Mac, Poser 8+

List what programs are needed to properly use this product, including the lowest compatible program version it has been verified to work in, ie Poser6+, Poser-2012Pro.

Needed Files – List any base figure or morphs essential for this product such as Victoria 4, v4 Morphs+, and so forth.

Product Link – An http:// format link to the product page for the above item(s) so the user can buy it if needed.

Installation Instructions – How to install the item. In most cases simply 'unzip to desired runtime' But if any setup is required this is where to list the steps.

Usage Tips and Limitations – Any tips or limits on the item such as 'does not work in DAZ Studio' and so forth

Morph List – A list of all morphs in the item.

File List – A list of all files in the product zip file.

The Runtime for this project

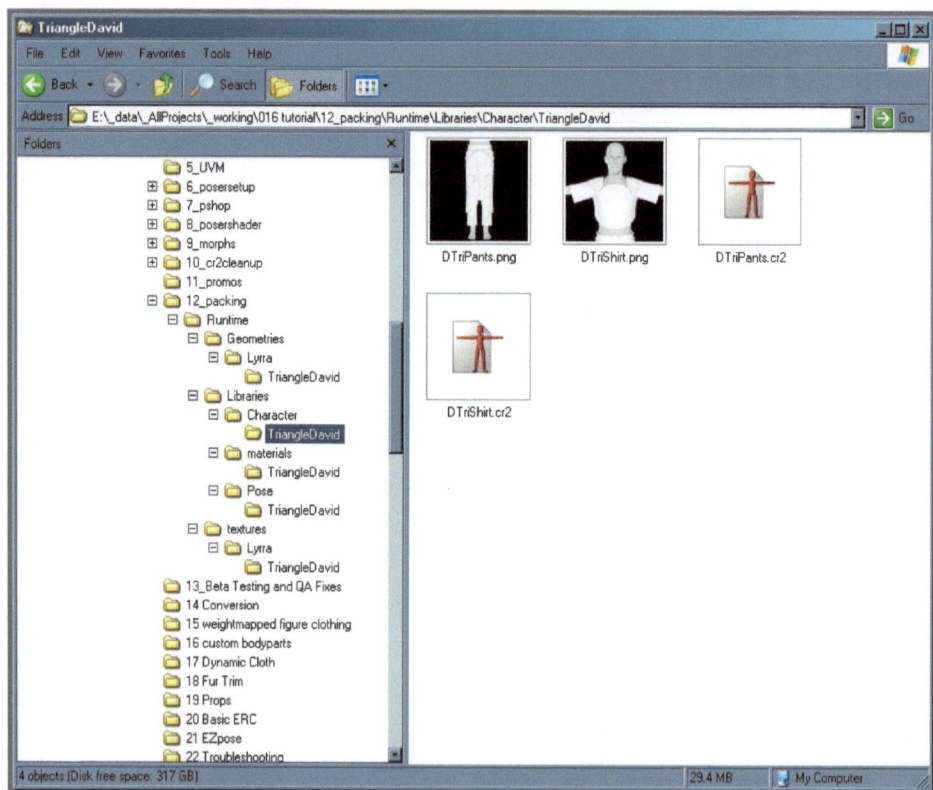

Chapter 13 –
Beta Testing and Fixes

Before releasing anything to the public, always have it

beta tested. And of course, then you have to fix any-

thing that might not be working properly, which can be

tricky

After your item is ready to send out, you will need to have it beta tested.. Most stores test items themselves, but it is always a good idea to have it tested yourself beforehand to avoid delays.

A good beta tester will test the item to make sure it installs properly, that it functions as describes and all parts of the item are contained with no extras. However they should not make comments regarding aesthetics or other value judgments unless requested. It doesn't matter if the item is purple or unattractive or for a figure they don't care for. All they are testing is for functionality – does it work as advertised.

Some things are not points of failure but may require a judgment call by the creator such as morphs that are too loose, shirts that appear vacuum fitted, and so forth. They are not wrong, they are possible aesthetic points. The creator may choose to disregard aesthetic opinions.

A recommended list of things to check for most clothing sets

Product Archive Integrity – The first thing to check is that the file unzips properly, with its runtime structure.

Runtime Structure – Then the runtime structure should be examined, to make sure all folders are spelled correctly and all parts of the product are where they ought to be. If a packing list is supplied it should be checked against the contents to make sure everything that is supposed to be there is, and that there are no extra files. Windows is especially good at including thumbs.db, and also various .bak (backup) files.

Functionality – After the basic check then the content should be installed into a Poser runtime. The first check is that the item loads and conforms to the figure. Each item should be tested separately.

1. Zero Fit - Load and conform on a zeroed figure. Check for fits on the default body shape. Check with and without textures. Also check a rendered version, as some poke throughs may appear or vanish when rendered.

2. Morphs - Check each morph supported by the clothing by dialing it on the figure. Check from all angles, and verify poke issues with renders. Save any renders to send to the clothing creator for fixes.

3. Bends - Set figure to default shape and zero pose. Check all 3 bends on every body part covered by the clothing. Render any issues. Make certain to check if any fix morphs exist and use them as needed. Note: JCM are often used as joint correctors, so keep an eye out for them.

4. Compound bends - Check compound bends with preset poses. Generally best

practice is to use those poses as supplied with the base figure such as the 'V4 General Poses'.

5. Textures - Check each material and pose file supplied. Load each and render to make sure each mat and pose file works as expected. Look for obvious and unattractive seams. Since clothing is made of pieces of fabrics, some seams are to be expected, and can increase realism. Texturing has a lot of judgment calls needed. You may want to mention such issues as stretched textures, inverted bump/displacements, and scaling issues.

A Beta Testers Report

After the testing the tester should send the report back. Hopefully it will say 'Its perfect. Send it on' But generally there is something that needs to be adjusted.

It is best to break the issues down by type: textures, pose issues, fit issues. Certain things in a product can be changed easily without reworking or adjusting anything else. However, some things that may need to be altered may require essentially remaking the entire product from scratch.

I have sent the David clothing set to an experienced tester. Here is the report I have gotten back.

Hi Lyrra,

I just finished getting my testing images in order. Not a lot of big stuff from what I could see.

The shirt is not set up to cross talk in older versions of Poser, although the pants are fine.

The pants load with the name Pants in the drop down, but the shirt loads as DTriShirt. These should probably be made consistent.

Textures passed and were great looking.

Fitting:

On load and conform in Zero Pose, Default Shape, there is a small poke through in the groin area. This poke is visible in most of the other morphs, so if it's fixed in Zero, it should probably fix in the rest.

Morphs that enlarge the thighs cause a poke in the inner thighs. SuperHero thighs overlap which may be hiding a Zero Pose poke in this morph. It is visible when the figure is posed. Adductors, Barbarian, Bulk, Hamstrings, Heavy, Pear Figure, Portly, Stocky, ThighFull, ThighInFull

Some of the larger morphs also had much smaller pokes on the outer thighs. Heavy, Pear Figure, Portly, Stocky, Definition.

Morphs that enlarge the chest/pecs cause small pokes on the chest near the neck band. PecShape 2, PecShape 3, PecShape 4, Pectoral.

Trapezius and Tone morphs causes pokes in the upper back.

Morphs that enlarge the arms, especially upper arms, cause pokes on the shirt near in those areas. Arms Heavy, Barbarian, Muscular, Deltoid.

Bulk morph has an unusual shape to the sleeves. They look a bit like very short Kimono sleeves.

Posing:

Collars bent forward cause pokes on the shoulder blade area of the back.

Collars bent upward cause pokes on the chest.

Combo poses of the shoulder/collar (David 3 Poses with limits on) showed pokes on the chest area and back/shoulder blade area.

Knee bends caused layers of the pants to poke through each other at the calf. The David figure's calves also poke entirely through the pants in places with knee bends.

Thigh bends cause poke through issues near the crease of the thighs.

(Attached are 35 images)

Evaluating the Report

Well as you can see, I didn't get a clean pass. Ah well. I expected at least one thing to fail, but as always my beta tester has found more than that. Now I need to take apart the report and the pictures and figure out what on the point of failure line I am starting with.

A point of failure line is a way of visualizing a process in stages, and determining what stages will need to be re-done if anything is changed at a certain point.

To understand this, contemplate the creation of the peanut-butter and jelly sandwich. Your first step is to obtain materials such as peanut-butter, bread, jam. Then you must obtain tools, plate and knife. Then you have the assembly process where you apply peanut butter to one side of one slice of bread and jam to one side of the other slice of bread, and then apply the peanut-butter and jam sides of the bread together, and gently set the result on the plate.

At any point in this process the entire thing could fail – if you have no bread, if you have no knife, if you apply jam to both sides of the bread and so forth. In that case you will need to go back one or more steps to repeat before you can successfully make your sandwich.

As you may have noticed by the previous several hundred pages of directions, making clothing for Poser is somewhat more complicated than making a sandwich.

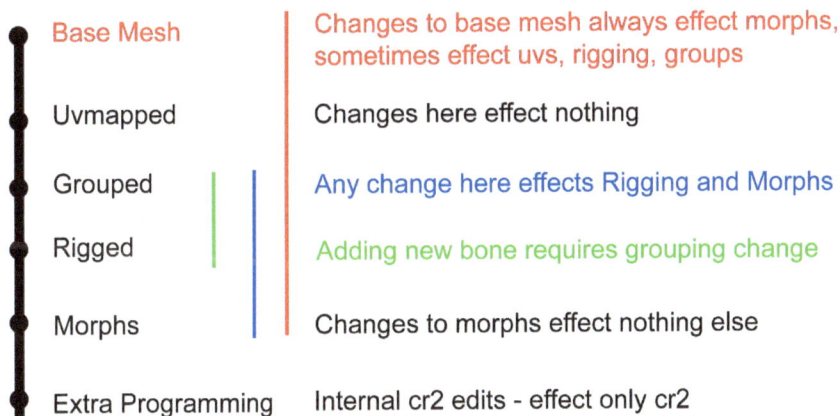

Base Mesh — Changes to base mesh always effect morphs, sometimes effect uvs, rigging, groups

Uvmapped — Changes here effect nothing

Grouped — Any change here effects Rigging and Morphs

Rigged — Adding new bone requires grouping change

Morphs — Changes to morphs effect nothing else

Extra Programming — Internal cr2 edits - effect only cr2

Changes That Effect Nothing Else

Texture changes - may slightly affect mats
Name of cr2, pz2,mc6
Internal cr2 changes

Therefor you have many, many more chances to fail, but below I have diagrammed the general steps of the Poser creation process.

The Point of Failure Line

Hopefully the illustration make it a little clearer but I shall attempt to explain anyways. The product has six main areas which are very interlinked. Base Mesh, Uvmapping, Grouping, Rigging, Morphs and Cr2 Programming. If you look at the colored lines you will get an idea of what is linked together.

The Mesh – if you make any changes to mesh such as fit, shape, style, etc you will almost always need to check or replace all morphs, adjust grouping, adjust rigging, recreate or adjust uvmaps & texture.

The Uvmaps – These can be effected if the base mesh is changed. If the uvmaps need to be adjusted then only the obj, and the corresponding texture maps need to be replaced or adjusted.

The Grouping – Sometimes it is necessary to adjust the grouping of the mesh if there are serious bend issue that cannot be fixed by any other method. Also if there is a last minute bone addition then the grouping must be changed to support it. This is usually a matter of regrouping the obj and replacing in the working folder. If a bone/group is added the rigging for it of course will also need to be added. If groups are changed all morphs will be broken.

Note: These days it is possible to transfer the morphs from one clothing item version to another using a utility such as Morphing clothes, or Poser's in-built tools in new versions.

Rigging – Most of the time rigging changes are simply joint tweaks to accommodate extreme poses or compound bends. However some times the existing grouping solution for the clothing is inadequate or the clothing requires additional bones for best use. Adding skirt handles or bones to adjust shoulder armour is quite common.

Simple rigging changes effect nothing but the cr2. Adding handles will require additional bones which may also require regrouping the obj, subject to the hazards caused by regrouping.

Morphs – The most common issue with morphs is pokethrough. All morphs are tested to a full value of 1, each morph on its own. Compound morph results are usually not checked (Ex: Voluptuous + Barbarian for example) unless they are special cases such as breast morphs for a certain fullbody morph. Most morphs can be removed, adjusted by whatever method and replaced. With the new morph brush it is now possible to adjust pokethrough issues live in Poser very quickly. Changing morphs does not change anything but the morphs resident in the cr2.

Cr2 Programming – Generally issues in the cr2 effect nothing else. Most of the issues will be in file calls, advanced programming, channel (dial) grouping and internal names.

Texture Issues – Issues with the texture are of course, with the textures. Occasionally they are mc6/pz2 file issues, or they can be issues with the actual image map. Changes will effect only the pz2, mc6 or jpg indicated.

File Names – Some file names can be changed with impunity such as cr2, pz2, pp2 and mc6. However any file that is referred to by any other file must be changed both in the file and the item looking for it. This includes .obj files, .jpg files and their complete file paths. If the product name is changed, then the entire filepath for everything must also be changed to reflect this. For example if you change the name of the obj from pants.obj to david_pants.obj the cr2 that uses that obj must have its file reference changed as well. If the product is changed from TriSet to DavidTriSet then every internal reference to that directory(ies) must be updated. (Geometry calls and texture map calls generally).

So with that in mind I have taken apart the report and sorted the issues to find out where I get to start with my point of failure. If I for example have to change the obj file, then every single thing dependent on it will have to be retested by myself and the beta.

Well the verdict is that the pants will need to have the obj itself adjusted, which means they will have to be tested entirely again in the next turn. The shirt however does not have an issue until the rigging stage. Most of the issues are with morph fits, as expected. I managed to overlook matching up the visible filenames – this doesn't change the functionality of the item. Crosstalk programming in the shirt needs to be added so the shirt works as expected in older versions of Poser without morph conforming. I had already done that on the pants to make sure the sash morphed as expected, since the auto-conforming will not pick up custom part names.

Making Repairs (Round one)

Adjusting the Obj

If you need to adjust the zero fit or base mesh of the item then you will need to replace the existing object with a new obj without disturbing the uvmaps or rigging. Significant changes also run the risk of disturbing the uv mapping and morphs.

As you can imagine it is usually best to avoid having to do this simply because remaking all the morphs can be nightmarish. These days there are some time saving tricks, but its still not much fun.

The issue here is a minor change. With luck I should be able to make my fix using the morph tool and exporting a new obj. Note: you can only use this trick once or twice on any given mesh due to the rounding issues. If you do this several times, as Poser exports the object the vertex coordinates keep getting rounded off and you will soon have even more issues than you started with.

You can also adjust the base mesh in your modeler. For a minor change you should be able to copy the uvs, groups and material zones back in via UVmapper. Some modelers will support a nondestructive import/export of the obj but mine

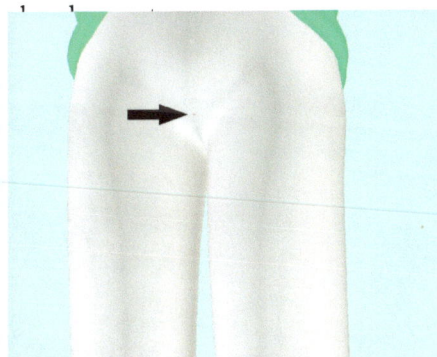

Yes. Its tiny. As you can see the tester helpfully added an arrow. It is best to test meshes without textures for exactly this reason. At regular zoom distance this issue can't be seen, which is probably how I missed it.

In theory I could make an always on fix morph and be done, but that is sloppy and some stores will not accept that sort of thing.

So I am going to have to modify the base mesh and carefully slide it back in without disturbing the morphs, groups, materials or rigging.

1   When making any kind of test or edit ALWAYS start Poser new, load a new scene, a new copy of the figure and load the morphs. This will help cut down on issues caused by memory issues, old obj cache issues, accidental changes that may have happened to the figure and who know what else.

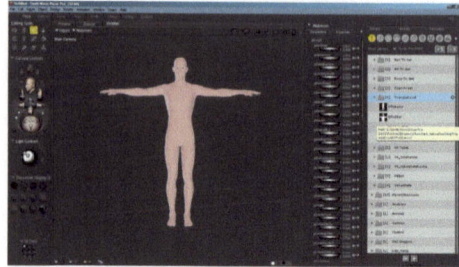

This is tricky enough already, reduce your variables.

2   I have loaded the pants and conformed. With the morph brush I create a new morph called 'fixit' and with a single swipe fix the issue.

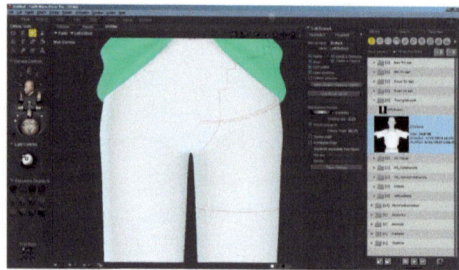

Unfortunately this was the easy part.

3   In order to 'bake' the change into the base mesh I will now need to export the item, keeping as much of its data intact as possible.

So in the Export option make sure to have just the pants selected, tick only the 'include existing groups' option and export. Give this obj a new name in this case d_tri_pants2.obj. This is a delicate operation and an iterated save will help you keep track and backtrack if needed. (And you probably will).

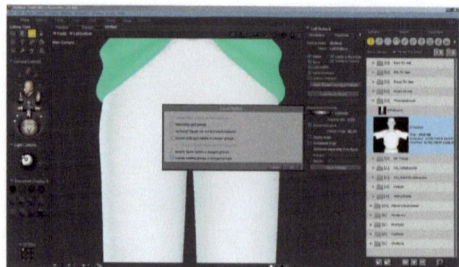

Chapter 13 –   Beta Testing and Fixes

4   Copy your new object to the working geometries folder.

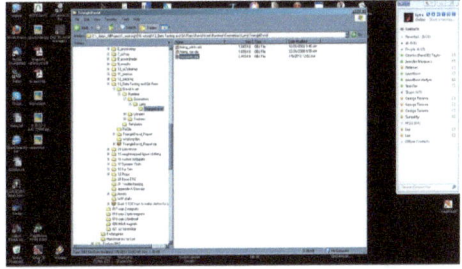

5   I use UVmapper to verify the object. First I check to see that groups, mapping and material exported properly.

The next test is to attempt to 'Import Uvs' from the original file. If it works, then all is well. Since morphs depend on the facets, this is a good fast test to see if they match.

However if you get the 'incompatible fact structure' error then something has changed.

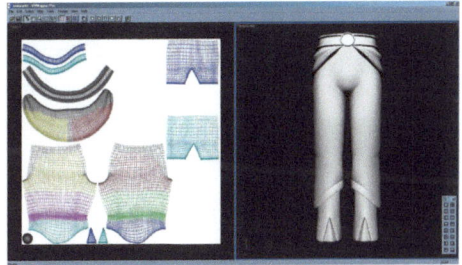

In this case, I exported while the sash was invisible and it did not export. (Oops) So I go back to my saved pz3 with the fixit morph and export again, this time with everything visible.

Now the vertex count matches, the uvs transfer and all is well.

6   You can work in a new copy of the cr2 or an old one for this next step. I simply switch the geometry reference call in the cr2 to point to d_tri_pants2.obj.

Now when I restart Poser and load a new fresh copy of the pants the modified base mesh should load.

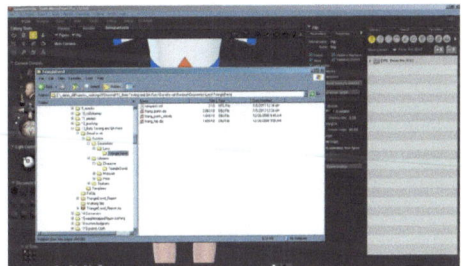

Adjusting the rigging

The Report

Collars bent forward cause pokes on the shoulder blade area of the back.

Collars bent upward cause pokes on the chest.

Combo poses of the shoulder/collar (David 3 Poses with limits on) showed pokes on the chest area and back/shoulder blade area.

Knee bends caused layers of the pants to poke through each other at the calf. The David figure's calves also poke entirely through the pants in places with knee bends.

Thigh bends cause poke through issues near the crease of the thighs.

Now that the base object has been successfully edited, I can move on to the next stage: rigging. Now I'm going to bet that many of these rigging issues are due to limitation of the David 3 joints. But they still need to be addressed. I will need to fix the ones that can be fixed with joint edits and then make correction morphs (either manual or automatic) to make everything else work.

A Joint Edit

1   I have verified the issue. The collars show no poke when bent back, but the forward bend does cause poke on the back of the shirt.

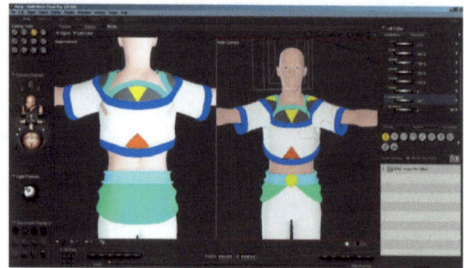

2   A simple adjustment of the front-back rotation of he shirt's collar fixes the issue. So I copy it to the other side and save the cr2. Remember rigging changes save in the cr2.

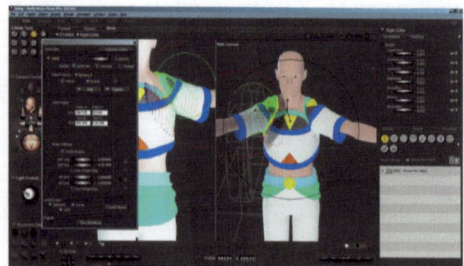

A Fix Morph

1   The first step is to verify the issues. Here I have bent one collar up and one collar down. The front and back views clearly show the pokethrough.

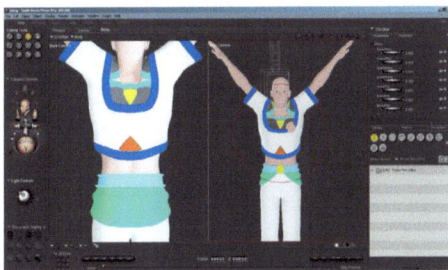

2   First I try adjust the joint on the collar to fix the poke. I can do it, but as you can see the entire side of the shirt inflates and pulls away from the figure. Not very attractive.

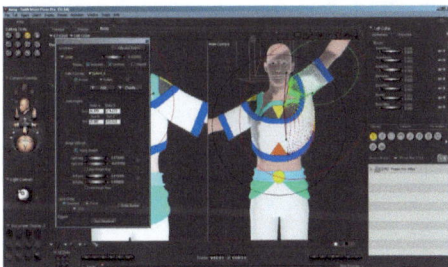

3   So instead of adjusting the joints, I will have to make 4 fix morphs. rCollarBendUp, lCollarBendUp, rCollarBendDown, lCollarBendDown.

Here I have made the collar down morphs using the morph painting tool.

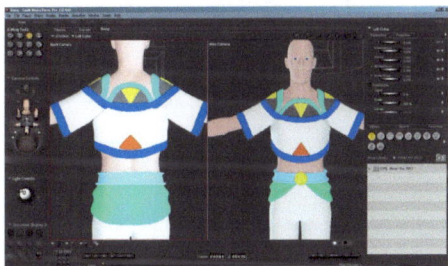

4   Here I have made one Collar Up morph.

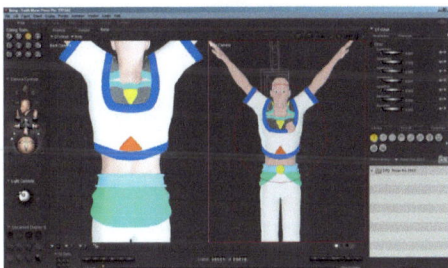

5   and both together. Now the morphs can either be left manual, for the user to dial themselves, or have coding added to turn them into JCM (joint controlled morphs) that will activate automatically.

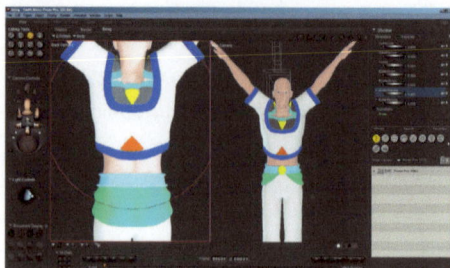

Because of the range of motion in the human shoulder, you will extremely often find corrective work is needed on the shoulder area.

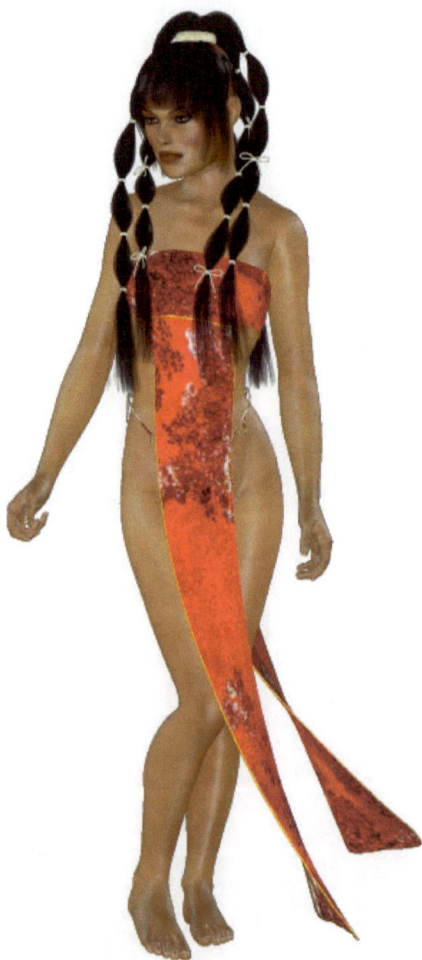

Gen X Dress

by Nerd

At first glance this dress seems very simple, a tight top and a long flowing skirt front and back. However the rigging is the impressive work here. In the cr2 you can see the ezpose dials, linked morphs, correction morphs and everything that contributes to the grace and ease of use of this set.

Chapter 14 – Conversions

Step by step walkthrough of four methods of converting clothing to different figures

Once you have made a clothing item for a certain figure it is usually only a matter of time before you consider converting it to fit another figure. There are several methods for converting clothing including various utility programs, the wardrobe wizard script in Poser, manual conversion in the modeler, magnet based conversion in Poser itself and the new Fitting Room. Each method has various strengths and weaknesses.

The two main tasks in a conversion are refitting the shape of the item and then changing the rigging to reflect the new figure. After that, then you will need to add fit morphs, correction morphs and so on just like in any fresh mesh.

In general it is always to convert from larger to smaller, never small to large, because what polys suffice for a child will not bend nearly as well on a full adult. It is also usually best to convert from male to female, and not female to male since the female breast shape is difficult to flatten out smoothly, though the new morphbrush does help with that.

Please remember to respect other peoples copyrights. Although it is possible to convert clothing made by someone else to different figures, you can only distribute it if you make it impossible to use the item without having the original mesh. In general the accepted method of this is via a file encryption method, which requires the original item to decode.

Liquid Knight on Sky 16 for Victoria 3

by Uzilite

I have no idea what the name of this piece means, but that hardly matters. The modeling and style speak for it. This sci fi set for V3 is the female counterpart to Major Cache. Both are strong examples of the sci-fi armor style.

Poser Only Method – OldSkool

The Poser only method relies on two things – scaling and magnets. After the obj is warped into the new shape the mesh is rigged to the new figure and work continues as usual.

1   I have loaded my new figure to convert to, michael4. I have zeroed out the pose, IK and morphs on the figure.

2   The d3 triangle shirt and pants obj are imported. As you can see David is a kind of short guy.

3   I have roughly scaled the shirt and pants to fit better on m4. Generally its a good idea to scale all axis at once to avoid distortion.

4   I have added two magnets to fit the sleeves and shoulders better. I will also need to adjust the fit on the shins. You can also use the morph brush, but I find for large area movements magnets make for a nice smooth transition.

5   After the mesh is refit each item is exported separately.

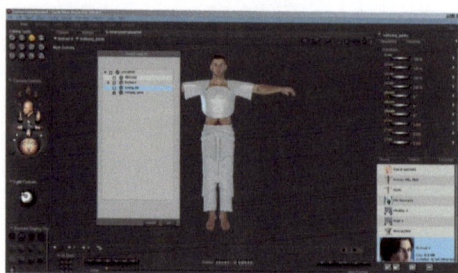

6   Since Michael 4 has different bodyparts than David some of the clothing groups need to be adjusted.

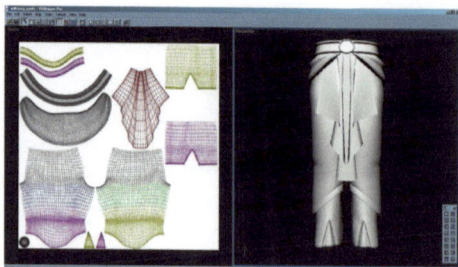

7   And now you are back at Chapter 6 – this is now a straightforward donor rigging job with the one custom bone for the sash. (Chapter 6)

Here is Mikey in his brand new outfit.

Poser Only Method – pp2014 Fitting Room

1   Load and zero your figure, in this case Roxy. Load the clothing. Do NOT conform.

2   Get the clothing fit as much as you can now. To do this use any and all of the following: rotations, scaling, moving the whole item, morphs to loosen and magnets.

It doesn't have to be perfect, but the closer you can get now, means the easier the fit room will be.

You can use magnets and painted morphs to refit the clothing at this stage as well.

3   I now go to the Fitting room. Like the cloth room, you will need to start a fitting session.

I start a new fit session and name it Shirt.

For Object select your clothing item. Deselect 'Zero Figure'. This will make sure all your scaling and moving is kept when the clothing is loading in here.

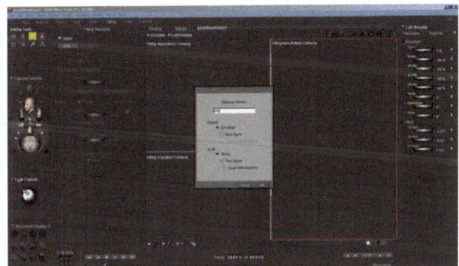

4   The session is loaded in. As you can see the top left box has the clothing item, with its vertices highlighted.

The bottom left box has the figure and the right box has the figure and the clothing together.

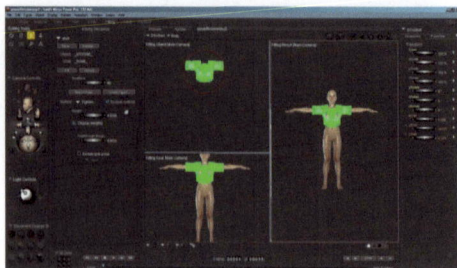

5   I am going to start with the default session settings – the fitting type is Shrink and the steps are 40. Some clothing may require more or less steps, or a different fitting approach.

Here is the result of the default settings.

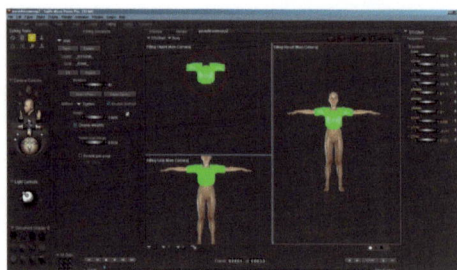

6   Now to create this as a new clothing figure. Choose 'Create Figure'.

The first step is to choose a name. Then there will be a slight delay as Poser thinks about things, and then an hierarchy window will open.

In the hierarchy window, which shows the donor figures rigging, choose all or some of the bones to include in your new figure. You can always choose to remove some later manually.

You can also choose to let Poser auto regroup the clothing, and auto create morphs in the clothing.

7   Once that is done you can delete the fitting session and return to the pose room.

Be aware that the old clothing will remain, here I have slid it to the side so you can see.

Now you must save the clothing cr2 to your library, which will also save the new obj to the same place.

As with any automated process, there will probably need to be some cleanup of joints and morphs. But as you can see, with minimal work its a fairly fast and easy way to convert any clothing item to any figure.

If you plan to use the fit room often, I strongly suggest you watch the tutorial videos and experiment with the other fit room settings.

Jack of Hearts for Michael 4

by Luthbel

Rogue Brotherhood for Jack of Hearts Textures

by Arien

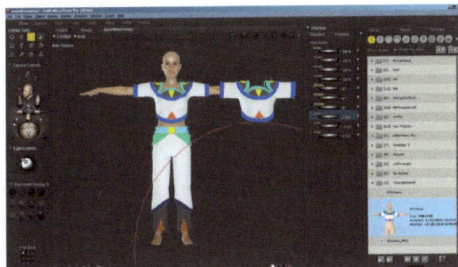

Full of detail and exquisitely textured this swashbuckling set for Michael 4 is well modeled and rigged. The textures by Arien add a wealth of detail and surfacing.

Poser Wardrobe Wizard Method

From version 7 upwards Poser has shipped with a python script called Wardrobe Wizard. You can also obtain WW as a standalone, as well as conversion kits for additional figures. WW does all the tedious and fiddly bits of the conversion for you, using its internal library of deformers and donor rigs.

WW as it ships with Poser can convert to and from a limited number of figures. To be able to convert to and from more figures, you will need additional licenses from philc.com.

However, like any automated utility sometimes the results aren't optimal. WW also has a number of interesting adjustment tools built into it, which can be helpful in other situations so I recommend having a thorough look through its features when you have a moment.

1   There is no need to load anything into the scene. Simply start the script. I have selected the triangle shirt and pants. You can see in the top box of the UI that 'multiple files' are selected.

Then I chose what runtime to save the converted clothing assets into in the second box.

In the Convert From box I chose v4, since I'm using the v4 conversion as my base (I have a limited number of WW licenses at the moment) and in the convert to box I chose Ben from p7.

In the bottom left you choose what type of clothing it is, and in the bottom right any other options you think are needed.

In this case I have selected high resolution to keep the detail sharp, close fit, Add full body morphs and Regroup.

After that I select ok and waited for about ten minutes for WW to do its thing. Since the slowest part of the process is analyzing the mesh, the next time I convert this clothing item with WW it will be much faster, since the analysis will be done already

And here is the outfit on Ben.

Now there is an issue with the sash of course, as there always is with custom parts in an auto conversion. The autogrouping has rigged the sash to left and right thighs, which will result in a mess the moment it is posed.

So before this can be used the pants will need to have the groups adjusted slightly and a bone for the sash added. And then the morphs, if any, will need to be regenerated.

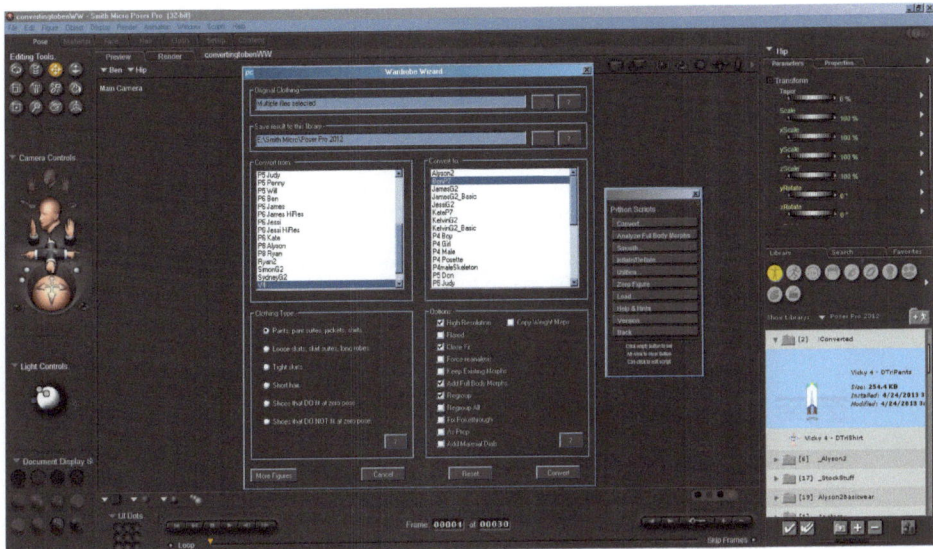

You can see how for simple clothing items this can be a nice fast process though.

Mummy Dearest for Victoria 4

by Lyrra Madril

This revealing fantasy style mummy outfit was much harder to make than it seemed at first.

The interlacing bandages across the body were modeled flat and tight to the figure. The cloth texture and folds are controlled with the displacement map.

The wrapped bandages on the feet were carefully painted to mimic the interleaved style of real mummy wrappings, although I'm fairly sure you won't be seeing this outfit in the museum any time soon.

Modelers Method

The modelers method is fairly straightforward. The one drawback to this method is that often you will loose uvmap compatibility, unless you take special care. This may or may not be a concern for you. Since you are literally reshaping the mesh in your modeling program you will have exactly as much control over the look of it as you did the first time you made it. You can also, if your modeler allows it refit the final mesh and not the lowres cage which should allow you to retain the maps. Another popular option is using a sculpting program such as Zbrush to reshape the mesh to the new figure.

1   I have set up a new figure in my modeler, in this case Ryan.

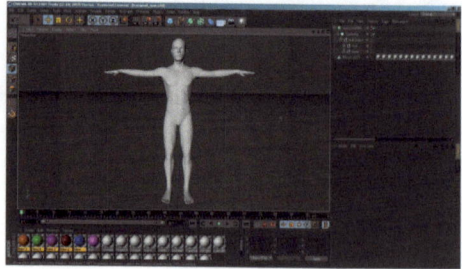

2   I opened my original David clothing c4d file and have copied the clothing straight over. You can already see what will need to be adjusted.

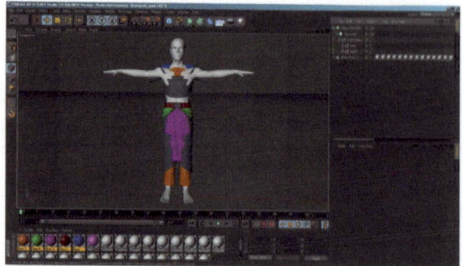

3   Now its a matter of manually refitting the clothing mesh low res cage around the new figure. So I start by turning off all the parts of the clothing and check each one as I turn them on.

Here the manual refit is done. Since the low res cage has so many fewer polys than the final mesh, it is very easy to make large changes without much work.

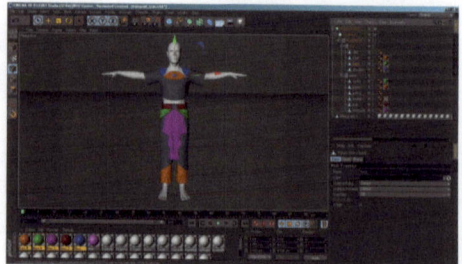

4   Export the clothing items separately. I use UVmapper to import the group and uv information over from the David version.

This only works on 'identical' mesh. So if you have added or removed polys it will not work, but its a nice quick trick if you can manage it.

5   And again we are back to Chapter 6, rigging from a donor file. The sash of course will need special handling once again.

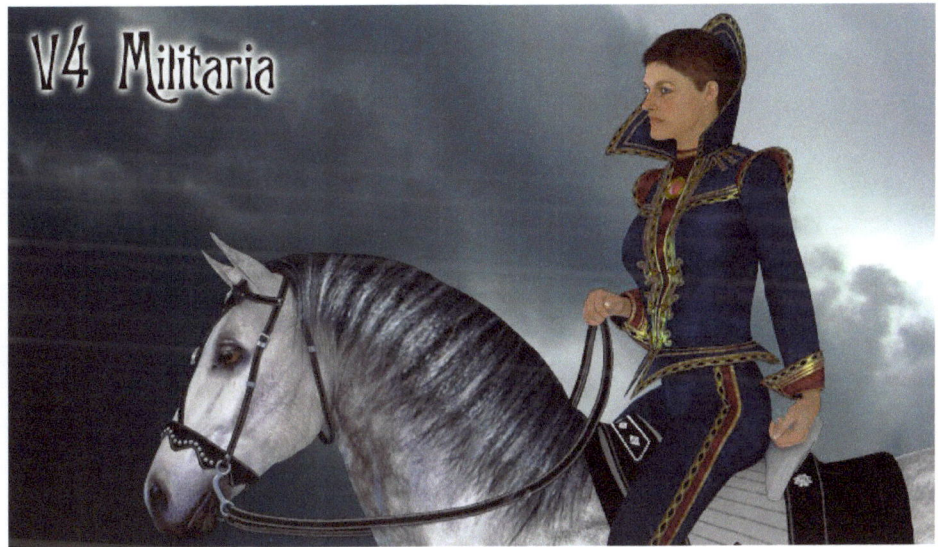

Militaria for Victoria 4

by Lyrra Madril

This outfit was style to mimic the European military uniform tradition, as is soon in both American military uniforms and many anime costume designs. The trim and decoration on the textures was created in Photoshop.

Chapter 15 – Poser 9+ Weightmapping

Recent versions of Poser have added weightmapping to figure, which requires clothing to be weightmapped to match

With the creation of Poser 8 and 9 weightmapping was brought to Poser. Rather than the previous method of simply using sticks and balls to define joints, weight-mapping additionally uses grayscale imagemaps to define inclusion and exclusion areas. This can give a amount of finesse that would otherwise be impossible.

When it comes to making conforming clothing though, it gets a little more annoying. The basic steps remain the same – create the clothing model and prepare your donor rig. However, you need to scrub out the existing weightmaps from the figured in addition to all the other stuff, as discussed in the 'Making a Base Conformer' chapter.

Once that is done the process continues.

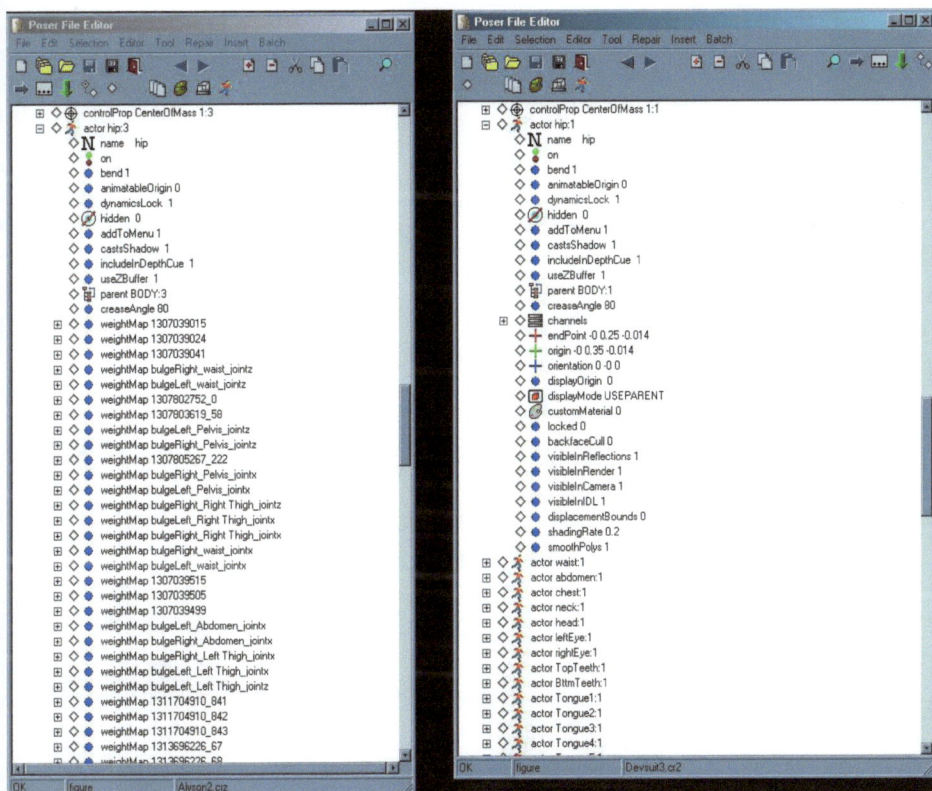

1   The clothing model is already made and prepped as usual with uvmaps. Here I have loaded Alyson2 and zeroed the figure.

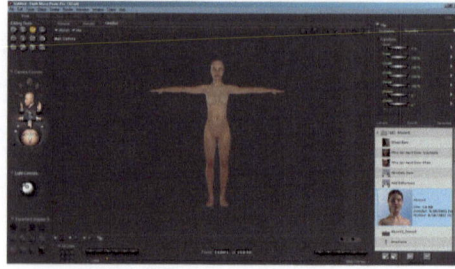

2   Now to import the mesh, make sure to untick all the import options. The clothing should load in and fit nicely around the zeroed figure.

Note: if you are making clothing for GN-DAnastasia for Alyson2 or any other heavily morphed character, remember you must always model and rig to the base figure.

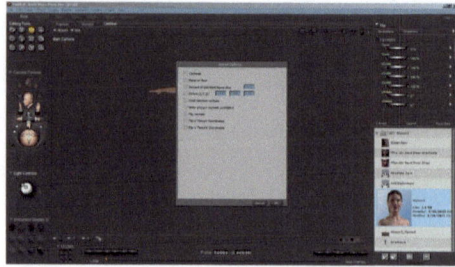

3   The dress is imported and fits the figure at default.

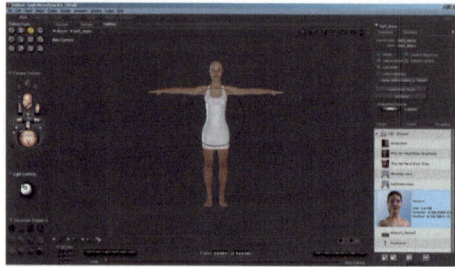

4   In the setup room I have selected the dress and applied the rig from my alyson2 donor rig.

You can choose to allow it to regroup the mesh or not on application. I chose not, since I have already adjusted the groups to make the skirt one part 'hip'.

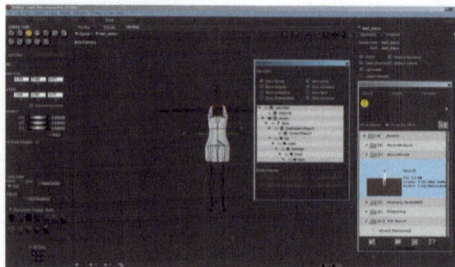

Chapter 15 –   Poser 9+ Weightmapping

5   Now it is a matter of testing and adjusting all the joints, just like any other conforming clothing item.

However since Alyson 2 has some newer technology used I'm going to go over those in the next section, so you know how to handle them.

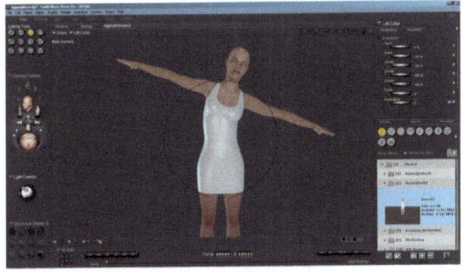

Adjusting nonstandard joints

Capsule zones

Any joint can have one or more capsules added to the joint zones, Shown here is one capsule on the thigh side-side rotation.

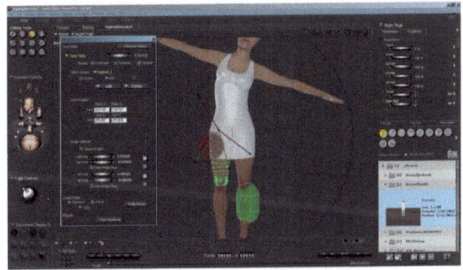

As you might guess capsule zones work pretty much the same as spherezones, but since you can significantly change the shape of he capsules you can obtain more finetuned exclusion and inclusion zones.

Shown here is another capsule on the thigh side-side rotation. As you can see the standard inclusion/exclusion arms still pertain.

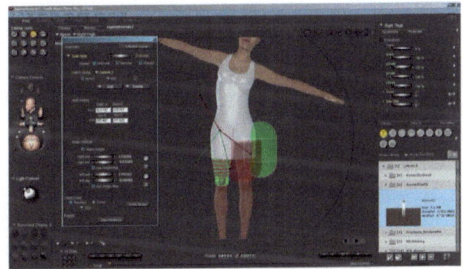

All Poser's rigging still can include types that have come before. For this reason most things that worked in previous versions still work in new versions of Poser.

Sphere zones

Here your classic sphere zone is visible. Notice that the capsule do not replace the spheres.

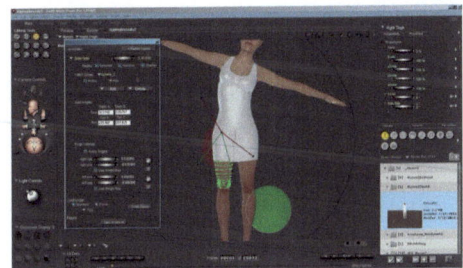

Any zone or weightmap can be activated and deactivated.

Chapter 15 –   Poser 9+ Weightmapping

Weight Maps

And of course any joint can have one or more weight maps. You cannot see the weightmaps themselves, but you can see the effects on the figure. Editing weightmaps is pretty much like using the morph brush.

The bulge settings can also be finetuned with weightmaps now.

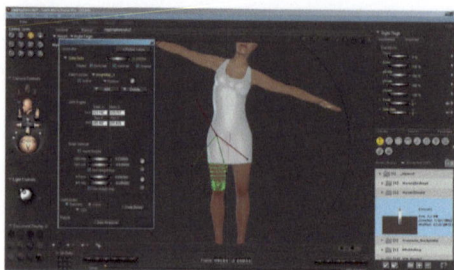

RollerGirl for Alyson2

By Ryverthorn

This outfit should be familiar to anyone using PoserPro2014. This conforming outfit for the weightmapped Alyson 2 figure was used for the box art for the program.

Poser's shader features helped create the look for the retro styled satin top and shorts. It was inspired by that 70's rollerskating look.

Chapter 16 – Custom Bodyparts

Not all clothing is the same shape. Some clothing items will need one or many extra bones in order to control the movement naturally

By and large most clothing can be handled with all the same parts as the regular figure has. However, as the clothing becomes more complex, there are times when you will need to add one or more custom bodyparts for various reasons. The three main types of custom parts are handles, regular extra moving parts like hoods, and strings of parts for articulated long wiggly things like scarves and chains.

There comes a point when the basic rigging of the figure is just not going to cut it for your clothing model. You may have extra armor plates, wings, scarves, long skirts … but they need to move and be articulated. This is when you are going to have to bite the bullet and venture into the setup room all alone to add one or more custom bones to your figure.

But do not despair, it isn't all that bad. Really.

In clothing generally you need to add either single bone parts or long strings. Single bone parts include both things like pauldrons, and sleeves but also the very common Body Handles (aka skirt handles) as used to create movement adjustments on long skirts. Long strings of parts are needed for long thin items like scarves, ropes, chains, loose belts and so forth.

I already demonstrated a single bone addition with the sash on the pants in earlier chapters. Here I will show adding both the mesh and the bones for skirt handles, and then creating the bones for a belt with a long articulated strap in front.

Skirt Handles

Because of the limitations of Posers rigging system, long skirts are often grouped entirely as Hip. Additional bones are added, so the user can use them to bend the skirt smoothly into position. This is not an ideal solution, but in many situations its works nicely. Here I will show preparing a long dress with the handles, and adding the rigging for them in the Setup room.

1   I have modeled a simple cote-hardie and belt from the medieval period. The belt will be handled in the second section of this chapter.

Export as obj files.

2   I have mapped and grouped the dress. As you can see on the template the entire skirt area is set to the Hip bodypart.

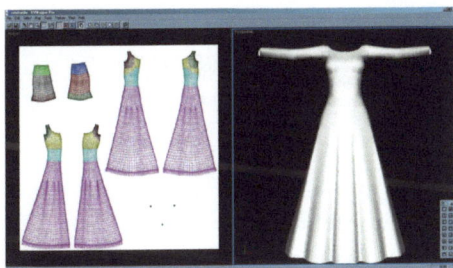

3   Load and zero the figure, in this case v4.

4   Import the object, with no boxes selected like usual.

Next comes the slightly fiddly part. In the Props folder is a folder named Primitives. This contains various simple objects like flat planes, cubes and spheres.

5   I could make the spheres in the modeler, but since I often find myself needing to add handles later I thought I'd walk you through this process.

If you rather make your handles in your modeler, go do that and then skip down to step 7.

I load, name and position eight spheres as follows

SitHip,and SitShin. These two handles will be zoned to control the entire skirt, and the lower skirt from the knee down. This makes sitting positions relatively simple.

Then I add four handles at the hem, lHem, rHem, bHem and fHem. These handles will be set to affect the lower parts of the skirt to move the 4 areas in and out as needed.

And lastly I add lLeg and rLeg, so that the thigh areas of the skirt can be adjust separately for walking poses.

6   Now export the clothing item with all the primitives. This will make it one object.

7   In UVmapper I set each handle to its own group as named above.

SitShin, SitHip, lLeg, rLeg, rHem, lHem, fHem and bHem

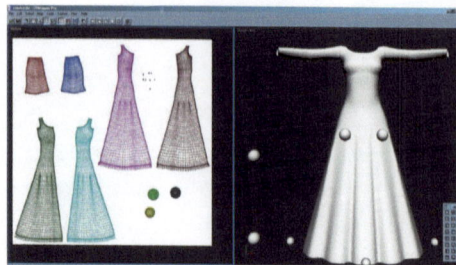

Also make sure to set them with a new material zones. I usually use Handles.

Chapter 16 –   Custom Bodyparts

8   Now back to a new scene with v4 in Poser to import the clothing again.

9   In the setup room load the v4 donor rig onto the cotehardie.

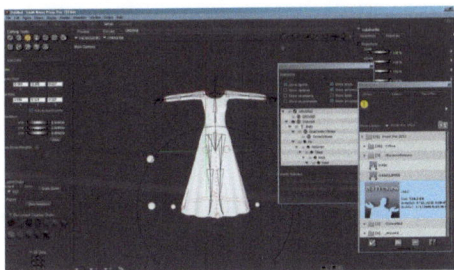

10   Now you will need to make new bones for each handle, just the same as you did when making the sash on the Triangle pants.

Start by selecting the hip and then draw a new bone in about the area of the handle. Name it, internal and external names, to match the handle it belongs to. Continue for all eight handles. Don't worry much about alignment, but the hierarchy is critical. They must all attach to Hip in order that the handles will all affect their parent part, Hip and bend the skirt.

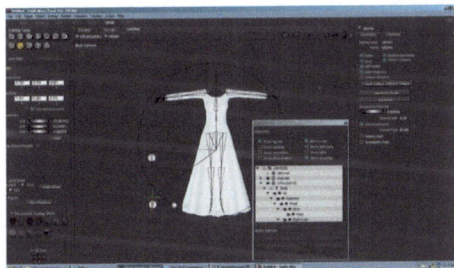

11   Now you can continue as normal, testing and adjusting each bend parameter on each bodypart.

Remember, any time you create a custom bone you may need to change its xyz order so twist follows the natural twist direction, and name all the bends something more informative than rotatex and rotatey.

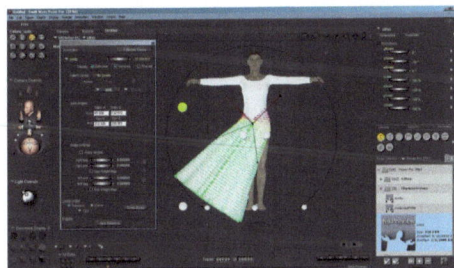

Dangly Bits

In order to bend a long thin item like a scarf or dangling belt you will need a string of bodyparts. The more sections you have, the more flexible the item is. Usually 10 segments is more than enough, but if your strap is very long you may wish to add more. In order to have smooth bends you need fairly dense mesh, so make sure to cut enough in while modeling.

The mesh will need to be grouped with all your segments in addition to the one common to the figure. When naming these groups it is market standard to start numbering at 1 at the base of the string and continue in order such as Belt1, Belt2, Belt3 and so forth. Utility programs also expect logical numbering sequences.

In addition most long straps and such have Ezpose controls added, which are a form of advanced cr2 programming. There are several utility programs to make this simply, most notably EasyPose Underground by Ajax. This adds dials to the main body of the item which control all the child parts of a long string at once, making it much easier to pose long things like belts and tentacles.

1   The cotehardie was often worn with a long belt. I chose one of the more simple styles and modeled it. It is simply a long strap and loop.

I have made sure to include enough polys in the long front strap so that the belt can be jointed and bend smoothly.

For a belt this long anything from five to ten groups should be plenty. Too few and it is stiffer, and too much is just overkill. Each group should be at least 4 polys or more tall after subdivision.

2   The belt after being mapped, grouped and materials set. As you can see in UVmapper each group has its own color and I have named them belt1, belt2 and so forth from the hip down.

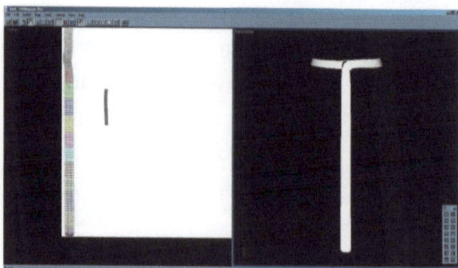

3   Load and zero the destination figure.

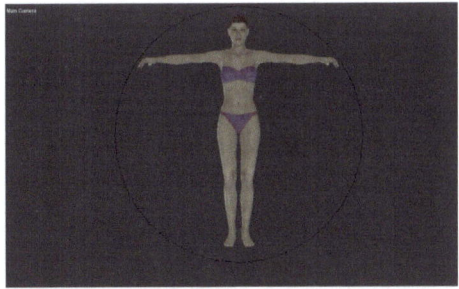

4   Import the belt, with no boxes ticked as usual.

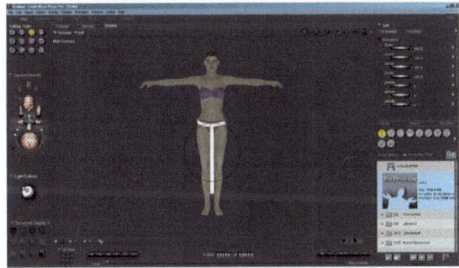

5   Select the belt and go to the set-up room. Load the donor v4 rig as usual. This will load the Hip you need as well as the rest of the figures bones.

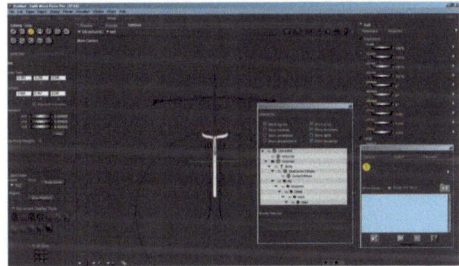

6   Just like any other custom part I start by selecting the parent group, in this case Hip. I then draw downwards to create a new bone which I rename Belt1.

Now select Belt1 and draw another bone below it. This bone should attach to Belt1. Name it Belt2. I don't worry all that much about alignment to the mesh at this point, just getting the hierarchy and names of the bones correct.

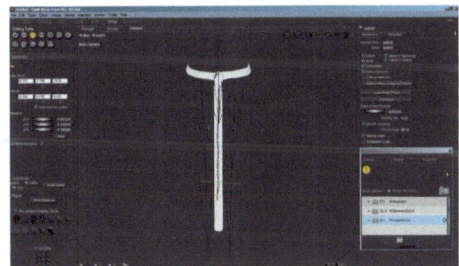

Chapter 16 –   Custom Bodyparts

7   After you have made a bone for each part return to the posing room. Now you can adjust each bone and all its bend zones.

Remember, any time you create a custom bone you may need to change its xyz order so twist follows the natural twist direction, and name all the bends something more informative than rotatex and rotatey.

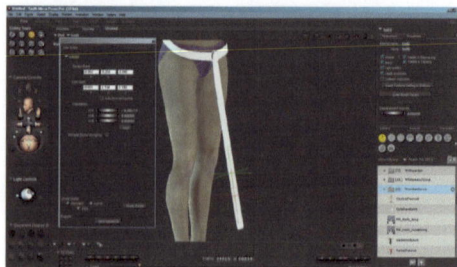

Ornate Kimono for Victoria 4

by Lyrra Madril

This was one of the most complex outfits I have ever rigged. The furisode style long sleeved kimono has custom rigging and handles on the sleeves, as well as handles and morphs on the skirt area like the v4 and m4 kimonos I made. The over robe with train however has nine easy pose sections and over a hundred body parts along with all their dials, morphs adjustments and whatnots. The long obi you can just see also has its own ezpose rigging.

Chapter 16 –   Custom Bodyparts

Chapter 17 – Dynamic Clothing

Creating, using and modifying dynamic clothing objects including hybrid dynamic/conforming clothing and converting conforming clothing to dynamic

Most commonly used clothing in Poser are conformers, rigged clothing items. However starting in Poser 5 it is possible to use dynamic cloth in Poser. Dynamic cloth starts with a regular obj format mesh file, in Poser it is set up with a cloth simulation in the Cloth room and then the fun part happens.

During a cloth simulation the vertexes in the cloth object are subjected to a series of calculations that include the tension and stretch settings in the simulation, as well as the collision objects per frame location to create a dynamically draped piece of mesh. Subjected to gravity, the motion of the body underneath and so forth, a dynamic cloth item has a natural fluidity that can be difficult if not impossible to recreate in a conforming cloth item.

However, dynamic cloth by its very nature has limitations. In order to gain fluid drapes it can be very high polygon and a high polygon object in a simulation can take a very long time. Also not all machines can handle cloth sims gracefully. Plus, there are modeling limitations that can make it a challenge to create dynamic cloth with crisp details and real illusion of solidity.

Modeling for Dynamics

Since dynamic cloth items will be draped in the simulator, the creator needs to be aware of certain constraints. In general, Poser clothing is made with quads, four sided polygons. However, if you drape a sheet of foursided polys you end up with odd diamond shaped crinkles on some folds. To avoid this, some modelers use either much smaller polys or tris, 3 sided polys. Both options radically raise the poly count of the model, which can make it harder to handle.

Another issue is the matter of crisp detail. Some details like seams will melt right out of a dynamic cloth item, so those should be created with displacement maps. However details like pockets, buckles, buttons and so forth will benefit by placing them in the Soft Decoration or Rigid Decoration cloth room groups. These grouping options will change how the simulator handles those items. Specifically items like buttons in the rigid group will follow meekly along with their cloth item without melting or distorting. Soft things like pockets, belts and belt loops should be Soft Decoration items, since they need to both move with the cloth item, but also to deform as they are draped.

It is generally not a good idea to roll edges on dynamic cloth items, however I have had decent results by assigning the rolled edge to a Soft Decoration group. This also tend to stiffen the hem. It is also best to avoid mesh that intersects itself, as that can cause simulation errors and crashing.

Full Dynamics

A full dynamic item will be completely simulated in the clothroom. I have already modeled the item, a nice 50's style halter dress for Alyson2. It has straps, a stiff belt buckle, a soft belt and a full loose skirt. An important thing to remember is that in order to dynamically simulate the effects of gravity the clothroom needs the fourth dimension. Time. You will need to set up a very small animation sequence in the cloth room in order to give the dynamic item the time it needs for the draping to be simulated.

So you will need to set up a very simple timeline if you are posing a figure . In the first example I will simply drape the dress to the figure. In the second example I will drape to a posed figure.

1   Prepare your clothing mesh. Load figure. In this case I have loaded the GND Anastasia morph and texture onto the figure as well.

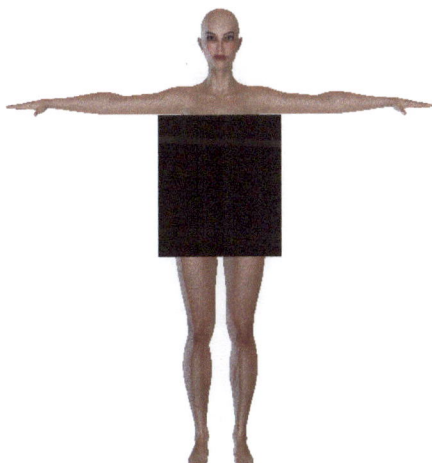

2   Import the cloth item. If you are starting with a preset dynamic cloth item it will be located in the Props section of the Library. Many preset items have already been draped once. This dress is hot off the presses, never touched by gravity.

3   Open cloth room. The cloth room controls are over on the right in sections. They are handily numbered in the order you need them. Most of it is greyed out since there is no active cloth item in scene yet.

The first step is to start a new Cloth Simulation. This lets Poser know that you want to run cloth dynamics and gets things set up.

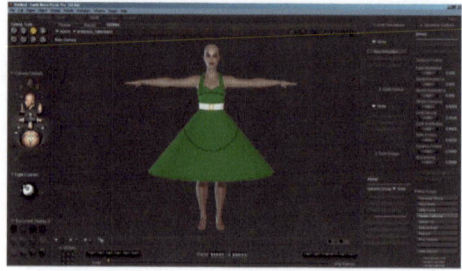

4   simulation range – choose the frames you wish the cloth to simulate in. For most basic uses I use the standard 1 to 30 frame range. If you have a complex simulation or pose you may need longer.

Additional options – I usually choose cloth self collision. This means that the program will track where the cloth impacts itself and use that as a collision. It can make the calculations longer but it prevents self intersections. The other options are in case you need an object pushing into a cloth item.

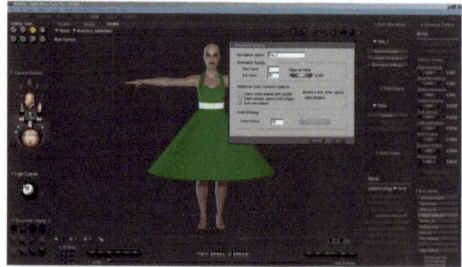

Cloth draping – you can choose to tack on additional draping time that will run before the posing animation is calculated. This can be handy to get a gravity drape before the figure starts moving.

5   Now select the clothing item and in the second section choose 'Cloth-ify'.

You will need to set collision objects, this tells the program what items the cloth will bounce off of. You want to at least add the figure, and probably the Ground as well. If the figure is seated, then add the seat as well.

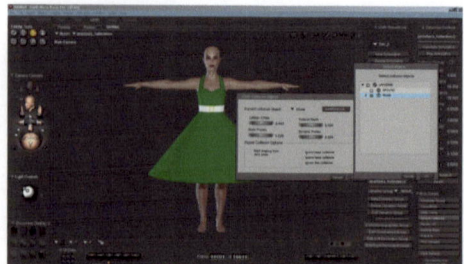

Chapter 17 –   Dynamic Clothing

You can choose to ignore head, hand and feet collisions. Since the hands have so many body parts often ignoring them can speed up calculations.

6   In section three you will adjust clothroom groups.

The cloth room uses its groups to determine how it simulates the mesh in the groups. The whole item is loaded into default by, you know. Default.

For this dress I select the Soft Decoration group and use Add Material to add the belt to it.

Then I add the Buckle to the Rigid Decoration group.

Lastly the straps are made choreographed, this will keep them from stretching or sliding off her neck.

7   And here is the dress after I have run cloth simulation. The skirt has relaxed in natural folds, the belt has dropped a little and the buckle followed along as it was supposed to.

At this stage you can export the obj for a nice predraped mesh for the user to clothify, or save it into the props folder for later.

Hybrid Dynamics

Some clothing items can work as hybrids. The clothing is conformed as usual, and then the dynamic portions are draped. This is usually done with long dresses, but can be done with any mesh. In this case I took the cotehardie from an earlier chapter and modified it slightly to be more dynamic friendly by removing the turned hem on the skirt. Other than that I made no mesh changes. The dress is rigged as a conformer. However, once the figure is loaded and the dress conformed then the Hip of the figure can be draped dynamically.

1   The figure is loaded and the clothing loaded and conformed. I select the dress, and enter the Cloth room to start a new simulation.

2   Now Poser sees the dress as a bunch of items since its a conformer, each bodypart is an item. So I select the Hip bodypart which contains the entire skirt and Clothify it. Set the collisions, so Poser will know to bounce it off v4 and the floor.

Set the groups – the button material is Rigid Decoration and I add the waist-band of the skirt to choreographed so it wont rip away from the bodice.

3   I set 30 draping frames before the sim. The sim started at the zero pose, and on frame 20 I set a seated pose. It continued draping to frame 30.

As you can see this isn't entirely smooth, it will take some more tweaking of the cloth parameters and perhaps a few dabs with the smoothing brush. The buttons have mostly survived the simulation, following along pretty much like real buttons would. Since this is a pose that is fairly impossible with standard skirt handles, the simulation gives me a much more natural fabric draping.

Converting to dynamics

Sometimes a conforming item has the look you want but refuses to be posed into position. Some items can be converted to dynamics and draped. Here I will go over part of the process. Since every item is built differently, you may have to do more or less work to make the dynamic conversion.

1   The first step is to examine the mesh for issues that would cause trouble in a dynamic simulation.

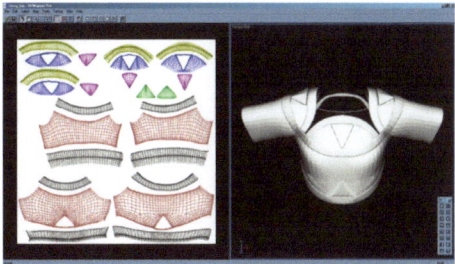

Self intersections – at any point does the mesh poke through itself? This is common when making pockets or belt loops. In this case, no. The shoulder tabs lay just inside the main part of the shirt.

Turned edges – are the edges of the mesh turned? If they are these polygons will need to be removed or the mesh will relax and unroll. This shirt has turned edges on the bottom, the top trim, the sleeves and the shoulder tabs.

2   You will need to isolate and re-move all the obvious problem areas. This is a good time to set groups up that will be used to make the clothroom groups later.

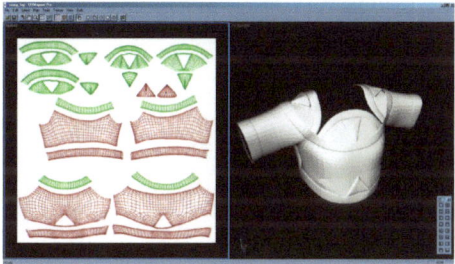

To keep the shoulder tabs from rip-ping off on this shirt I will need to add the tabs and the top band of trim on the shirt to the Choreographed group.

3   Here I have David loaded and have imported both my treated clothing object meshes.

4   I clothify both items and set
their collisions.

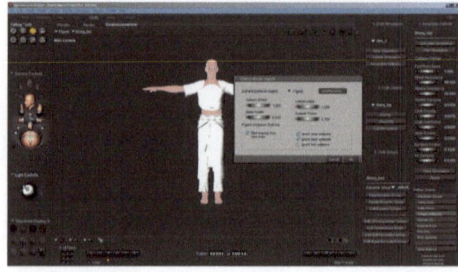

5   Cloth room groups are created
using the groups I made in UVmapper.
On the pants the belt is Choreographed,
the sash is soft deco and the belt is rigid
deco. The top of the sash, the top of the
swag and the tops of the insets are set to
Choreographed so they don't rip apart.

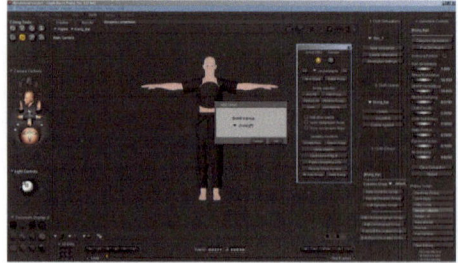

6   I have posed the figure a little
bit and draped the clothing. Oddly
enough not a great deal has changed.

This method can be more work but
can also be a powerful addition to the
flexibility of your clothing collection.
For example converting and dynamically
draping many long dresses makes for
many more posing options.

It can also be used to convert clothing,
or to make clothing on the floor or a
hanger.

Chapter 17 –   Dynamic Clothing

Chapter 18 – Fur Trim

Covering four different methods to creating fur trim on

Poser clothing

Humans have used fur to accent and edge clothing for as long as we've been wearing it. So at some point you are going to have to tackle this surprisingly tricky adornment. There are four methods to creating fur trim in Poser. The simplest of course is to paint it on the texturemap and hope that does the trick.

For the more adventurous you can try the following three methods, each with their advantages and disadvantages.

Displacement

Pros – easy to make, good for short fluffy fur like rabbit and mink. Easy to change to non-fur. Can be put anywhere as it is texture map based. Can even be done purely with shaders, no maps.

Cons – can look bad very easily. Longer 'fur' can be clipped at edges with large bucket sizes (rendering preferences). Must remember to render with displacement on.

For this type of fur it is as simple as adding the displacement via noise, either on the texturemap or in Posers shader room. Map based displacement will work in any application that uses displacement, like Poser or DS.

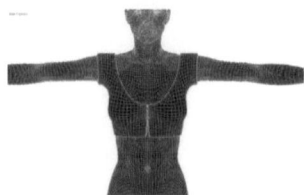

This is the base mesh of the shirt.

This displacement uses an image map.

This displacement uses the Noise node for the displacement.

Dynamic Hair

Pros – Uses the Poser dynamic hair for realistic short to super long fur. Can look amazing. Easy to remove. Growth groups can overlap for more natural partings.

Cons – can only be used in Poser, and can make even a simple render take a long time. Intimidates users.

Poser's dynamic hair room can be used to 'grow' hair on most anything. In this case we are going to grow hairs to make the fur edging. You can add hair to anything well after its been modeled.

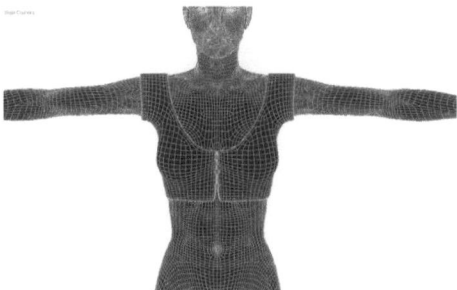

This is the same mesh as the displacement above.

And here with hair groups grown from the Trim material.

Mesh Based Transparency

Pro – renders fairly quickly. Can look realistic if well done. Good for long to super long fur.

Con – easy to texture badly. Sheets of transparency eat up polygons and increase render time dramatically. Transparency layers must be built during the mesh creation phase. Can cause render artifacts with complicated light and ao settings.

The layers of mesh will need to be made in your modeling program. Depending on the fluffiness of the fur required you can make your fur in several ways. Generally one or two solid sheets and then one or two strand sheets do the trick. The rest of the illusion is created with transparency maps to cut the fur shapes out of the planes. This is the same trick as is used for modeling hairs, but much simplified.

Here the shirt is prepared with mesh groups for the transparency. If you look you can see the edges of the three layered sheets.

And here, rendered with the layers of transmapped fur.

Cloaked Mage for Victoria 4

by Lyrra Madril

This simple one piece dress with cape was inspired by a Russian dress by Erte. However this version is aimed more at fantasy renders. The fur trim on the dress was mostly done via displacement. The fur trimmed boots use the alpha sheet method of overlapping transparency layers.

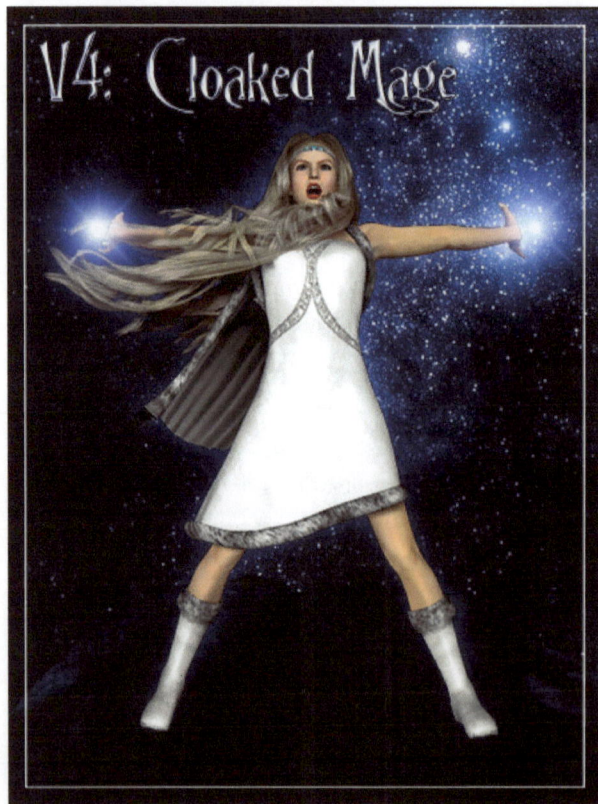

The cape has custom rigging with several parts and ezpose controls to make it easier to pose. The skirt has custom rig handles.

Chapter 19 – Props

Covering the basics of creating, modifying and saving

props with a focus on clothing items and accessories

Many clothing sets can be accented with prop items. This can be as simple as s knife in a sheathe, or as complex as a full set of matching jewelry. For the most part making a prop is very simple. Some complexities arise when dealing with hand-held props. In addition, making MAT pose files that will apply to a prop take a special line of code, materials however work perfectly normally. Props can contain morphs, made pretty much the same as in a rigged figure.

Smart Parent props are prop items that were saved when parented to a specific bodypart of a figure. When they are reloaded, they will automatically glue them-selves back in place. This is a useful option for hand-held items such as guns and swords which can be difficult to jiggle into positions. If you make a hand-held prop you may wish to include Hand poses for ease of use.

Groups of props parented to one item can be saved. This is useful for such things as items in a basket, or a knife in a sheathe . Props can also be included when saving a rigged figure, such as a rigged swordbelt and the prop sword parented to it.

A Simple Prop

1   First to show how to set up a simple prop in Poser I have modeled this very normal modern barstool.

2   Uvmap and set materials as nor-mal. Since this figure will not be rigged, I have set it as one group 'chair'.

3   Import the object into Poser. Since I already sized it relative to A2 in the modeler I am not worried about size.

However, if you are not certain about how big the item is in the modeler you can choose the import option '100% of figure size' this will make it approximate-ly 5 feet tall, going by the original Poser 4 figures. You can then adjust as needed in Poser, and export and re-import to fix the size.

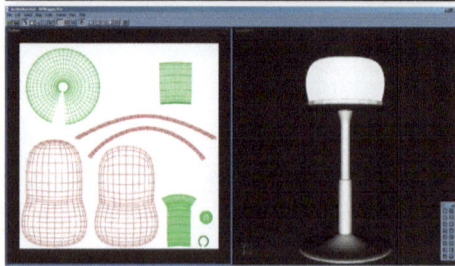

4   Set up the shaders, as simple or complex as you like for the item.

5   Save the item to the props folder. Now if only you will ever use this, you are done.

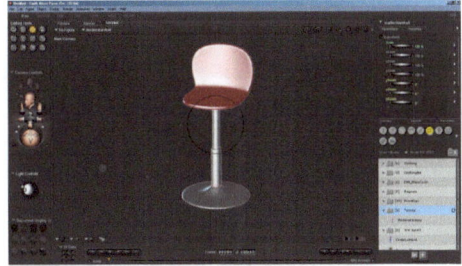

6   But since Poser inserts the props geometry into the pp2 file, most stores request exterior geometry calls be inserted into the pp2.

This will take a moment in a text editor – you must remove the custom delta information and put in a standard geometry call. Poser File Editor has a simple tool included for this process.

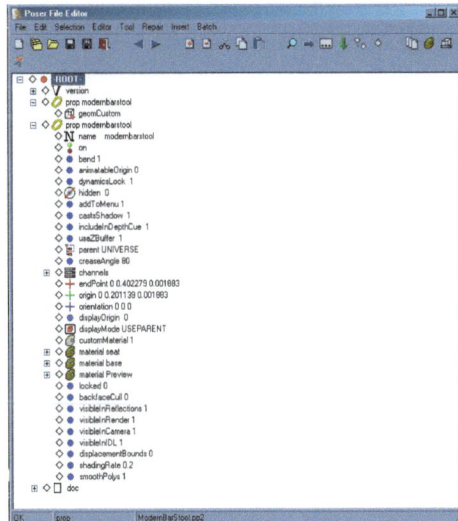

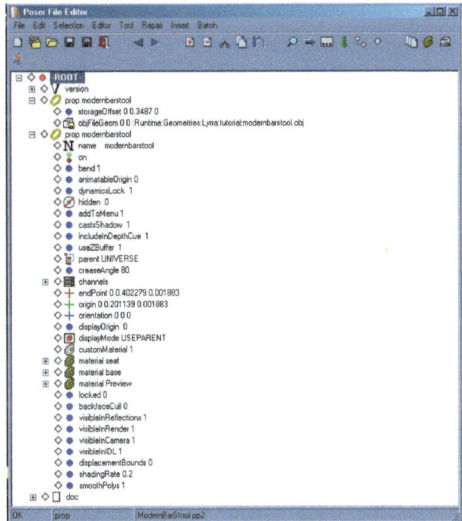

A Smart Parent Prop

1   Once you have got the hang of
normal props, smart props are not all
that different.

Model the item as normal. Since most
smart props are accessories or hand-held
items, I usually model them with a figure
in the scene as reference.

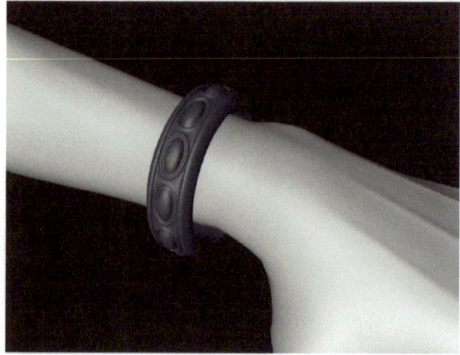

2   Uvmap, then set as one group
'bracelet' and set materials. I chose to
make the inset gems in 2 groups, so
users can have alternating colors if they
like.

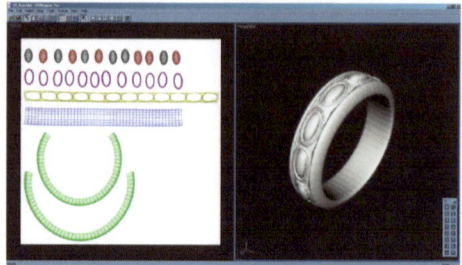

3   Import the object to Poser.
Load your reference figure.

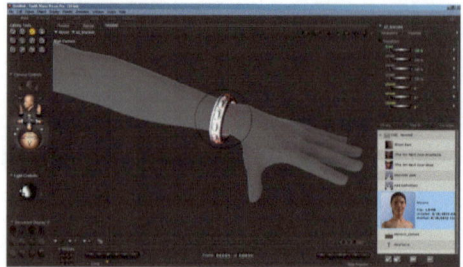

4   Set up the shaders on the item.

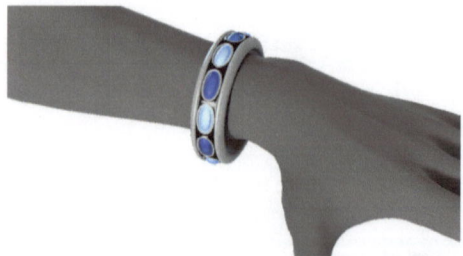

5   Now select the item and in the Object menu set its parent to be the lForearm. This will glue the item to the arm. Now when you bend the figures arm the bracelet will go with it.

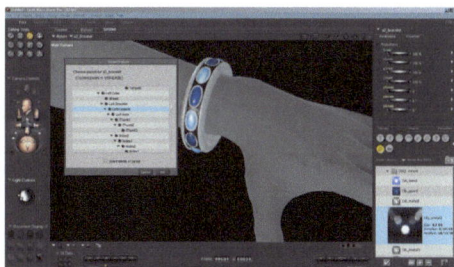

6   Select the bracelet and save as a prop. It will ask you if you want to save as a smart prop. Say yes.

Now the parenting information will be active any time you load the item into a scene with a figure loaded. As long as the figure bodypart name is the same (lForearm), the parenting should take.

7   And lastly extract the embedded geometries as mentioned before.

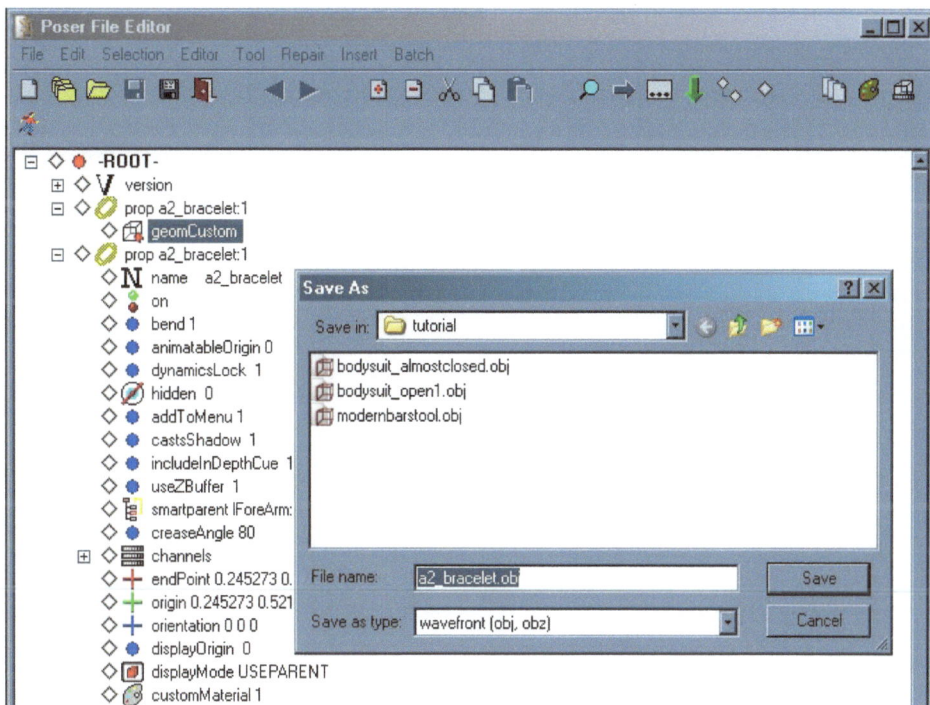

Mat Poses for Props

1   Most users still prefer MAT poses. However making mat poses for props take one more edit than making regular ones.

Set up your materials as usual.

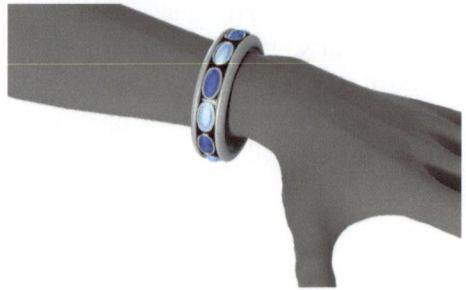

2   Save all your materials as mc6 presets in the Materials folder of the library.

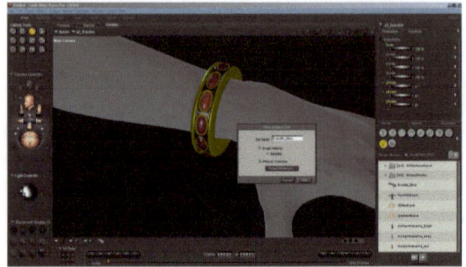

3   Now in file manager copy them to the Pose folder. Change the file suffix to pz2.

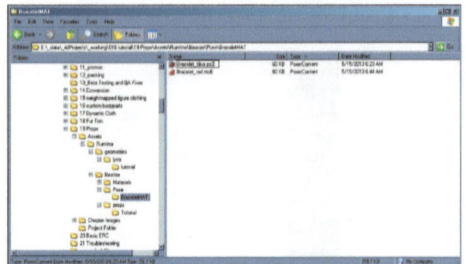

4   Now you will need to open each pz2 and change the lines from mtlcollection to figure

```
{
version
      {
       number 7
      }
mtlCollection
      {
```

to
```
{
version
      {
       number 7
      }
figure
      {
```

and save, thats it.

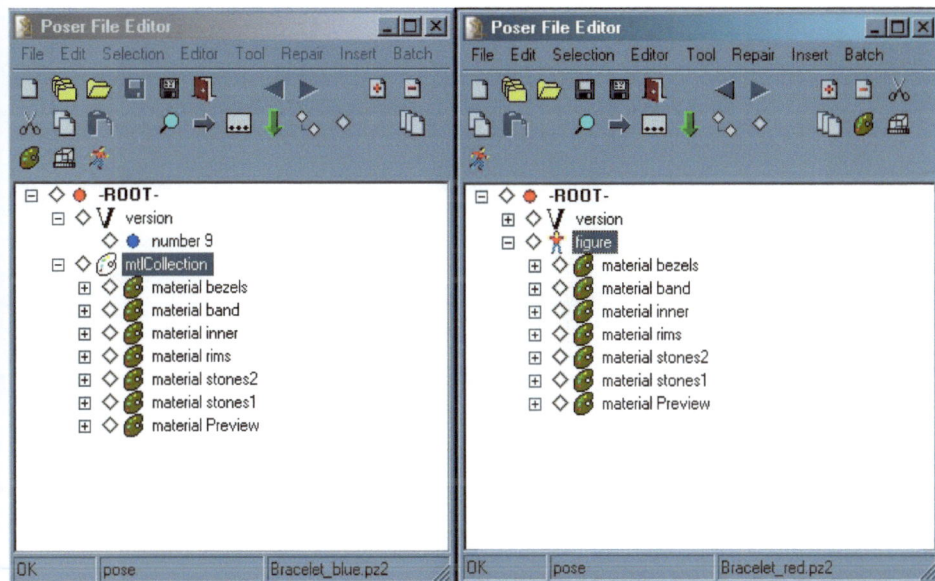

Chapter 20 –
Advanced cr2 Programming

Getting under the hood of a cr2 and adding or rewriting

sections of code to change the figure and morph behav-

iors

Once you have mastered the basics of cr2 creation and modification, you can now start to delve into the more complex, under the hood programming. Most clothing items do just fine without them, but some can benefit from judicious use of these tricks. These subtle or sometimes not so subtle coding additions can radically change the behavior of joints and morphs in a figure. A single line of code in the right place can make a correction morph activate when an arm is bent, make clothing automatically dial to fit figure morphs or even create a cascade of rotation changes to bend a long strand of parts with one dial.

There are more subtleties of Poser syntax programming that can be used when editing pz2 format files to create all sorts of programming instructions: adjusting joint parameters via a pose, switching uvmaps, inserting and removing morphs, even python script calls for even more complex programming. However this chapter will focus on those programming actions most commonly used for making clothing items.

Super Conforming

Shortly after the Body channel and FullBodyMorph dials were added users noticed a strange behavior in Poser. When a clothing item was loaded that contained morphs of the same name as the figure, the morph dials got locked to the controls of the figure. The dials on the clothing no longer did anything, but when the figure morphs were activated the clothing morphs did too. This was both useful and annoying. Useful in that it certainly saved time, but annoying in that Poser was indiscriminate about what it would crosstalk to – if you loaded two characters the dials of one would slave to the dials of the other, unless you loaded a special 'crosstalk null' figure in between.

As Poser further evolved, this 'crosstalk' bug was removed. Of course users, now accustomed to the ease of automatically conformed morphs, asked for the functionality back. This was provided by a code modification in the morph channels of the clothing, which, if the figure was selected when the clothing was loaded, would enslave the clothing morphs to the figure as before. But much more reliably.

Now of course in the most recent versions of Poser there is a figure parameter option of 'conform morphs' which has the same functionality, but still allows user adjustment of the morphs on the clothing. However, where the clothing figure has bodyparts that do not exist in the figure, some code adjustments still need to be made so the whole thing functions as expected.

There are many names now for this phenomena – super conforming, auto conforming, crosstalk. They all mean the same thing in the end. When the clothing is loaded and conformed the figure's dials control the clothing morphs.

Poser 4-7 The Old Fashioned Way (it always works)

1   Open your clothing cr2 in Poser File Editor or a text editor. Find the morphs in the channels of each bodypart. You will see two lines.

```
Figure 4
Body:1
```

The figure number may change, but that doesn't matter. The code lines need to be changed so the clothing morph looks to the figure for control, and not to its own master dials.

```
Figure 1
BODY
```

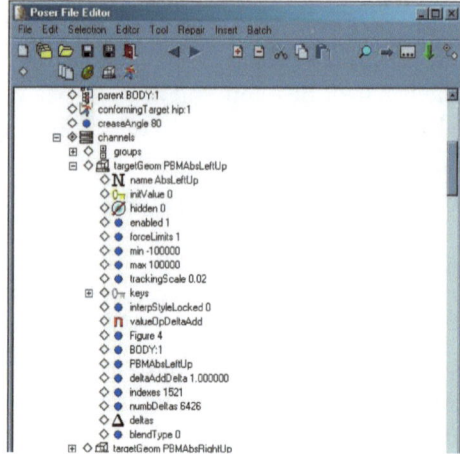

2   Here I have changed the morph channel entries - and ONLY those - to read Figure 1 instead of 4. Most characters default to 1 when first loaded in a scene unless other rigged figures are present. I have also changed Body:1 to BODY, allcaps. Now when the clothing item is loaded onto the figure the morphs will superconform. This works in every version of Poser I have tested it in from 4 to Poser Pro 2014, and doesn't matter if the figure has the same bodypart name or not which is an issue with PP2014 morph conforming.

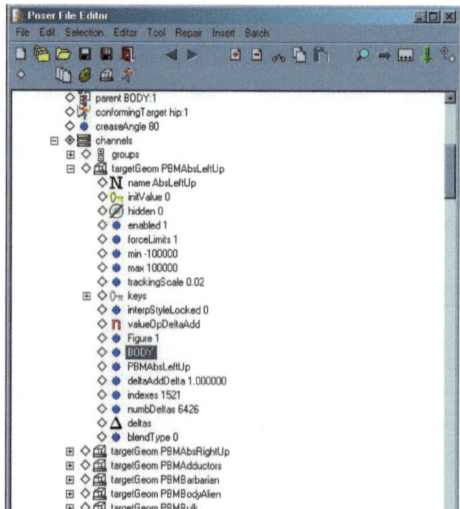

JCM – Joint Controlled Morphs

Morphs started out very simply, you controlled them by turning the dial on the bodypart. Then the Body was added and with it the lines of code in the bodypart morph that enslaved it to a control dial elsewhere. With this example and knowledge, of course, content makers experimented with exactly what they could hook dials up to.

There are a lot of things that don't work, I've found a few myself. But there is also a variety of things that do work. One of the most commonly used nowadays is the Joint Controlled Morph. This describes a morph that has code lines added so that it is activated by the values in a rotation setting somewhere on the figure or clothing.

Joint controlled morphs are the magic fixit. Many clothing makers use them to make morphs that fix issues in certain poses. The fix morph self activates when certain dial rotations hit specified limits, without any need for the user to adjust them. JCMs are very popular with figure makers to overcome some of the less than natural bends created by most rigging systems. In conjunction with weightmapping it can lend a very realistic set of bends and deformations as a figures moves.

A simple joint controlled morph adjustment

1   On the right is a view, in Poser File Editor, of a normal morph channel. This happens to be a body morph on a figure, but the structure is identical on any standard morph. I will explain the line entries you will most likely have to edit.

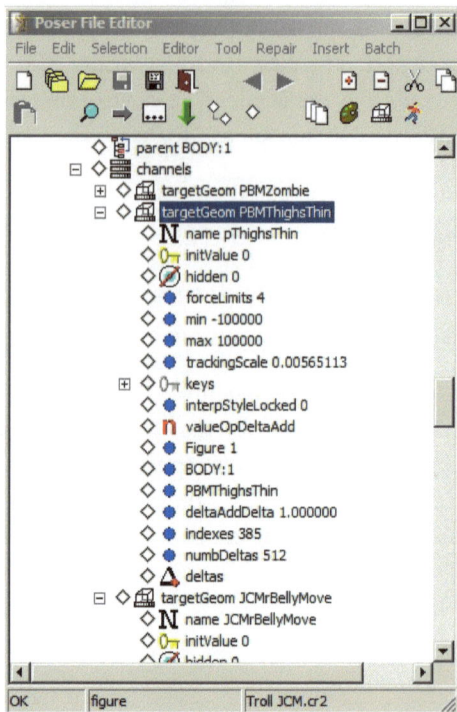

targetGeom This is the name of the dial as it shows to the user in Poser.

name The internal name of the morph and what Poser actually looks at for conforming and suchlike.

initValue Initial value, what value this is set to be default, usually 0.

hidden   is this morph hidden. This is a binary setting either 0 for not hidden, or 1 for hidden.

min The minimum value the morph can be dialed to.

max The maximum value the morph can be dialed to, also known as the limit.

valueOpDeltaAdd This is the start of the control section. You can have several control sections in a morph if you get fancy, but generally there is only one controller.

Figure 1 The figure number of the controller, this can change. If you loaded this in fourth in a scene it will load as 4.

Body:1 The group name of where the controller is, in this case the Body channel of Figure 1.

PBMTHighsThin The name of the controlling dial, this will of course always change depending on the morph name.

DeltaAddDelta This is the start of the actual morph data information section.

deltas The actual morph obj information as converted to text. In a text editor this is a giant string of gibberish. PFE shrinks it down to one line which I find much more manageable.

2   This is a JCM or Joint Controlled Morph with all its JCM coding.

It looks pretty much the same until you hit the valueOpDeltaAdd lines. As you can see there are two, which means this morph can be controlled by two different things.

In the first valueOp section the controller is in figure 1, this figure, in the bodypart group rButtock. The next line is the name of the controller channel, in this case xrot, or X rotation channel.

This means that when the rButtock on this figure is bent it will activate the joint controlled morph at a value controlled by the last line in this section deltaAddDelta.

This is the Influence Value. The value is a number which usually found by dividing the full setting 1 or 100% by the value at which you want it to be fully activated.

So for a rotation channel you usually want 1 / 45 where 1 is the full value and 45 is the degree rotation at which the morph should be fully active.

You can stick a JCM in a translation or scale dial as well, but that is much less common in clothing. For more information on this please see Rbtwhiz Poser ERC documentation center on rbtwhiz. com.

The second valueOp section in this morph details the control of the morph by the xrot or bend of the rThigh.

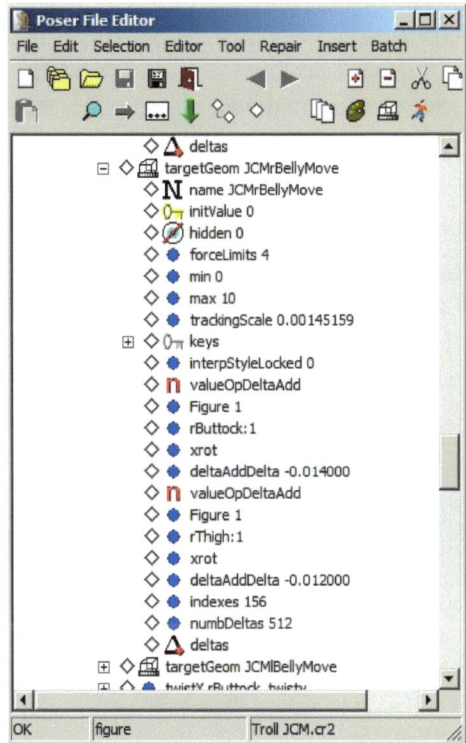

Poser File Editor

File Edit Selection Editor Tool Repair Insert Batch

◇ △ deltas
⊟ ◇ 🖳 targetGeom JCMrBellyMove
    ◇ N name JCMrBellyMove
    ◇ 0⌐ initValue 0
    ◇ ⊘ hidden 0
    ◇ ● forceLimits 4
    ◇ ● min 0
    ◇ ● max 10
    ◇ ● trackingScale 0.00145159
⊞ ◇ 0⌐ keys
    ◇ ● interpStyleLocked 0
    ◇ n valueOpDeltaAdd
    ◇ ● Figure 1
    ◇ ● rButtock:1
    ◇ ● xrot
    ◇ ● deltaAddDelta -0.014000
    ◇ n valueOpDeltaAdd
    ◇ ● Figure 1
    ◇ ● rThigh:1
    ◇ ● xrot
    ◇ ● deltaAddDelta -0.012000
    ◇ ● indexes 156
    ◇ ● numbDeltas 512
    ◇ △ deltas
⊞ ◇ 🖳 targetGeom JCMlBellyMove
⊞ ◇ ● twistY rButtock twisty

OK   figure   Troll JCM.cr2

EZPose

It doesn't take very long before you find that posing a long string of objects, like a rope or scarf, manually is a complete nuisance. Wouldn't it be so much nicer if you could just bend all the parts with one controller?

Well of course you can. Eventually. You have two methods, either you can connect all the Bend dials to a master control via ERC or you can get into the intricate back and forth of cascading dial controls. Ezpose is a system created by Ajax where the dial controls are cascaded along a string of parts. In ERC A controls b, c,d,e. In Ezpose A controls B, B controls C, C controls D and so forth. In more sophisticated EZPose controls like Wiggle, additional types of ERC and dependencies are used as well for some very sophisticated effects.

It is possible to code Ezpose command strings by hand, but honestly most people don't have that kind of patience. In general, most people use a tool, the most common is of course Ezpose Underground by Ajax.

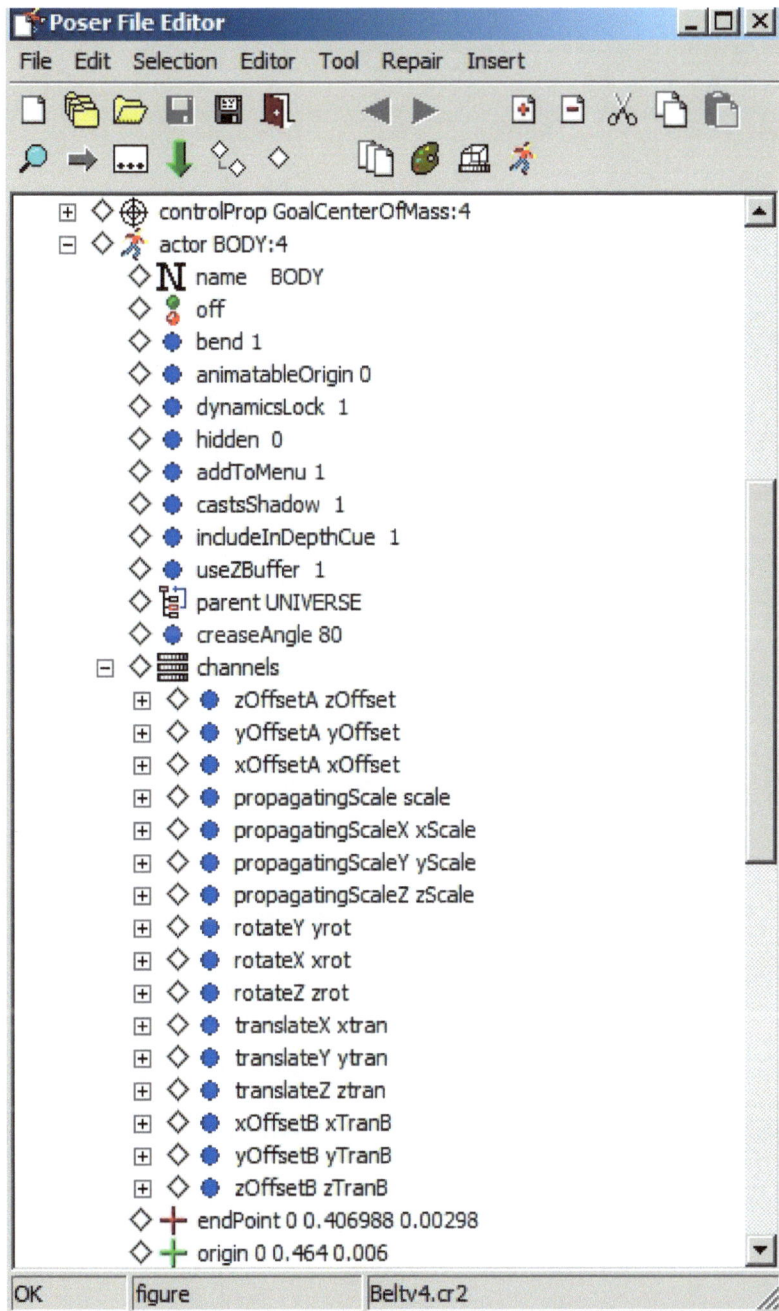

This is a perfectly normal bodypart channels section with the standard offset, scale, rotation and trans dials.

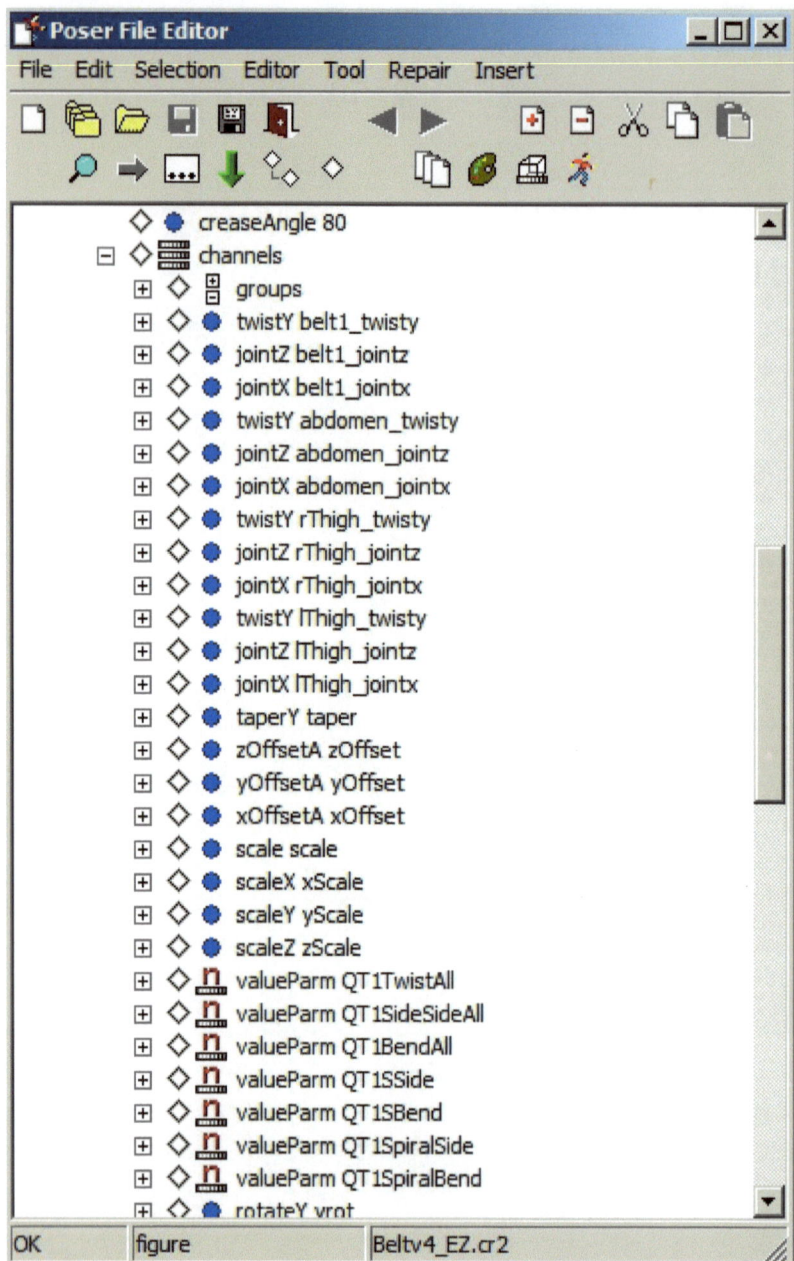

This is a bodypart channels section with the addition of several new dials. These start with valueParm and then the name of the dial. This is the internal dial name, usually containing a unique prefix to help avoid internal programming conflicts.

These lines will be in all the bodypart channels of the parts they effect. This causes the dial change to change all the parts at once.

How to add Ezpose with EPU

As you can guess adding several thousand lines of intricate code manually is no fun, although it can be done. I generally use a utility program called EZpose Underground. There are other utility tools which will also do this.

1   This is the opening menu screen of EPU. As you can see it has a fair number of options. When you load a cr2 into it, it will pick up data from the file itself.

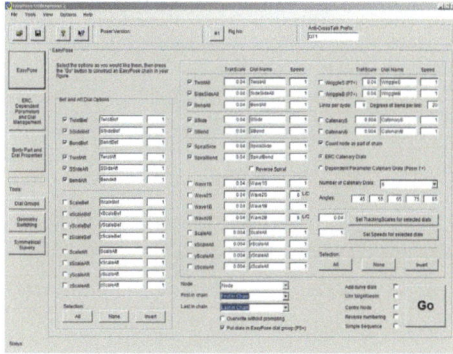

2   Here I have loaded my belt from Chapter 16. Since it has 10 bodyparts its a great candidate for EZpose.

The program picked up the Poser version number, some options are disabled for lower program version such as catenary dials.

Each dial I want to create has a check mark next to it, so the standard one in the top middle section, then the before and after dials in the top left section. I didn't add waves, wiggles, catenary or scaling dials.

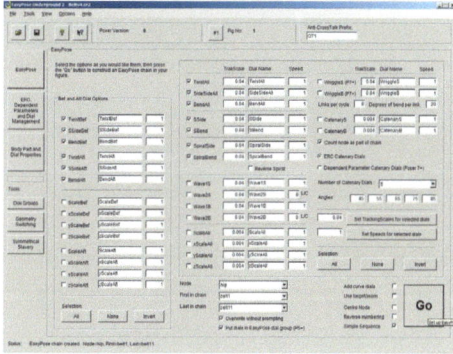

The important bit is down on the bottom middle. Node is the bodypart you want to control dials to go, in this case Hip. First and last in chain are obviously the first and last bodyparts. This is why we number bodyparts as I did in Chapter 16. EPU can follow from belt1 to belt11 easily. I set my last option for 'simple sequence' and now I'm ready to hit the Go button.

Now Save As a new file, I usually add EZ to the file name. Always save as, so you can check and make sure you got everything set up properly. If you made a mistake, go back to your original and try again.

Dependent Parameters in Poser 7 and Higher

In Poser seven the Dependent Parameters tool was added. This very versatile tool allows you to build advanced morph and joint behaviors directly inside Poser. Most parameters that are wired up to another such as jcms, fbms, and most ERC, can be created using the Dependent Parameters Editor, as well as new possibilities such as animated joint centers as part of a morph. However, parameters built by this feature do not always translate well to other programs or earlier versions of Poser.

Here is a quick example of 'teaching' a morph setting by using the Dependent Parameters Tool.

1   I have loaded David and con-formed the triangle shirt I made earlier. As you can see with the right collar bent to -50, I need the correction morph activated.

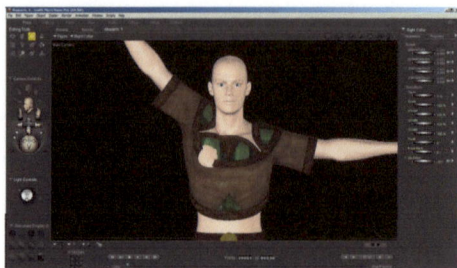

2   I have removed everything but the shirt from the scene. This makes it easier for me to select the right things during the next process, and also frees the shirt from being conformed to David.

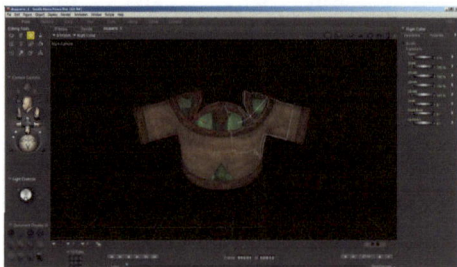

3   Right click on the dial you will use as the controller, in this case the Bend channel of the rCollar. Select the 'Edit Dependencies' tool.   When the tool starts nothing is happening. As you can see the value of the control dial is at 0, it is NOT teaching, there are no dependent parameters listed, and the graph is a flat line. This is good.

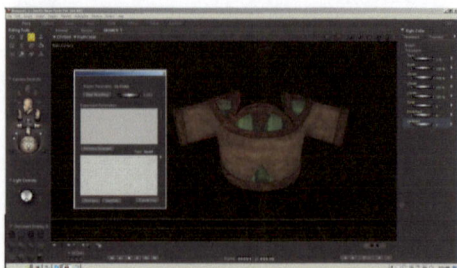

4   Pay careful attention to every thing you do after you start teaching. Try not to touch anything but the two dials you need to so do not move the camera, scale, or move anything else. I advise saving first. Its very easy to crosswire things at this stage.

Push the Start teaching button.

Set the bend on the rCollar to -50.

Select the Body of the shirt and set the rCollarUp morph to 1.

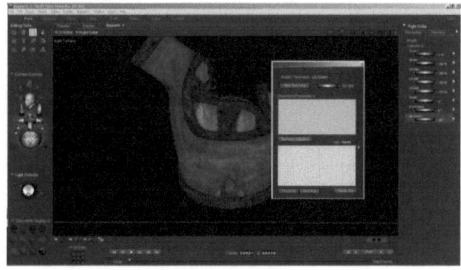

5   Now set the rCollarUp morph to 0.

Set the Bend on the rCollar to 0.

Press Stop Teaching.

If all has gone well you will see a dependent parameter listed in the editor " Body::rCollarUp" and the graph now has a diagonal line. If you have not managed to set a start and end value, you will get no line or a flat one and your morph will not behave properly.

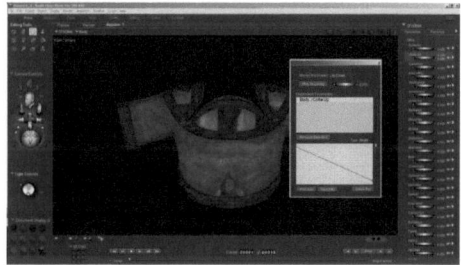

Now when I bend the rCollar of the shirt the joint will automatically turns itself on and off.

To have it follow the Body of David I will need to open it in PFE and change the controller to the figure body and not the shirt body.

Chapter 21 – Troubleshooting

Anything that can go wrong, will go wrong

- Murphy

If all goes well and the laws of chance favor you, your item will work properly and you will never need this chapter. However, since that happens very rarely, here is a list of common issues and how to solve them.

1. Sharp edges appear mushy in Poser

Cause: This is usually caused by Poser's automatic smoothing making a mess of sharp corners. It also can cause black smudges on edges of previewed or rendered objects.

Solution:

Option 1 – try adjusting the edge crimping

Option 2 – Split the corner vertices in UVmapper. Note: this will break any morphs already made and may cause issues with displacement. OldSkool method.

Option 3 – Add more edge loops close to the effected edge. This can often reduce the effects of oversmoothing and reinforce the edge

2. The object imports too large/small/out in space

Cause: You scaled or moved something while modeling

Solution: Re-export the figure, reload it into your modeler and check your clothing mesh on that. Refit as needed, re-export and try again.

3. The object appears inside out

Cause: Your normals are inverted

Solution: Flip the normals in Poser on import, in UVmapper or in your modeler

4. The object renders black

Cause: Your normals are inverted

Best Solution: Flip the normals in Poser on import, or in UVmapper or in your modeler

Quick solution: In the material room tick of 'normals always forwards. This will increase rendering times.

5. The clothing obj on import doesn't fit at the zero position and shape

Cause: You modeled over a morphed or posed figure.

Solution: Export the figure with no morphs and in the zero position or load from the figures obj file. Check your clothing obj against this. Refit as needed and re-export.

6. The setup room errors on exit 'this object contains ungrouped polygons'

Cause: You have ungrouped polygons or groups with no corresponding bone.

Solution: Check your spelling of group names and custom bone names. Check groups in UVmapper or similar.

7. The item jumps when conformed

Cause: Your donor rig was not zeroed, with IK off.

Solution: select the conforming item and zero rotations. Then Memorize Figure in the figure menu and re-conform.

Solution: if the first option doesn't do it, check your donor rig for any rotations and IK. Then re-apply the clean rig to the clothing.

8. The shoes jump when conformed

Cause: Your donor rig was saved with IK on.

Solution: Disable IK in your donor rig, then re-apply the clean rig to the clothing.

9. Making High Heels work

Cause: High heels are modeled to a bent foot position.

Solution: Group the entire shoe to Foot and supply a foot pose.

10. The item does not fit in the zero position and shape when conformed

Cause: The clothing was modeling to a morphed or posed figure.

Solution: Check the base figure for hidden 'always on' morphs, jcms, or magnets. Deactivate if needed. Zero rotations, re-export. Check clothing in modeler against new figure for fit.

Cause: Poser is flubbing the mesh smoothing, figure smoothing and mesh smoothing don't mesh and cause pinprick poke through

Solution: Best solution is to fix in the modeler. You can also make an always on Fix morph, or slap a displacement map on there.

Cause: The donor rig was saved with rotation or IK on.

Solution: Check donor rig, zero rotation and turn off IK. Re-apply to mesh

11. When I load my clothing nothing happens

Cause: Your cr2 is looking for an object that isn't named or located where it thinks it should be

Solution: Check your cr2 and your object location name to make sure they agree

12. When I load my clothing parts are missing

Cause: Your cr2 is not calling all groups in the clothing item

Solution: Usually a typo in a group name, Check for capitalization

13. When I load my clothing it turns weird colors

Cause: Your cr2 has no Materials section in the figure area. Poser picks a random color out of its hat

Solution: Resave the cr2, this will create the Materials section as needed. Set all materials to a color that is not toxic pink or bilious green and continue.

14. When I bend one part other parts of the clothing fly off

Cause: Some mesh polys are grouped to the wrong group

Solution: Check your groups. Make sure you haven't missed some polygons here or there

15. Reversed bone syndrome

Symptom: When the part is bent the bottom of it stays put and the top rips away from the garment.

Cause: Poser glued the custom bone on backwards. It often does this on end segments.

Solution: In the joint editor switch the position of the green and red crosshairs. This should reverse the bone so it bends properly.

16. Dyslexic bones

Symptom: You bend the left arm and the right clothing mesh moves.

Cause: Dyslexic creator has named the left and right part-names reversed sides.

Solution: open the obj and correct the names. Reload cr2, which should load the corrected obj.

17. Disobedient children syndrome

Symptom: You bend the parent part such as thigh and the shin just stays put.

Cause: sometimes caused by a grouping error. If the mesh is grouped correctly it can be caused by Poser being stupid.

Solution: Check for possible grouping error in the obj. If obj is fine, then save cr2 and file, close Poser and reopen to check.

18. The leg bone is attached to the chest bone

Symptom: you move one group and another unconnected part bends as well.

Cause: your hierarchy is mixed up.

Solution: Check to make sure the hierarchy is proper and matches the figure, and all custom parts were created and attached in the right places.

19. Cracking bends

Symptom: The bodyparts crack at the joints when bent

Cause: bodyparts set to not bend in parameters

Solution: retick Bend in parameters

Cause: missing weld statements in figure section of cr2

Solution: rerig entirely or copy and paste weld statements into each breaking bone in the figure section, which can be fiddly.

Cause: groups touching are not parent and child but parent and grandchild or child and child

Solution: regroup the mesh following the grouping rules more closely

Cause: mesh grouped into bodyparts in modeler was moved

Solution: Vertices on seamlines must be in exactly the same place. Align or weld and try again

20. Offcenter twist warping

Symptom: When twist is applied to a part it warps into a spiral mess

Cause: the end and start of the rotation do not match the mesh location, bodypart is not straight up/down or in/out

Solution: adjust the start and end of the rotation with the joint editor. You may need to edit the rotations of the start and end points

21. Bar? What Bar?

Symptom: You can't see any twist bar but the bend and side-side look normal

Cause: Poser has decided that the Start and End are the same number. Manually change one to a different number so you can see the bar. Now that you can see it, you can grab the ends to move them.

22. Backwards Twist

Symptom: Bodypart twist makes the clothing twist and the part stay put.

Cause: your twist bar is on backwards. This can go on backwards even if the bone is right way round.

Solution: The red end should be towards the parent part and the green facing away. If it isn't, grab one end and pull it past the other and it will flip.

23. The cr2 loads some other random object

Symptom: I go to load my saved item and some other random thing shows up instead.

Cause: Poser is stupid and the object had a common name such as shoes.obj so Poser picked the first shoes.obj it found.

Solution: Rename your obj to something more unique. Most stores require this anyways.

24. My texturemaps load wrong

Symptom: the MAT or material when applied loads a non-related texturemap.

Cause: Poser is stupid and the imagemap had a common name such as black.jpg, so Poser picked the first black.jpg it found

Solution: Rename your texturemaps to something more unique. Most stores require this anyways.

Symptom: the texturemap when loaded leaves white gaps all over the mesh, it does not match up.

Cause: this isn't the right map for this mesh.

Solution: Make sure you loaded the correct map. Check the map against the objects uv's to make sure the map was made for the correct version. Make sure the correct obj is loading into Poser.

25. My texture maps are hashed up

Symptom: The mesh looks fine and bends fine. However when the map is applied it loads in patchwork squares, some reversed as well as black squares

Cause: We don't know. Something horrible happened between the modeler and Poser. Its possible it has something to do with flipping normals

Solution: Sometimes you can reorder the vertices to match an earlier version and fix the mapping issues. Mostly, you will need to remap the mesh and adjust the textures to the new map.

26. My item has extra material zones in it

Symptom: When I look in the material room I see material names that are not in my model

Cause: The cr2 has picked up materials from either an incorrectly applied MAT pose or material, or your donor rig wasn't cleaned out entirely

Solution: Edit the Material area in the Figure section of the cr2 to remove the extras. Poser File Editor has an automatic fix tool for this. Check your donor cr2 to make sure the materials section has been removed

27. Every bodypart/group is a different color

Symptom: when you load the clothing every part comes in a different horrible color and then Poser crashes or freezes

Cause: You did a search and replace of 'figure:1' to 'figure' in the entire cr2 instead of just the morph channels

Solution: search and replace 'figure' to 'figure:1' and hope that puts it back. If not, re rig.

28. Why cant I find my morphs

Symptom: I know I made morphs in the figure but I cant see dials for them

Cause: You forgot to make an FBM dial in the body for your morphs.

Solution: Follow the instructions for making FBM's manually

Cause: Your morph channels and morph names in the Group of the morph channels are not the same. Caused by manually moving morphs from one cr2 to another in Poser File Editor or a text editor.

Solution: Delete all Groups from the cr2. Poser File Editor has a filter to do this automatically. Poser will regenerate the Groups for the morphs automatically on load.

Cause: Poser has stuck them into an Other group in the cr2.

Solution: Find where it has hidden them in the groups. Rename or edit the group listing.

29. The morph is there but doesn't work

Symptom: you turn the dial and nothing happens.

Cause: It is crosstalked and locked to the figures dials.

Solution: In general, as long as it responds to the figures dials you can ignore it, this means crosstalking is working properly.

Cause: You have a bad or empty morph.

Solution: delete and reload if needed.

Cause: looping dependency, the morph is slaved to itself so Poser ignores it.

Solution: Remove or recode your dependencies.

Cause: You set Minimum and Maximum to the same number.

Solution: Change the numbers.

30. Parts of my morph aren't working

Symptom: the morph when dialed or crosstalked doesn't dial on all parts.

Cause: A bodypart was left out when the FBM coding was created.

Solution: Add the missing lines of coding in the morph for that bodypart.

Cause: Poser's automatic morph conforming only works on bodyparts that match the figure. Custom parts need manual coding inserted.

Solution: Add the missing lines of coding in the morph for custom bodyparts.

31. My morph has sharp edges in weird places

Cause: The morph is not there in all bodyparts it crosses

Solution: Check the morph is named properly, and has all its ERC coding set up correctly. Add morph if missing.

Cause: The morph isn't dialing in all bodyparts

Solution: Check the morph is named properly, and has all its ERC coding set up correctly. Add morph if missing.

Cause: some other morph is dialing in addition

Solution: Check your morph and make sure you didn't bake another one into it by accident. Check the morph that is also dialing and make sure a stray ERC line hasn't crept into it.

32. Doubledialing

Symptom: The morph works when dialed or controlled by the figures morph, but it dials to double the normal strength, exploding or shrinking the clothing

Cause: Double dialing is usually a programming error. Usually it means that two morphs or controls are activating the morph at the same time, effectively double its strength

Solution: Proofread your coding to make sure that only one entry is calling this morph. You can use the Dependent Parameters tool to trace linkages in Poser

33. This morph won't crosstalk

Symptom: You turn the dial on the figure and the clothing morph doesn't do anything

Cause: Something is not connected properly

Solution: Check that the morphname is the same on the figure as on the clothing. Check that the FBM calls the bodypart morphs on the clothing properly. Check that the 'Conform morphs' option on the clothing is selected.

Cause: You turn the dial on the figure and the morphs on the custom bodyparts do nothing

Solution: Custom bodypart morphs will not automatically conform. You will need to add the extra code snippet that slaves the morph to the figure. Please see chapter 9.

34. Wrong number of vertices

Symptom: I went to load the morph I created outside Poser into the clothing and it failed with the error message 'Incorrect number of vertices' or similar.

Cause: Your morph has a different number of vertices than the destination figure. This could have been caused by a welded/unwelded mismatch, or by edits made during the morph creation or export process.

Solution: Check the figure and the morph. Try 'welding vertices' in UVmapper. Check that the item you started with matches the item in Poser. If you used any edit to the clothing item except moving vertices/polys in and out then you have changed the mesh and the morph will never work.

35. The morph worked but the mesh flies around at partial values

Symptom: The morph loaded fine. It looks great at 1 and at zero but at any other value the mesh is crumpled/torn/in orbit.

Cause: Poser calculates morphs in linear translations. Any vertex travels the straightest point from position B to position B. This may not be aesthetically pleasing.

Solution: Make several morphs, in stages instead of just one. It is possible, if you are brave, to ERC link them together into a smooth whole. However in general most users are happy with several variation morphs they can use.

36. The morph looks fine/wrong until its rendered

Symptom: When you activate the morph it look fine but pokes through when rendered.

Cause: Something in the shader maps is changing the mesh.

Solution: Turn off your displacement and render to verify. To fix adjust displacement setting or map.

Symptom: When you activate the morph it pokes through all over but looks fine when rendered.

Cause: Preview smoothing is not the same as rendered

Solution: Do nothing. If the preview poke bothers you, adjust the morph

37. Seeing ghosts

Symptom: I have transparency maps on an item for whole or partial transparency. But when I render it I see ghostly edges of the item, usually in a light color.

Cause: You have specularity on the item that is not being masked. You have invisible yet shiny mesh.

Solution: Remove the specularity from the ghosting area or create and apply a specularity mask. Generally the transmap can double up.

38. My transparent objects render black on the inside

Symptom: I have leaves, hair or feathers that are simple flat sheets of mesh. They look fine in the preview, but when they render any polygon facing away from the camera is very dark or black

Cause: Poser sees all mesh as one sided infinitely thin material. If the normal on the poly is facing away from the camera, Poser renders it like it was in shadow.

Solution: In the material room tick 'all normals face forwards'. This will force the material to render as if the normals always face the camera. This can make renders take a long time. Use sparingly.

Solution: Use the alternate diffuse channel as well as the regular and set them to half strength

39. My item renders fine plain but after texturing parts sink into the figure

Symptom: The item fits fine at zero pose and when rendered without shaders. When the texturemaps are applied and rendered the mesh sinks into the figure

Cause: One or more of your displacement maps are going inwards instead of outwards

Solution: Edit your displacement maps either in your image editor or via node maths

40. Mesh ripped apart at strange places after render

Symptom: The item fits fine at zero pose and when rendered without shaders. When the texturemaps are applied and rendered the mesh breaks at material edges or at hard corners.

Cause: You have a displacement map that cross material edges at a non zero value and the materials have different displacement setting.

Solution: Match up the displacement settings or modify the displacement map.

Cause: You have a displacement crossing an edge at a non 0 value where the verts of the mesh have been split

Solution: Weld the verts or set the displacement to a 0 value (black).

41. 180 Y bug (Poser 6 and below)

Symptom: Everything loads and fits fine. But when I rotate the figure to exactly 180 degrees on Y, so it faces away and the clothing flips to face forwards.

Cause: This is a known Poser maths bug. It was fixed as of Poser 7.

Solution: Change the rotation to 180.1 or 179.9 or upgrade and /or patch Poser.

www.ingramcontent.com/pod-product-compliance
Lightning Source LLC
Chambersburg PA
CBHW040929030426
42334CB00002B/7